SUBSTANCE ABUSE AND DEPENDENCE

Substance Abuse and Dependence

An Introduction for the Caring Professions

Edited by

HAMID GHODSE

DOUGLAS MAXWELL

St George's Hospital and
Medical School, London

MACMILLAN
PRESS
Scientific & Medical

First published 1990

Published by
THE MACMILLAN PRESS LTD
Houndmills, Basingstoke, Hampshire RG21 2XS
and London
Companies and representatives
throughout the world

Filmset by Wearside Tradespools,
Fulwell, Sunderland

Printed in Hong Kong

British Library Cataloguing in Publication Data
Substance abuse and dependence.
1. Addiction
I. Ghodse, Hamid   II. Maxwell, Douglas
616.86
ISBN 0–333–45858–3
ISBN 0–333–45859–1 pbk

Contents

The Contributors

S. Das Gupta
Consultant Psychiatrist,
Drug Dependence Centre,
St Mary's Hospital,
Praed Street,
London W2 INY

Nicholas Dorn
Development Director,
Institute of Study on Drug
    Dependence,
1–4 Hatton Place,
London EC1N 8ND

James Edeh
Senior Lecturer,
Psychiatry of Addictive
    Behaviour,
St George's Hospital and Medical
    School,
Cranmer Terrace,
London SW17 0RE

Roger Farmer
Consultant and Honorary Senior
    Lecturer in Psychiatry,
University College Hospital Drug
    Dependence Clinic,
Hampstead Rd,
London NW1 2LT

Hamid Ghodse
Professor and Director,
Psychiatry of Addictive Behaviour,
St George's Hospital and Medical
    School,
Cranmer Terrace,
London SW17 0RE

Michael Gossop
Head of Research,
Drug Dependence Clinical
    Research and Treatment Unit,
The Maudsley Hospital,
Denmark Hill,
London SE5 8AZ

Andrew Johns
Senior Lecturer,
Psychiatry of Addictive Behaviour,
St George's Hospital and Medical
    School,
Cranmer Terrace,
London SW17 0RE

Spencer Madden
Consultant in Charge,
Mersey Regional Alcohol and Drug
    Dependence Unit,
Countess of Chester Hospital,
Liverpool Rd,
Chester CH2 1BQ

Douglas Maxwell
Consultant Physician and Reader in Medicine,
St George's Hospital and Medical School,
Cranmer Terrace,
London SW17 0RE

Judith R. Morgan
Consultant Psychiatrist in Charge,
St Giles Hospital,
St Giles Rd,
London SE5 7RN

John Strang
Director,
Drug Dependence and Clinical Research Treatment Unit,

Bethlem Royal Hospital,
Monks Orchard Rd,
Beckenham,
Kent BR3 3BX

Gerry Stimson
Senior Lecturer,
Dept of Sociology,
Goldsmith's College,
New Cross,
London SE14 6NW

Brian Wells
Consultant Psychiatrist in Charge,
Drug Dependence Treatment Unit,
St Stephen's Hospital,
Fulham Rd,
London SW10 9TH

Acknowledgements

The editors wish to extend their sincere appreciation to all the contributors who have worked so hard to make this publication a reality. Despite the many demands upon them, they have been generous with their time, their enthusiasm and their many skills. We are also grateful to the publishers for their part in the production of this book and in particular to Mr David Grist for his patient co-operation. We should also like to thank Ms Melanie Sharp and Ms Cynthia Scott for their secretarial assistance.

Introduction

Hamid Ghodse and Douglas Maxwell

Drug abuse has always been an international problem because it has never been possible to confine drugs to their places of origin. Whenever and wherever man has travelled, he has taken his drugs with him and the associated drug-taking practices have spread too. Modern methods of transport and communication have increased and facilitated this dissemination. More people than ever before travel, more people than ever before are exposed to the drug-taking practices of other cultures, and the drugs themselves, particularly in their modern, potent forms, can be transported easily and safely. This, of course, applies to all drugs, both licit and illicit, and although attention tends to be concentrated on the illicit spread and use of heroin, cocaine and cannabis, there is also a vast global trade in legal, recreational drugs—tobacco and alcohol—as well as in products such as tranquillisers and hypnotics which have legitimate medical uses but which are also drugs of abuse and dependence.

The scale of global drug problems generated concern as long ago as 1909 when the First International Drug Conference was convened in Shanghai. Since then, there has been an extensive international programme of legislation, latterly under the auspices of the United Nations, and between 1912 and 1972 twelve multi-lateral drug treaties were concluded. The Single Convention, signed in 1961 and amended by the 1972 Protocol, consolidated legislation on narcotic drugs and the 1971 Psychotropic Convention extended the drug control system to newer, synthetic and psychoactive drugs. Both of these conventions aimed to reduce drug abuse by controlling very strictly the supply side of the drug economy: they license the production, manufacture, internal and international trade, prescribing and storage of the substances covered so that legitimate trade and production are limited to the required amounts, and diversion into illicit channels is prevented. Although this sort of control is undoubtedly necessary, it has become apparent that international supply control is not a sufficient response and that prevention, or at least reduction, of the illicit

1

demand for drugs of abuse is also essential.

The urgent need for a policy of demand reduction has been accentuated by the arrival of the Acquired Immune Deficiency Syndrome (AIDS), because in many countries drug abusers who share syringes, needles and other equipment form a major route of transmission for the human immune deficiency virus (HIV). Indeed, in some countries the majority of cases of AIDS/HIV infection have occurred because of the use of contaminated injection equipment. Infected drug users can transmit HIV sexually as well as by sharing injection equipment, and infected females can transmit the virus to their unborn child so that drug abusers form the route of access for HIV into the general population. Because there is no effective treatment for AIDS, and no vaccine against it, it poses a very serious public health problem. Thus, for the first time in many countries, it is in the public interest to fight drug abuse using all available means. Previously, drug abuse and drug dependence had been perceived only as personal problems, with the individual concerned being seen at best as an unfortunate victim, but often, because of the perceived volitional component of drug taking, as suffering the deserved consequences of earlier folly. Now, because of the threat to public health, there is far greater determination to attack drug dependence, and the increased political will to act against it was reflected by the convening in Vienna in 1987 of the Ministerial Conference on Drug Abuse and Illicit Trafficking. As well as the traditional concern with controlling the supply and suppressing illicit traffic, the conference had a much broader mandate—to intensify and extend the scope of international co-operation into new areas such as demand reduction and the treatment and rehabilitation of drug users.

In the light of these developments, this book is timely and appropriate. It is the first British multi-author textbook on drug abuse, and nearly all the authors are closely involved on a daily basis in the course of their work with those who abuse drugs. Thus they bring to this work their 'hands on' experience of drug abuse in the UK. This is important because, although drug abuse is a global problem, conditions and problems vary locally and the British perspective will be welcome to practitioners of many disciplines.

The scope of this book extends from the epidemiology of drug abuse in the UK and the pharmacological properties of the common drugs of abuse to drug prevention strategies and the law relating to drug abuse. There are chapters on important conceptual topics such as the nature of dependence and the course of drug abuse, as well as chapters on the management of many different aspects of drug abuse—all based on the personal experience of the authors and their critical interpretation of the literature. Alcohol is not treated separately but is included in each chapter as and when appropriate. It is hoped that this combination of theoretical background material and practical guidance will be of particular interest and useful to the many professionals of different disciplines who are currently involved in caring for drug abusers. It must be emphasised that the order of the chapters is unrelated to the importance of their content. In particular, prevention, which is the subject of the penultimate chapter, is undoubtedly the topic of the greatest importance and significance today.

1

What is Dependence?

Andrew Johns

Synopsis

Dependence is easier to recognise than it is to define. Images of young men in squats injecting heroin, of the well-heeled snorting cocaine or of the inebriate under the railway arches may be reinforced by television, by press reports or by walking down the streets of any large town or city. Similarly, patients with drug- and alcohol-related problems form much of the day-to-day workload in casualties, general practice surgerics and hospitals. Despite the enormous diversity of these patients and their problems, they have one thing in common. The solvent inhaler, the heroin user and the heavy drinker all misuse various substances and show signs of dependence upon them. This chapter is concerned with current views of the nature of that dependence, how it arises and its significance for the individual and for society.

Introduction

What is a drug?

A drug in its broadest sense is a chemical other than those required for the maintenance of normal health, which on administration alters biological function. Drugs may be further differentiated on the basis of their effect on bodily systems, and those that alter mood, cognition and behaviour are termed 'psychoactive'. However, there is no sharp boundary between psychoactive drugs and others, since substances used mainly for their effects on the central nervous system may have actions elsewhere. Opiates not only induce euphoria and analgesia but also reduce gut motility, and amphetamines produce marked tachycardia. Psychoactive drugs may be therapeutic or non-therapeutic agents, and some psychoactive substances are used for both purposes. Opiates may be taken in the form of pharmaceutical preparations such as diacetylmorphine, or as raw opium and illicit heroin powder. However, some psychoactive drugs are less likely to be self-administered than others. Chlorpromazine and antidepressants are psychoactive drugs and yet rarely become drugs of dependence, because their central effects are not experienced as being pleasurable or rewarding—i.e. they have low reinforcement potential. In summary, a drug of dependence is a non-medically used psychoactive drug which is centrally rewarding and likely to be self-administered.

What is drug misuse?

Some of the terms which apply to drug use and users are notoriously value-laden, for whether a substance is described as 'used' or 'misused' depends not only on the pattern of consumption, but also on the attitudes of the observer. It is therefore important to use neutral terms where possible and to define patterns of use clearly. In place of 'addict' or 'alcoholic' a preferred phrase is 'problem drug or alcohol user', which emphasises that the focus of concern must be wider than the actual dependence on a substance. Although the phrase 'drug misuse' is widely employed, this is ambiguous, for an examination of some of the concepts behind this term reveals patterns of misuse which may be differentiated according to their consequences. The WHO recommends the following (Edwards *et al.*, 1981):

(a) Unsanctioned use: use of a drug that is not approved by a society, or a group within a society. When the term is used, it should be made clear who is responsible for the disapproval.
(b) Hazardous use: use of a drug that will probably lead to harmful consequences for the user—either to dysfunction or to harm. This concept is similar to the idea of risky behaviour.
(c) Dysfunctional use: use of a drug that is leading to impaired psychological or social functioning (e.g. loss of job or marital problems).
(d) Harmful use: use of a drug that is known to have caused tissue damage or mental illness in the particular person.

The Royal College of Psychiatrists' (1987) definition of drug use also draws on outcome criteria:

> Drug misuse is any taking of a drug which harms or threatens to harm the physical or mental health or social well-being of an individual, or other individuals, or of society at large, or which is illegal.

The drunken driver who injures a pedestrian, or the housewife who takes large amounts of diazepam to get through the day and the young man who injects illicit heroin are all covered by this definition, which is broadly framed to encompass the wide range of problems which may follow the inadvisable use of psychotropic drugs.

What is dependence?

Some of the problems involved in defining the state of dependence may be illustrated by using a clinical example. Take the case of a young man who smokes half a gram of heroin a day. He has done so for many years and finds that any interruption of this habit leads to physical and mental distress. Many would say he is 'dependent' on heroin. It may be thought that the everyday meaning of this term is clear and that there is no need for much elaboration. But further consideration will show that the expression and severity of this state of dependence is powerfully shaped by a variety of internal and external factors. These include psychological aspects of functioning, such as the ability to tolerate discomfort, and the personality of the individual. There is also an interactive or dynamic contribution, in that the relationship between an individual and his peers and society as a whole will shape the expression of a state of dependence. For these reasons, a rounded description of dependence draws on physical, psychological and sociological factors. In 1964 the World Health Organization recommended the use of the term 'drug dependence' and offered the following definition:

> A state, psychic and sometimes also physical resulting from the interaction between a living organism and a drug, characterised by behavioural and other responses that always include a compulsion to take the drug on a continuous or periodic basis in order to experience its psychic effects, and sometimes to avoid the discomfort of its absence. Tolerance may or may not be present. A person may be dependent on more than one drug.

While this formula neatly encapsulates some of the core features of dependence it also contains concepts that need further explanation. Firstly, the relationship between the physical and psychological aspects of dependence is often misunderstood. At a fundamental level, drugs of dependence act on the brain to produce physical effects which have psychological manifestations. But this is too simple a view because chemical activity and psychological drives are not yoked together like horse and cart. Indeed each may, in turn, lead the other. For example, the severity of opiate withdrawal symptoms is influenced by factors such as anxiety and expectation (Phillips *et al.*, 1986). In this case psychological factors precede and influence the expression of a physical state. On the other hand, withdrawal from cocaine can induce intense depression, and here psychological factors follow the physical use of a substance. Concepts such as physical and psychological dependence should not therefore be regarded as polar opposites, or even as the main elements of dependence, but as different views of the same phenomenon, one expressed in terms of cellular functioning, the other in terms of thoughts, feelings and drives. With this in mind, the concept of drug dependence may be examined in the light of the contribution of physical, psychological and sociological factors.

Physical or biological factors

In the next chapter 'tolerance' and 'withdrawal syndromes' are described in relation to individual drugs of misuse, whereas this section is concerned with the contribution of these factors to the phenomenon of dependence.

Tolerance
Drug users seek central effects from their drugs, which, although reinforcing and generally pleasurable, upset the chemical equilibrium within the brain. The nervous system responds in such a way as to reduce the effects of repeated drug administration. This leads to a state of 'tolerance' in which the drug user finds that higher doses of a drug are required to produce a given effect. Most people would be drowsy if given 20 mg of diazepam as a single dose, but a benzodiazepine misuser may take more than 100 mg of diazepam a day and remain awake. The heroin user with a long-established habit may inject doses equivalent to hundreds of milligrams of opiate which would be lethal to a non-tolerant individual.

Neuroadaptation
There are many mechanisms which have been proposed to explain the development of tolerance, and most invoke a physical response at the neuronal level with the result that tolerance has long been regarded as an aspect of 'physical dependence'. The phrase 'physical dependence' is misleading as it is not always accompanied by further drug use. Surgical patients given opiates to relieve pain may experience withdrawal symptoms. As they do not show drug-seeking behaviour or wish to take drugs, they could hardly be described as physically dependent. As an alternative term the WHO (Edwards *et al.*, 1981) suggested 'neuroadaptation', which is a reflection of the ability of brain cells to adapt to the presence of a drug. This is usually the most important element in the build-up of tolerance, and leads to the presence of a characteristic withdrawal syndrome if drug use is discontinued.

Withdrawal states
If neuroadaptation follows the use of a drug, then withdrawal leads to decompensation or rebound symptoms. Withdrawal symptoms have characteristics which tend to counterbalance the effects produced by the drug itself. Withdrawal from stimulants such as cocaine and amphetamines leads to lethargy, sleepiness and low mood. Depressant drugs like alcohol and

benzodiazepines are associated with excitatory withdrawal symptoms such as agitation, tremor, fits and, possibly, hallucinations. Withdrawal states are often dysphoric but are not always associated with marked physiological symptoms: those of cannabis and nicotine are relatively slight.

Although the physical aspects of dependence are powerful influences on drug-taking behaviour, they do not tell the whole story, nor is the relationship between them fully understood. For example, tolerance and withdrawal are in many ways related but do not always go together. Some drugs such as pentazocine give rise to little tolerance, cannabis induces tolerance but no clear withdrawal state, whereas marked tolerance and withdrawal may follow the use of opiates and barbiturates. Physical withdrawal symptoms are not the touchstone of dependence, for dependence may occur without withdrawal and withdrawal without dependence. The contribution of physical symptoms to the state of dependence can only be appreciated when set in the context of psychological and social factors.

Psychological factors

The acquisition and maintenance of dependence are markedly influenced by a range of psychological factors such as learning and personal characteristics. For example, if an animal in an experimental situation is able to obtain its own injection of cocaine by repeatedly pressing a lever, then it may be encouraged to do so several thousand times to obtain a further amount of the drug. In this case, dependence on cocaine is an operantly conditioned behaviour, i.e. behaviour is controlled by its consequences. Those consequences that increase the frequency of a behaviour are termed reinforcers. Food, sex and drugs are said to have 'reinforcement potential'. Expectation of drug effect and withdrawal are also important. A shy young man may find that taking alcohol or amphetamines reduces anxiety, and in consequence uses these substances more frequently in social settings. Aversive withdrawal states such as those of opiates and benzodiazepines are powerful reinforcers of further drug-taking behaviour.

Other learned factors related to environmental stimuli become cues or triggers for craving and withdrawal states. It is common for alcohol users to report that craving is increased by a host of environmental cues, such as a chance meeting with drinking companions, the close proximity of an off-licence to the workplace, or even a particular time of day. An injecting drug user may find that in the first few months of abstinence the sight of a needle or syringe alone may provoke physical symptoms of withdrawal and act as an environmental reminder for his own drug use.

Individual personality characteristics undoubtedly contribute to the onset and maintenance of dependence, but there is no evidence for an 'addictive personality'. Although people differ in their desire to experiment, their need for stimulation and their responses to adversity, some individuals do appear to use drugs or alcohol for these reasons. Still at the level of personal factors, the way in which a drug user thinks of himself and his addiction may be relevant. If the user of heroin sees himself as an 'addict' and believes that this is a life-long state, this will tend to perpetuate his dependence.

Sociological factors

Both the acceptance of drug use by an individual and the immediate availability of drugs are predominantly determined by peer groups and other social factors. Roles such as those of 'skaghead', 'addict' or 'dealer' may be rewarding for some people in that they contribute to a sense of personal identity or identification with the cultural subgroup. For these reasons, the task of coaxing a drug user away from dependence is less likely to succeed if the social context of drug use is ignored.

The Dependence Syndrome

If the compulsive drive or craving for drugs is known as 'dependence', then the drug-taking behaviours which follow are described as the 'dependence syndrome'. In 1981 the World Health Organization gave a check-list of the main criteria necessary for the assessment of the dependence syndrome.

- A subjective awareness of compulsion to use a drug or drugs, usually during attempts to stop or moderate drug use.
- A desire to stop drug use in the face of continued use.
- A relatively stereotyped drug-taking habit, i.e. a narrowing in the repertoire of drug-taking behaviour.
- Evidence of neuroadaptation (tolerance and withdrawal symptoms).
- Use of the drug to relieve or avoid withdrawal symptoms.
- The salience of drug-seeking behaviour relative to other important priorities.
- Rapid reinstatement of the syndrome after a period of abstinence.

The key feature of the syndrome is the compulsion to use drugs, which results in an overwhelming priority or 'salience' being given to drug-taking behaviours. This is shown by heroin users who argue that nothing else matters and who persist in taking to the point of overdose and, on occasion, death. Commoner examples are those of the alcohol-dependent businessman who neglects his work in order to drink, and the haste of some cigarette smokers to replenish their supply.

Evidence of any single criterion such as neuroadaptation is insufficient to categorise drug-taking behaviour as drug-dependent. The whole picture has to be taken into account, and the relative contribution of each criterion considered, including some assessment of overall severity. At its most extreme and recognisable, the syndrome corresponds to the compulsive drug-taking behaviour previously described and has personal consequences that may threaten life. However, there is no sharp cut-off point that allows less severe cases to be readily distinguished from non-dependent but recurrent drug use, for dependence on drugs is not always a disability.

In summary, the dependence syndrome comprises three components:

(1) An altered biological state as shown by the phenomena of tolerance, withdrawal and the reinstatement of these after abstinence.
(2) An altered behavioural state as shown by prominence of drug-seeking behaviour and stereotyped pattern of drug use.
(3) An altered subjective state as shown by impaired control and craving.

Criticisms of the concept of the dependence syndrome

As formulated by the WHO the concept of the dependence syndrome has been enormously influential. The key elements have been incorporated with modifications into the two main international classifications of mental illness in current use. These are the DSM-III-R and the ICD-10 (American Psychiatric Association's *Diagnostic and Statistical Manual*, 3rd edition, revised, and the *Tenth Revision of the International Classification of Diseases*). But despite its general acceptance, the dependence syndrome has also received much criticism and comment (Heather *et al.*, 1985). The main objections may be summarised as follows.

It is argued that the use of the term 'syndrome', and also its full description, betray the view that dependence is an illness or disease. This has considerable implications, for, as suggested by labelling theory, changing the name of a behaviour actually changes the behaviour in question. A drinker may then assume a 'sick role' and, as his personal responsibility for his 'deviant behaviour' is diminished, be expected to cooperate with medical treatment. Furthermore, it is suggested that the syndrome is defined in tautologous terms. Evidence exists only for an 'altered psychobiological state' and for features such as tolerance, withdrawal symptoms and the reinstatement of these after abstinence. Research findings do not support 'loss of control' and other subjective factors.

In addressing these points it may be agreed that there are medical connotations of the term 'syndrome', but the full description is an attempt to describe a 'psychophysiological–social' phenomenon. Dependence is essentially a form of behaviour for which personal responsibility is retained, and it is a matter of observation that change may follow social, medical and non-medical interventions. In further support there has been much research, especially in the alcohol field, into the validity of the syndrome. A number of questionnaires have been developed to assess its usefulness, and the severity of the syndrome appears to predict attendance at a treatment clinic, craving for alcohol after a 'priming' drink and failure to control drinking following relapse (Edwards, 1986). It is an interesting finding that measures of the alcohol dependence syndrome provide good prediction of reinstatement in alcohol users, but equivalent measures for drug dependence are not yet so useful.

Alternative models of habitual substance abuse

Although the concept of the dependence syndrome may dominate our attempts at understanding and classifying substance misuse, alternative models have been proposed. In general, these draw little on medicine, being largely influenced by psychological and sociological principles.

Social learning models

Social learning theory is a set of concepts which are said to be relevant to all human behaviour, whether moderate or excessive, and to apply to a wide range of 'addictive behaviours' such as drug and alcohol use, excessive gambling and eating. For example, alcohol is taken by the social drinker and the problem drinker alike, because of the expectation that pleasant consequences will follow. Some of these are learned from parents, peers, books and television while others are learned through direct experience. Although alcohol is widely available, not everyone has the experience of heavy drinking, for the likelihood of this depends on a wide range of psychosocial factors including occupation, personality and subculture. Learning to drink heavily may therefore result from exposure to certain alcohol-oriented environments and the expectation of rewarding consequences, or, to put it another way, through a variety of psychological and social cues. A sort of selective attention leads to drinkers anticipating pleasurable effects while trying to ignore distant punishing consequences, such as threatened loss of job or ill-health.

As a heavy drinker begins to experience problems, a set of negative expectations develop so that there are strong reasons to want alcohol and strong reasons to avoid it. This ambivalence reflects an approach–avoidance conflict which is experienced as a compulsion to drink. The drinker may say to himself, 'I want that drink, even though I'm desperately trying not to.' Sometimes a state of 'learned helplessness' supervenes in which no attempt is made to stop drinking because it has been learned from previous experience that it is futile to try. This is an example of impaired cognitive control, that is, the ability to regulate consumption by thinking, goal-setting and making commitments.

Many aspects of social learning and impaired control are drawn together by Allan Marlatt (Marlatt and George, 1984) who has proposed a cognitive–behavioural model of 'relapse prevention'. The escalation of initial drug use into continued use is described as a two-stage process. Factors which trigger resumption of use are seen as different from the causes of continued drug taking. As in the dependence syndrome mode, 'craving' and 'loss of control' are important determinants. Marlatt suggests that the likelihood of one lapse becoming a full relapse is determined by an 'abstinence-violation effect'. Briefly, if a drug user attributes a lapse to factors that are seen as uncontrollable, such as being 'ill' or having a moral weakness, then hopelessness follows and the probability of further relapse is increased. This model has been very influential and has generated new approaches to the management of substance misuse (Saunders and Allsop. 1987).

Other models

Though unsupported either by research findings or clinical experience, the 'disease' model of dependence is widely held by many drug and alcohol users and by a significant body of treatment and counselling agencies. The disease concept suggests that there is a fundamental pathological process leading to an illness which may be called alcoholism or drug addiction. The core pathology is assumed to be a physical and mental process leading to a permanent degree of craving, which implies that the illness is life-long. Recovery, it is argued, can only be sustained by a commitment to abstinence within a structured programme of group support, such as that of 'AA' and 'NA' (Alcoholics Anonymous and Narcotics Anonymous), which in a residential setting may be called the 'Minnesota Model' (Cook, 1988).

Room (1985) has suggested that dependence could be located at any one of five areas of functioning: the physiological, the psychological, the level of interpersonal interaction, the level of social worlds and the cultural level. Although this analysis takes views of dependence beyond the individual into the realms of social forces, it has had limited influence. The American anti-psychiatrist Thomas Szasz has argued that heroin and cannabis have largely ceremonial functions within society and that 'drug problems' follow proscriptions on drug use. This polemical view results partly from a lack of a historical or socio-cultural perspective and has not proved fruitful.

A brief history of the concept of dependence

Present concepts of dependence rest on the attempts of each generation to understand why some individuals habitually overindulge in the use of drugs and alcohol. Over the years this behaviour has been described in concepts drawn from theology, personal morality, medical science and, more recently, psychology and sociology. A study of history shows that responses to dependence within a society are partly determined by the terms used to define the problem.

In seventeenth and eighteenth century Britain, alcohol was generally regarded as safer to drink than water and essential for good health. Opium was available and widely used for medicinal purposes. Habitual overindulgence was of course recognised, but regarded as a social evil and a personal vice. Public drunkenness was not regarded as a major problem, and although the courts could punish offenders it was assumed that processes of social control within communities would contain overindulgence. The prevailing philosophy was that of rationalism, which stated that men always acted freely in accordance with principles of rational self-interest and that if anyone broke accepted rules of proper conduct they did so knowing that punishment could follow. The drunkard had therefore chosen to be drunk.

A great change of outlook occurred at the end of the eighteenth century, when the scientific method was applied not only to the material world but also to the explanation of human drives and actions. Human behaviour was seen as determined by forces outside the individual's control and yet susceptible to scientific explanation, with the result that habitual drunkenness was explained by the disease of addiction. Dr Benjamin Rush of Philadelphia (1745–1813) and his counterpart in Britain, Dr Thomas Trotter (1760–1832), an Edinburgh physician, each wrote highly influential tracts in which addiction to alcohol was described as 'a disease of the will'. Rush considered that once a 'craving' for strong spirits had developed, the addict could not resist the impulse to drink. Drunkenness was not seen as a vice or personal weakness, since the sufferer had lost control over his drinking. Both doctors came to suggest that the only remedy was complete abstinence from drink, and so the 'Temperance Movement' was born. By the early 1830s, Temperance Societies were active in the United States and Britain. It was believed that the essence of alcohol addiction lay not in the vulnerability of individuals, but in the addicting nature of alcohol itself and so a complete legislative ban became their goal. There was no opposition to provision for treatment, and help for 'inebriates', as they came to be called, formed a major part of temperance activity (see Heather and Robertson, 1985).

Interestingly, the application of the disease concept to the use of opium was slower to occur. In the England of the 1850s, opium could be bought in any grocer's shop, and regular users or 'opium eaters' were acceptable in their communities and rarely the subject of medical attention. Opium was used mainly by the working classes, and it was only when this was seen as an example of lower-class deviance that its sale became regulated by the Pharmacy Act of 1868 and further legislation in the 1890s. In the last decades of that century the disease of 'morphinism' was described in medical textbooks, and addiction became a new medical specialty. However, this was a disease defined in psychological terms with strong moral overtones. Both morphinism and alcoholism were regarded as the product of 'diseased cravings and paralysed control' and the product of 'moral bankruptcy or insanity'. Though opium eating was medicalised, failure to respond to treatment was seen as failure of personal responsibility, which in turn was ascribed to a hereditary moral weakness (Berridge and Edwards, 1987). In the early years of this century, and especially after the repeal of Prohibition in the United States in 1933, interest in addiction waned. Addicts and alcoholics were still regarded as morally reprehensible, partly to blame for their misfortune and undeserving of medical attention.

The following decades saw the rediscovery of the disease concept and the subsequent reinvolvement of medicine in the care of substance misusers. Much of this was influenced by Dr E. Jellinek, who, in the late 1940s, established the Yale Center for Alcohol Studies. Jellinek defined alcoholism as 'any use of alcoholic beverages that caused any damage to the individual or society or both'. He emphasised the criteria of 'loss of control' (gamma alcoholism) and inability to abstain (delta alcoholism), and described the phases of alcohol addiction as those of a chronic and progressive disease. In his later work, 'loss of control' became identified with 'physical dependence' involving increased tolerance, withdrawal symptoms and craving, which was thought to characterise addiction to heroin and other 'hard' drugs. The disease concept was also adopted by Alcoholics Anonymous, whose approach has been previously described. In retrospect it appears that the disease model did not arise solely from pure scientific considerations but also out of the concern that the alcoholic and drug user deserved better treatment. The function of this approach was to legitimise addicts and the actions of those who helped them. While research in the addictions flourished in this climate, the man in the street with an alcohol or drug problem continued to receive cursory attention from medical services and even less help from any other source.

By the 1950s it was apparent that the use of the terms 'addiction' and 'disease' not only meant that drug or alcohol addiction was regarded as a stigma but also failed to acknowledge the contributions of the social sciences and hindered the proper development of services. In 1952 the WHO used the concept of 'dependence' for the first time, framing this largely in social and psychological terms. However, 'dependence' on a drug such as alcohol was seen as less serious than an 'addiction' to opiates. This confusion became of concern to the WHO Expert Committee on Addiction-producing Drugs, which recommended in 1964 that both 'drug addiction' and 'drug habituation' should be replaced by 'drug dependence' (see page 2). The provisional description of the alcohol dependence syndrome offered by Griffith Edwards and Milton Gross (1976) has been enormously influential. The key features, such as compulsion to drink, prominence of drink-seeking behaviour, tolerance, withdrawal symptoms and reinstatement after abstinence were adapted and incorporated in the WHO definition of the 'dependence syndrome'.

Like a chameleon the concept of dependence has shown itself capable of adaptation to a changing scientific background. The predominant influence is currently that of psychology, but there are emerging disciplines, such as molecular biology, which may gain ground in the future.

The aetiology of dependence

To say that the causes of dependence are multifactorial is not only trite but true, for a state which is described in 'psychophysiological–social' terms is unlikely to have just one aetiology. Although numerous theories have been proposed at almost every level from the cellular to the social, three broad levels of explanation may be characterised as 'constitutional', 'individual' and 'environmental'. Constitutional or biological approaches are concerned with inherited predispositions. Individual factors range from the neurochemical to the psychological, and include interpersonal functioning. Lastly, environmental factors relate aetiology of dependence to social or cultural variables such as the quality of parenting, peer influence and the availability of drugs.

Constitutional factors

The notion that hereditary factors may contribute to dependence has had a long history. Victorian eugenicists had argued that inebriates inherited a form of constitutional weakness, but there was no science of genetics to test the theory. It has, however, been repeatedly observed that some forms of addiction, notably alcohol abuse, appear to run in families. The question then arises: is there reliable evidence to support this view, and, if so, what is the mechanism?

Twin and adoption studies

Over the past 80 years, more than a hundred studies have shown that alcoholism is three to five times as frequent in the parents, siblings and children of alcoholics as in the general population (Cloninger, 1987). Families with a history of alcohol abuse are therefore easily found, but it is necessary to separate nature from nurture to tease out a possible genetic component. This may be done in two ways. One approach is to compare identical and non-identical twins. If the identical set are more alike or 'concordant' for alcoholism, this points to a genetic basis. Another way is to study adopted persons who had alcoholism in their biological family but not in their family of upbringing. However, the results obtained from twin studies are inconclusive (Goodwin, 1984). Two major studies have demonstrated a higher concordance rate for alcoholism among identical twins; however, another study did not support these findings and a fourth was equivocal.

From 1970 onwards, Goodwin (1984) carried out a series of adoption studies in Denmark to examine the contribution of genetics to alcoholism. It was found that chronic alcoholism was about four times more likely in 55 adopted-away sons of alcoholics than in 78 such sons of non-alcoholics; however, alcoholism in adopted-away daughters of alcoholics was not significantly increased above the incidence in adopted controls. More recently, Bohman (Cloninger, 1987) studied 2000 adoptees born between 1930 and 1949 by inspecting official registers in Sweden for entries indicating alcohol abuse and criminal offences in the adoptees and their biological and adoptive parents. There was a significant correlation between abuse of alcohol in adopted-away sons and their biological parents. Criminality in the biological parents did not predict either criminality or alcoholism in the adopted-away sons.

It is a consistent finding in many studies that alcoholism in biological parents predicts alcoholism in their sons raised away from home. Conversely, children reared by alcoholic adoptive parents are not at increased risk of alcoholism. There is also some evidence for the category of 'familial alcoholism' in which there is not only a family history, but also early onset and more severe symptoms. Having demonstrated that there is a genetic component to alcoholism, it then becomes pertinent to consider how genes may affect behaviour in this way. One way is to look at the variability of the enzymes that break down alcohol, and another has looked for inherited vulnerability factors in high-risk individuals.

Genetic polymorphism of alcohol-metabolising enzymes

Alcohol is metabolised in the liver by two enzymes, alcohol dehydrogenase and aldehyde dehydrogenase, which together determine how quickly alcohol is broken down. The activity of these enzymes therefore influences tolerance to alcohol, onset of withdrawal symptoms and many other aspects of the alcohol dependence syndrome. It is now clear that marked differences in alcohol elimination rates between individuals can be explained by genetically predetermined differences in the efficiency of these two enzymes (Grant, 1988). There are 20 inherited variants or isozymes of alcohol dehydrogenase but few are of clinical importance. Only two isozymes of aldehyde dehydrogenase (ALDH) are found in the liver, and the high-affinity form, designated ALDH-2, plays a crucial role in the breakdown of alcohol.

The most important finding has been that 50% of Japanese and Chinese have a completely inactive variant of ALDH-2 but none of the Caucasian or Negroid populations so far screened have shown this deficiency. A genetic mutation leading to a substitution of just one amino acid in the structure of the enzyme leads to inactivation. If ALDH-2 is inactive, then taking alcohol leads to an accumulation of acetaldehyde and a toxic reaction of facial flushing, vasodilation and tachycardia. It can be predicted that individuals with the inactive form of ALDH-2 will be discouraged from alcohol abuse by the adverse reactions and this is found to be the case. The frequency of alcoholism in Japanese with inactive ALDH-2 is significantly lower than in individuals with the normal enzyme. In this case there is a clear relationship between a genetic variant of an enzyme of alcohol metabolism and drinking behaviour.

'Vulnerability' studies

Adoption studies show that children of alcoholics can be considered a high-risk group for the future development of alcoholism. A number of studies have looked at these high-risk individuals and found some interesting results. One approach has been to identify young men who are not yet alcoholic but who have alcoholic parents. The non-alcoholic sons of alcoholics show greater tolerance for alcohol than do matched controls with a similar drinking history. This tolerance is not due to personality factors or to the ability to break down alcohol, and is reflected in improved psychomotor coordination and less subjective intoxication after a standard drink. In other words, after taking alcohol the sons of alcoholics are less clumsy and feel less drunk than the sons of non-alcoholics (Schuckit, 1984). These responses may be seen as a marker for individuals at risk, reflecting an inherited ability to tolerate some of the effects of alcohol. Other markers may include electroencephalographic (EEG) responses to a given stimulus. One such wave, the 'P300', shows a characteristic latency in individuals at risk, and also in their alcoholic parents. Long-term follow-up studies will be necessary to establish which of the individuals at risk actually develops a drinking problem.

It may be considered surprising that genetic factors have been shown to contribute to a complex behaviour such as alcoholism, and furthermore that individuals who are at risk may be identified in some families and some racial groups. Looking to the future, newly developed techniques such as 'genetic fingerprinting', which allow the precise identification of individuals and their characteristics, will greatly improve the power of family and group studies of alcoholism and possibly of other forms of addictive behaviour. It is simply not known whether any of these findings may be applicable to drug dependence, for there has been a paucity of biological research in this area.

Individual factors

In looking for the causes of dependence, individual characteristics appear to make the greatest contribution. Though originating at the molecular level, these characteristics are modified by learning and subsequently expressed as behaviour. Personality, temperament and interpersonal factors are also highly relevant.

Neuropeptides and opiate receptors

In the early 1970s, Kosterlitz and his workers in Aberdeen isolated some simple pentapeptides from the brain of the rat, which had the remarkable property of imitating the effect of morphine on other animal systems. In other words, the brain produces its own morphine-like chemicals which are collectively called the endogenous opiates or neuropeptides and were subsequently classed as the endorphins and enkephalins. It was later found that these neuropeptides act on opiate receptors scattered throughout the central nervous system and in a wide range of peripheral sites. Specific opiate antagonists such as naloxone and naltrexone have been synthesised, which act by having a very high affinity for these opiate receptors. Consequently effects of morphine such as respiratory depression following overdose can be reversed by administering an opiate antagonist.

The neuropeptide/opiate receptor system is now known to mediate a wide range of behaviours which are modified by morphine, such as analgesia, central reward tolerance and dependence. For example, giving endogenous opiates has been shown to lead to tolerance after just one injection, and withdrawal symptoms follow cessation of chronic administration in animal models (Hendrie, 1985). Also, the finding that naloxone can precipitate withdrawal in dependent animals strongly implicates the involvement of opiate receptors in this phenomenon.

It has been suggested that the exogenous opiates induce tolerance and dependence through an interaction with endogenous opioid mechanisms. For example, exogenous opiates may inhibit the synthesis and release of endorphins. Tolerance develops when the resultant decrease, or down-regulation, of endorphins induces a need for greater doses of exogenous opiate in order to maintain homeostasis. Neuroadaptation occurs and endorphin production is further reduced. If the exogenous opiates are stopped, the dependent system is devoid of all opiate inhibitory influences and enters a state of withdrawal. But evidence for this model is hard to find. The expected down-regulation of endorphins following chronic morphine use has not been demonstrated, and brain endorphin levels do not appear to be different in morphine-dependent rats.

Could changes in opiate receptor levels explain the acquisition of tolerance and dependence? It is clear that chronic administration of an

opiate antagonist leads to the up-regulation or increase in the number of
opioid receptors. However, it has been more difficult to demonstrate the
expected down-regulation in response to chronic morphine use, suggesting
that this is not an absolute requirement for the development of dependence.

There are neuropeptides which do not act on opiate receptors directly,
but appear to modify the phenomena of dependence. For example,
oxytocin facilitates the development of dependence on morphine, and
adrenocorticotrophin (ACTH) has some effects that may antagonise
endorphins. Hendrie (1985) proposed that aspects of the opioid withdrawal
syndrome may be due to the excitatory effects of ACTH at opiate
receptors.

Benzodiazepines and benzodiazepine receptors

In parallel with the isolation of opiate neuropeptides and receptors, the site
of action of benzodiazepines was investigated in order to understand some
of the mechanisms of benzodiazepine dependence. Ten years ago, specific
binding sites for benzodiazepines were found on the same protein as
receptors for GABA (gamma-aminobutyric acid), the main inhibitory
neurotransmitter in the brain. Among the many functions of the GABA–
benzodiazepine receptor complex is the mediation of anxiety. Benzodiazepines and 'benzodiazepine agonists' exert a powerful anxiolytic effect on
binding to the receptor, by enhancing the inhibitory effects of GABA.
Another class of drugs called 'benzodiazepine inverse agonists' have the
opposite action: by reducing the action of GABA they have the behavioural effect of increasing anxiety (File, 1988).

Although the mechanisms underlying benzodiazepine tolerance and
withdrawal are not known, there is some evidence for the existence of
endogenous inverse agonists which may have a role in the acquisition of
dependence. It is suggested that the withdrawal anxiety which follows the
cessation of chronic benzodiazepine administration is due to the revealed
action of these inverse agonists. A third group of drugs, called benzodiazepine antagonists, act at the same receptor site blocking the effects of both
benzodiazepine agonists and inverse agonists. Flumazenil is an example of
such an antagonist and may have therapeutic value in managing the
symptoms of benzodiazepine withdrawal.

Neurochemical reinforcement mechanisms

It is known that the repeated use of drugs of dependence partly results
from their powers of positive reinforcement—i.e. their use leads to
pleasurable feelings which in turn increase the likelihood of further

self-administration. There is now considerable evidence suggesting that addictive drugs derive their reinforcing effects by pharmacologically activating brain mechanisms involved in normal motivation and reward.

Animal studies have shown that electrode placement at a wide variety of sites within the brain is positively reinforcing. But stimulation in the lateral hypothalamic level of the median midbrain bundle and also in the ventral tegmentum is especially reinforcing. This functional connection has been called the 'ventral tegmental reward system', and the main site of action within it is the nucleus accumbens. Release of the neurotransmitter dopamine within this system is the critical event involved in reinforcement. The simplest model suggests that dopaminergic activation within the nucleus is rewarding and that any event that enhances dopaminergic transmission in this area of the brain should also be reinforcing.

There is good evidence that psychoactive stimulants, alcohol and opiates all activate the ventral tegmental dopamine system which leads to reinforcement. However, these substances act differently within the system. The use of stimulants such as amphetamines and cocaine leads to a functional increase in the levels of dopamine and other neurotransmitters within the nucleus accumbens. Opiates and alcohol, on the other hand, increase the firing of dopamine cells within the ventral tegmental area (Bozarth, 1988).

Effects of learning on opiate action and tolerance

A common analogy for the interaction of a specific receptor site and its drug is that of a lock and key, with the implication that this is a purely mechanical matter of fit. It is difficult on the basis of this model to account for the observation from animal work that behavioural manipulations affect the ability of naloxone to reverse some effects of opiates. The studies employ the technique of drug discrimination, in which a mouse may be trained to discriminate between an opiate and saline. This effect is susceptible to reversal by opiate antagonists such as naloxone. However, the ability of naloxone to reverse drug discrimination has been shown to vary with certain behavioural manipulations, such as altering the level or timing of the training doses of the given opiate. Other work has shown that contingencies which follow the training dose also influence the later response of an animal to a drug.

These studies, taken with other evidence summarised earlier (see page 9), illustrate some of the complex interactions between drug, receptor site and the individual, which influence the acquisition of dependence. At a higher level, the contribution of personality, mental illness and attitudes has received much attention.

Personality factors

Character flaws are often ascribed to an individual who has become dependent on drugs or alcohol. The popularly expressed view that 'there must be something wrong with them' is supported by numerous studies which suggest that the personality of a drug or alcohol user is in some way inadequate or immature. However, relatively few of these have used objective tests and proper selection criteria.

Many researchers have applied a standardised personality inventory to populations of substance misusers. The Eysenck Personality Inventory (EPI) as applied to opiate users shows that they do not appear to differ from normals on extroversion, but score higher on neuroticism than normals but lower than neurotic or alcoholic patients. Eysenck defined 'psychopath' as an individual who scores high on both the extroversion and neuroticism scales of the EPI, and on this criterion the scores of opiate users do not show the 'psychopathic pattern'. In the United States, the Minnesota Multiphasic Personality Inventory (MMPI) is the more widely used instrument, and some studies have found that opiate users score more highly on MMPI scales of psychopathic deviance. But this result could also be accounted for by greater delinquency in opiate users compared with non-users (Mott, 1972). Use of standardised measures of hostility has shown that institutionalised drug users show high levels of both hostility and self-punitiveness that may represent a generalised trait. Non-institutionalised users are probably more like the general population.

Much of the research in this area is flawed by the application of broad measures of personality to narrowly selected groups of subjects, such as young, institutionalised men. Nevertheless, while there is no evidence for an 'addictive personality type' common to substance misusers, there are indications that they show more 'neuroticism' and 'hostility' than do non-users. It is also a consistent finding that drug users are of average or above average intelligence, but this is scarcely a unique trait.

Another approach has attempted to link specific individual drives with patterns of addictive behaviour. Cloninger (1987) identified two types of alcohol abuse on the basis of alcohol-related symptoms and personality traits (see Table 1.1).

The development of type 1 'loss of control' alcoholism (the gamma alcoholism described by Jellinek) is associated with traits of a passive-dependent or anxious personality. These are the triad of: (i) high reward-seeking behaviour (that is, an individual who is emotionally dependent and sensitive), (ii) high harm avoidance (that is, one who is cautious, pessimistic and inhibited), and (iii) low novelty seeking (that is, one who is rigid and fussy about detail).

In contrast the development of type 2 'inability to abstain' alcoholism (the delta alcoholism of Jellinek) is associated with a triad of traits characteristic of an antisocial personality: (i) high novelty seeking (that is,

Table 1.1 Distinguishing characteristics of two types of alcoholism

Characteristic features	Type of alcoholism	
	Type 1	Type 2
1. Alcohol related problems:		
Usual age of onset (years)	After 25	Before 25
Spontaneous alcohol-seeking (inability to abstain)	Rare	Common
Psychological dependence (loss of control)	Common	Rare
2. Personality traits		
Novelty seeking	Low	High
Harm avoidance	High	Low
Reward dependence	High	Low

an individual who is impulsive, exploratory and excitable), (ii) low harm avoidance (that is, one who is confident and uninhibited), and (iii) low reward dependence (that is, one who is socially detached, independent and unemotional.

These groups should not be considered as discrete entities because many alcohol users have some features of each type. Rather, they are polar extremes of personality traits that vary continuously. Women predominantly develop loss of control (type 1), with later onset and more rapid progression of medical complications. Both types of alcoholism are common in men, but type 2 is more characteristic of those in hospital treatment.

A neurobiological learning model

Cloninger has attempted a synthesis of the neurological, psychological and pharmacological aspects of dependence in proposing a neurobiological learning model (Cloninger, 1987). Three main personality traits are characterised as novelty seeking, harm avoidance and reward dependence.

(1) 'Novelty seeking' refers to a heritable tendency towards frequent exploratory activity in response to novel or appetitive stimuli. It may reflect the activity of the dopaminergic ventral tegmental reward system previously described. Individuals with this tendency may find the use of opiates, stimulants and alcohol especially reinforcing.
(2) 'Harm avoidance' refers to a heritable tendency to respond intensely to aversive stimuli, thereby facilitating learning which inhibits behaviour, in order to avoid punishment or novelty. The functional basis of this system may be serotonergic neurones, especially within the septo-hippocampal system. Benzodiazepines (see page 20), other anti-anxiety drugs and alcohol are thought to act by enhancing GABA

inhibition of serotonergic neurones. Clinical and family studies show that low harm avoidance is associated with alcohol-seeking behaviour and high harm avoidance with susceptibility to loss of control.

(3) 'Reward dependence' occurs when learning is facilitated by a brain system that is activated primarily by onset of a reward or by threat of punishment. Noradrenalin may be the major neurotransmitter within this system, and the major pathways involve the locus coeruleus in the pons with projections to the entire cerebral cortex. It is suggested that individuals with low basal firing rates in this system are expected to respond to signals of reward, such as social approval. There is evidence for the hypothesis that reward dependence reflects neuroadaptive processes that are critical in the acquisition of tolerance to the sedative effects of alcohol and in susceptibility to 'loss of control' alcoholism.

Psychopathology and dependence

In considering the relationship between psychopathology and dependence it is important to distinguish correlates from causes. Certain disorders such as affective illness occur more frequently in substance misusers than in the general population, and this is a correlational relationship. In general terms, psychopathology does not appear to be an important predictor of substance use. As demonstrated, the results from family and genetic studies indicated that certain personality traits may be associated with the choice of drug used and patterns of use. There is a large body of work from the United States which suggests that 'antisocial personality disorder' is the most prevalent diagnosis being reported in up to 50% of substance misusers. The DSM-III diagnostic criteria used are broadly framed, and similar results are not found in studies conducted in this country.

The presence of concomitant mental illness undoubtedly modifies the course of addictive disorders, but there is no more specific association. For example, individuals whose predominant mood state is depressive in type may resort to stimulant drugs or to alcohol in order to 'self-medicate' symptoms. Psychotic symptoms such as hallucinations or delusional states may cue the use of anxiolytic drugs but this is uncommon. Of greater clinical importance are the many psychopathological disorders which appear to result from states of dependence (see Chapter 9). In summary, mental illness is rarely a true aetiological factor for dependence, but their coexistence has a profound effect on course and outcome for the individual.

Social and environmental factors

Life-event studies

Though addictive behaviours are related to criminality, unemployment, and family and social disruption, there is controversy about which is cause and which is effect. Rounsaville and co-workers (1982) tested the hypothesis that events which precede the onset of illicit drug use may be an indicator of different patterns of later drug-taking behaviour. By analysing the detailed life-records of nearly 400 opiate users, the following three groups were identified:

(1) an initial childhood trauma group, whose delinquent activity and drug abuse came only after substantial disruptive events occurring in childhood (31% of the sample);
(2) an early delinquency group in whom regular antisocial and delinquent activity preceded initial drug use (24% of the sample);
(3) an initial drug use group for whom criminal activity and disruptive life-events happened after the start of illicit drug use (45% of the sample).

They found that those drug users in the initial childhood trauma group were more likely to receive later diagnoses indicating severe personality difficulties such as antisocial personality disorder. These drug users fit the pattern described by psychoanalytic theorists who argue that disrupted parenting can lead to later vulnerability to depression, low self-esteem and disintegrative reactions under stress. The delinquent group later had more arrests than other drug users and were less likely to experience psychiatric disorder. They also seemed more able to cope than the initial childhood trauma group. The third group, whose initial drug use preceded either disruptive life-events or delinquency, were not as deviant or disturbed as those in the other two groups. But they clearly had their problems, mostly related to arrests for drug offences and to depressive symptoms.

This study does not attempt to discover 'why' these individuals first used drugs, but the results do show that the severity of problems surrounding current drug use may be related to previous experience of difficulty in upbringing and early criminality.

Social background and deprivation

It is a matter of observation that there are important differences between social classes in their use of drugs and alcohol, which are probably due to factors such as the availability and acceptability of certain drugs within a subgroup. Economic cost is not the sole determinant: for example, use of cocaine is reported among affluent city types and also in the unemployed youth of Southwark. Where drug use is prevalent, it is strongly associated with socio-economic deprivation. A study of heroin users in the Wirral found that 70% were unemployed and there were significant positive correlations with indices of deprivation such as overcrowding, single-parent households, households with three or more children and no access to a car (Parker *et al.*, 1987). However, the causal contribution of socio-economic deprivation has yet to be determined.

Availability

People use drugs and alcohol because they are there. But not everyone exposed to them does so and it is likely to be the same concurrence of individual factors, combined with acceptability and availability, which determine use. Some environments are more conducive to drug use than others, and in prison, for example, inmates who have never used any drugs before will often take indiscriminately whatever is available to them. The availability of alcohol and drugs in a society is determined by a range of factors from government policy to the activities of local drug dealers, all of which are responding in some way to an expressed demand for mood-altering substances.

Alcohol is our 'favourite drug' and its availability is determined by restrictions on sale and its price relative to personal disposable income. The recent liberalisation of pub opening hours led to an increase in the use of alcohol by some groups, and the overall consumption of alcohol is known to be very 'price sensitive'. Many drugs of dependence may be legitimately prescribed, and so the practices of the medical profession profoundly influence the availability of these drugs both for individuals and society. In the 1960s there was much concern over a small number of London physicians who created a local epidemic of heroin dependence by massive overprescribing. The same era also saw increases in the availability of prescribed amphetamines and barbiturates, to which the medical profession responded by adopting a voluntary ban on these drugs in some areas. This was followed by a national reduction in prescribing habits, and amphetamine prescriptions fell from four million in 1966 to one million in 1976. Barbiturate misuse has also fallen dramatically over the same period: it is now rarely prescribed and in consequence is less available. Use of these older sedatives has now been supplanted by the consumption of benzodiazepines, which account for over 90% of all sedative–hypnotic prescriptions. Licit availability of these drugs leads to one in five adults taking them in any one year, and illicit use is very common by, for example, opiate users. Availability of the more important drugs of abuse such as heroin, cocaine and amphetamines is such that, despite the efforts of customs and police, they are so readily obtained in most towns and cities that if a young person wishes to experiment with their use there is likely to be little obstacle to his or her doing so.

Peer influence and culture

Most young people are introduced to various forms of non-medical drug use by the encouragement of friends and associates of their own age and background. The activity of taking a drug then assumes a significance which goes beyond the immediate pharmacological effect and which in some way serves to reinforce the identity of the group. For example, the use of cannabis may have the function of inducing relaxation and group cohesion at a student party and the expression of cultural and religious values in a Rastafarian setting. Within a group, the use of drugs may become ritualised and acquire a jargon of its own. Use of this jargon then identifies an individual as a member of the wider subculture of drug users. In a culture with rapid changes of attitude and lifestyle, the use of various drugs and alcohol can become subject to 'fashionable' influences. Solvent abuse by young people appears to vary considerably in extent between various schools and towns and also from year to year. Patterns of alcohol use are especially influenced by trends within the advertising industry, which is currently targeting campaigns at the young and at women in particular in an effort to increase drinking by these groups. Religious beliefs also influence the acceptability and consumption of alcohol within a society. Among members of the Jewish faith, alcoholism is relatively rare as drunkenness is rejected and the ability to tolerate drink carries no status. Drinking alcohol has a ritualised place in this culture, which discourages overindulgence.

Sociological theories

Various sociological theories have attempted to look for causes of addiction in the quality and nature of the interaction between an individual and society. 'Deviancy amplification' occurs when society reacts against substance misuse by categorising it as 'deviant' and by introducing controls. The new social restraints lead to an intensification of the deviance, which in turn prompts greater social controls and so on. An application of this theory is seen in the stereotyping of drug users and their fixed and stereotyped views of police and treatment agencies, and in the frequent references by many countries to a 'war on drugs'. However, the notion that controls necessarily increase consumption is arguable.

Durkheim's concept of 'anomie' has also been applied to addictive behaviour. It is suggested that if people within a society fail to attain their objectives, such as status or influence, by legitimate means, they may use illegal or deviant methods instead. Drug use is then seen as a valid way of life which legitimises the user and imparts a sense of identity and role.

Conclusion

When presented with the tragedy of a young man drinking himself into a state of physical illness and mistreating his family, or a woman from an affluent background squandering her resources on heroin, there is a temptation to reach for the easy answers in response to the question 'Why did this happen?'. The causes seem so many and so intertwined that we try to keep things simple and commonly seize on one explanation, chosen almost at random. 'It is the fault of her family . . .', 'He has a weak personality . . .', 'She was always a rebel . . .', are frequent explanations. Yet the enormity of the task of trying to explain the causes of dependence in an individual should not preclude an attempt at understanding. This is important not only in appreciating the predicament of the individual drug or alcohol misuser but also in planning strategies for change. Effective therapies are more likely to develop if views on causation are clear.

References

Berridge V. and Edwards G. (1987) *Opium and the People: Opiate Use in Nineteenth-Century England*, 2nd edn (New Haven, CT: Yale University Press).

Bozarth M.A. (1988) Opioid reinforcement processes. In *Endorphins, Opiates and Behavioural Processes*, eds Rodgers R.J. and Cooper S.J. (Chichester: John Wiley), pp. 53–74.

Cloninger C.R. (1987) Neurogenetic adaptive mechanisms in alcoholism. *Science*, **236**, 410–415.

Cook C. (1988) The Minnesota Model in the management of drug and alcohol dependency: miracle, method or myth? Part 1. The philosophy and the programme. *Br. J. Addiction*, **83**, 625–634.

Edwards, G. (1986) The alcohol dependence syndrome: a concept as a stimulus to enquiry. *Br. J. Addiction*, **81**, 171–183.

Edwards G. and Gross M. (1976) Alcohol dependence: provisional description of a clinical syndrome. *Br. Med. J.*, **1**, 1058–1061.

Edwards G., Arif A. and Hodgeson R. (1981) Nomenclature and classification of drug- and alcohol-related problems: a WHO Memorandum. *Bull. World Health Organization*, **59**, 225–242.

File S.E. (1988) The benzodiazepine receptor and its role in anxiety. *Br. J. Psychiat.*, **152**, 599–600.

Goodwin D.W. (1984) Studies of familial alcoholism: a review. *J. Clin. Psychiat.*, **45**, 14–17.

Grant D.A.W. (1988) Genetic polymorphism in the alcohol metabolising enzymes as a basis for alcoholic liver disease. *Br. J. Addiction*, **83**, 1255–1259.

Heather N. and Robertson I. (1985) *Problem Drinking: The New Approach* (Harmondsworth: Penguin).

Heather N., Robertson I. and Davies P. (eds) (1985) *The Misuse of Alcohol: Crucial Issues in Dependence, Treatment and Prevention* (London: Croom Helm).

Hendrie C.A. (1985) Opiate dependence and withdrawal—a new synthesis? *Pharmacol., Biochem. Behav.*, **23**, 863–870.

Marlatt G.A. and George W.H. (1984) Relapse prevention: introduction and overview of the model. *Br. J. Addiction*, **79**, 261–273.

Mott J. (1972) The psychological basis of drug dependence: the intellectual and personality characteristics of opiate users. *Br. J. Addiction*, **67**, 89–99.

Parker H., Newcombe R. and Bakx K. (1987) The new heroin users: prevalence and characteristics in Wirral, Merseyside. *Br. J. Addiction*, **82**, 147–157.

Phillips G. T., Gossop M. and Bradley B. (1986) The influence of psychological factors on the opiate withdrawal syndrome. *Br. J. Psychiat.*, **149**, 235–238.

Room, R. (1985). Dependence and Society. *Br. J. Addiction*, **80**, 133–139.

Rounsaville, B.J., Weissman M.M., Wilber C.H. and Kleber H. (1982) Pathways to opiate addiction: an evaluation of differing antecedents. *Br. J. Psychiat.*, **141**, 437–446.

Royal College of Psychiatrists (1987) *Drug Scenes: A Report on Drugs and Drug Dependence by the Royal College of Psychiatrists* (London: Gaskell).

Saunders B. and Allsop S. (1987) Relapse: a psychological perspective. *Br. J. Addiction*, **82**, 417–429.

Schuckit M.A. (1984) Subjective responses of alcohol in sons of alcoholics and control subjects. *Arch. Gen. Psychiat.*, **41**, 879–884.

WHO (1964) Thirteenth Report of WHO Expert Committee on Addiction-producing Drugs. *Tech. Rep. Ser.* No. 273. (Geneva: World Health Organization).

Bibliography

Edwards G. and Busch C. (eds) (1981) *Drug Problems in Britain: A Review of Ten Years* (London: Academic Press).

Meyer R. E. (ed.) (1986) *Psychopathology and Addictive Disorders* (New York: Guilford Press).

Royal College of Psychiatrists (1987) *Drug Scenes: A Report on Drugs and Drug Dependence by the Royal College of Psychiatrists* (London: Gaskell).

2

Effects of Drugs of Dependence

Spencer Madden

Synopsis

The chapter deals with the short- and long-term effects of psychoactive drugs, particularly their effects on the brain, mind and behaviour. In discussing harmful results it should be noted that harm can ensue from misuse of a drug which affects the mind, although dependence on the preparation may not have developed. Misuse is here viewed as the non-medical use of a drug for its seemingly pleasant mental effects. Unintentioned damage can arise from casual, even single misuse, e.g. infection following non-sterile injection or accidental injury while intoxicated. There are many substances whose effects on the brain and mind can lead to misuse and dependence, but they can be grouped into a relatively small number of categories.

Tolerance and dependence

The repeated intake of most of the psychotropic drugs produces tolerance to their effects. Progressively larger amounts are then taken to ensure the desired results. Tolerance arises from three mechanisms: altered disposition of a drug within the body, diminished responsiveness of neurones directly affected by the substance, and homeostatic adjustments of neuronal systems not immediately disturbed by the compound.

The first process, of pharmacokinetic change, involves acceleration of drug metabolism. Psychotropic drugs undergo most of their metabolic inactivation within the liver. Their biotransformation is hastened by induction of the responsible enzymes. More rapid metabolism of drugs is quantitatively less important than the second process of pharmacodynamic changes in the nerve cells. The alterations counteract the acute effects of drugs on neuronal function. The neuroadaptive changes persist for some time after the particular drug is withdrawn; they then manifest themselves in an abstinence syndrome. The withdrawal discomfort can lead to further drug intake for its temporary relief; a state of physical dependence is thus established. Little is understood about the third process which determines tolerance, but learning responses play a role. The stimuli for the acquired responses include not only alterations of cerebral activity, but also external cues; tolerance develops more rapidly in laboratory animals if drug administration is repeated in a constant environment.

Between drugs of the same category (that is, between drugs whose effects on neuronal activity and mental processes carry strong similarities) cross-tolerance can occur, so that the repeated intake of one compound leads to tolerance to other drugs within its class. Cross-dependence also arises: the abstinence syndrome from sudden cessation of a particular drug is suppressed by consumption in adequate doses of a comparable substance.

Opioids

An opioid is a drug whose effects resemble those of morphine. An opiate is a substance that is naturally present in opium or that can be derived from opium by chemical manipulation. Morphine and codeine are found in opium; heroin is obtained by a simply achieved alteration of morphine. There are also preparations with morphine-like effects which are synthesised from sources other than opium; methadone (Dolophine) and pethidine (meperidine; Demerol) are examples. Strictly speaking, therefore, 'opioid' is a more generic title than 'opiate' although the two terms are sometimes used interchangeably.

Opioid drugs interact with certain receptor sites on neurones to exert an inhibitory effect on nerve impulses. There are naturally occurring substances in the nervous system which act on the same sites in a similar way; these endogenous opioids are members of the enkephalin, endorphin and dynorphin groups of peptide compounds. Repeated administration of an exogenous opioid drug leads to suppression of endogenous opioid activity; removal of the drug then produces an excitability of nervous tissue that is revealed as an abstinence syndrome and that lasts until endogenous activity returns to normal.

The well-known calming effects of opioids on the mind are enhanced by intravenous injection or by smoking. Heroin in particular when taken by these routes produces an intense if transient impression of pleasure. The feeling, or 'flash', can invoke a strong desire for its repetition. Repeated consumption of opioids leads to tolerance and to physical dependence. The tolerance is sometimes extreme, with a regular user able to survive otherwise lethal amounts.

There is a characteristic withdrawal syndrome which, with heroin, begins after a few hours of drug cessation, reaches a peak during the second and third days, and then subsides so that after a week the individual is largely, though not entirely, recovered. The withdrawal features from methadone are slower in onset, less severe in intensity, but more prolonged. Lassitude, anxiety, depression, restlessness and insomnia are prominent. There is an increased flow of saliva, nasal secretion and lachrymal fluid; sniffing, sneezing and running eyes develop. Pains occur in muscles, bones and joints. Anorexia, nausea, vomiting, colicky abdominal pains and diarrhoea ensue. The pupils are dilated; there is frequent yawning. The subject feels alternately hot and cold. The skin takes on a gooseflesh appearance which, combined with coldness, gives rise to the epithet 'cold turkey'. There is a slight rise in temperature and blood pressure; pulse rate may be increased or decreased.

Among opioid misusers mythology prevails about the severity of the abstinence syndrome. It is possible that the condition may be physically serious for those who are elderly or weakened by concomitant disease, but otherwise the discomfort can be likened to an uncomplicated episode of influenza—a condition that is unwanted but ends in recovery. Cross-dependence arises between opioids and forms the basis in treatment for substitution of an illicit or injectable drug by a legal or oral alternative.

The opioids may be administered by the four classical routes of ingestion: eating, sniffing, inhalation from smoking and injection. The choice is narrowed by the particular opioid and its preparations, and is of course affected by fashion. Heroin 'sublimes' when heated; that is, the drug passes from the solid to the gaseous form without an intervening liquid state. Therefore when powder containing heroin is warmed on metal foil the drug rises as fumes, leaving (usually though not always) the impurities behind. The heroin is then inhaled for rapid absorption through the vascular bed of the lungs. The method, which originated in the Far East, is known as 'chasing the dragon'; the user pursues the ascending smoke which is fancifully likened to a dragon's tail. 'Chasing' has the advantage of freedom from the medical hazards of injection and from the legal risks of possession of injection equipment containing traces of illicit drugs. The practice has the disadvantage of appearing relatively innocuous to the newcomer.

A major hazard from the intravenous injection of an opioid is overdosage. Acute opioid poisoning may be accidental or suicidal; it is also suspected that unusually potent preparations have been sold or given to particular users with homicidal intent. Death can be so quick that the subject is found lifeless, with needle and syringe still in the arm, and perhaps showing froth around the lips from oedema of the lungs. Opioid overdose should be strongly suspected by the combination of coma, pinpoint pupils and depression of breathing.

Injection into subcutaneous tissue or muscle, or leakage of injection material from a vein, can induce local tissue damage or infection that is due to contamination with adulterants and organisms rather than to the drug itself. The same applies to the important systemic complications of opioid use, including viral, bacterial and fungal infections. Unusual sequelae such as heroin nephropathy, transverse myelitis of the spinal cord, peripheral neuritis and acute myopathy have been tentatively attributed to immune reactions towards adulterants in illicit preparations. Additives include barbiturates and methaqualone to impart a psychoactive effect; quinine to simulate the bitter taste of heroin; and coffee, gravy browning, face powder and other materials to bestow the brownish colour so beloved in some countries by heroin dealers and their clients.

Specific opioids

An easily effected manipulation of morphine produces diacetylmorphine or diamorphine, better known as heroin. The drug passes more rapidly than morphine across the blood–brain barrier into cerebral tissues where it is hydrolysed to morphine. Both drugs are excreted and detected in the urine as morphine glucuronide. The greater part is excreted within a day, but traces are detectable for over 48 hours. Methadone has a long half-life in the plasma of one to one-and-a-half days; its effects are less euphoric though more prolonged than those of heroin.

Codeine and other weak substances such as pholcodine are available in proprietary cough medicines and analgesic mixtures that are subject to misuse and dependence. Dihydrocodeine (DF118; Paracodin) is prescribed in tablets or as ampoules for injection; the tablets, intended for swallowing, can be crushed and injected. Dextropropoxyphene (propoxyphene) is available in analgesic preparations that are associated with dependence and, more worryingly, with deaths from overdosage.

Pethidine (meperidine; Demerol) is prescribed for the relief of pain but is liable to misuse and dependence; the drug is unusual because high dosage can produce excitation, tremors, dilated pupils and convulsions. Dextromoramide (Palfium) and dihydromorphone (Dilaudid) are drugs of misuse and dependence. Dipipanone (Pipadone) and the antihistamine cyclizine (Marzine) are the active ingredients of the proprietary composition, Diconal; until prescribing regulations in the United Kingdom were tightened, misuse, dependence and overdoses from the preparation were frequent. Drug misusers sometimes invent their own combinations of an opioid with a sedative or stimulant drug.

Opioid antagonists and agonist–antagonists

It has already been noted that opioid drugs, and the endogenous opioid-like peptides whose actions they simulate, interact with receptor sites on neurones. There are three main classes of opioid receptor; the activation of a particular receptor subspecies leads to a specific spectrum of results.

Certain opioid drugs can combine with one or more type of recognition site in a manner which competitively blocks the binding and so antagonises the action of an opioid that is agonistic (active) at that site. The same drugs may have an agonistic effect on an alternative receptor class. Additionally an opioid can exert a weakly agonistic and partial action on a receptor locus, but by its presence competitively interferes with a more powerful drug at the same site. Through these rather complex interactions an opioid may be able to exert an antagonistic influence on other opioids or show both agonistic and antagonistic properties.

Naloxone (Narcan) is a pure antagonist used in the treatment of opioid overdosage, in the experimental assessment of opioid agonism and (because it precipitates withdrawal features in persons taking opioids) in the diagnosis of opioid dependence. Nalorphine (Nalline) and levallorphan (Lorfan) are predominantly antagonistic drugs but exert some agonistic effects, notably depression of breathing, in the absence of a stronger agonist. Pentazocine (Fortral, Talwin) is an agonist–antagonist analgesic which can cause dependence, and which induces withdrawal symptoms in persons dependent on other opioids, including methadone. Buprenorphine (Temgesic) is a weak agonist available as ampoules or as tablets for sublingual use; the tablets can be misused by injection and also by sniffing. Because it is a partial agonist it produces abstinence features in persons severely dependent on opioids, but can itself lead to dependence.

Cyclazocine and naltrexone block the euphoric results of heroin and have been used in the treatment of heroin dependence. Cyclazocine produces unwanted effects of sedation, dysphoria, hallucinations and illusions; its discontinuance provokes withdrawal features of dizziness or fainting though without craving or drug-seeking behaviour. Naltrexone, which is a long-acting, pure antagonist, lacks these side-effects and appears more advantageous.

Designer drugs

Compounds similar to pethidine (meperidine; Demerol) and to the stimulant drug mephentermine (Wyamine) have been synthesised specifically for misuse. Naturally their dissemination and intake take place without the years of careful investigation that precede the release of a product from the pharmaceutical industry. Ill effects, notably parkinsonism, have arisen. The commercial availability of the chemical precursors of designer drugs can be inhibited by legal regulations.

Sedatives

The drugs described in this category have all been shown to provoke misuse and dependence. They share an abstinence syndrome in which anxiety, tremulousness, convulsions and hallucinations can develop. This drug class, perhaps more than others, is subject to changes in the popularity of its individual members. The vicissitudes stem from eventual recognition by doctors of their disadvantages as much as from shifts in other socio-economic determinants of drug acceptability and availability.

Alcohol

Further chemical synonyms, not employed hereafter in this section, are ethyl alcohol and ethanol. There is animal and human experimental evidence to indicate that in small amounts, found in a standard drink or less, the drug has a stimulating effect on the central nervous system. Quantities that are usually imbibed exert a depressant action. Since the cerebral functions that evolved late in evolution to ensure caution and social control are affected first by alcohol, the substance has a disinhibiting as well as a euphoric result. Large amounts are more obviously sedative, with impairment of concentration, speech and locomotion. Coma can ensue, with death from depression of the brain centres controlling circulation and breathing, or from inhalation of vomit. Intoxication can also lead to accidents; a head injury may be misdiagnosed as drunkenness, with a fatal outcome from lack of treatment.

Alcohol produces, as an acute effect on neuronal membranes, a disorder or fluidity that inhibits the transmission of nerve impulses and so depresses the nervous system. Repeated exposure to alcohol promotes a neuroadaptive change, with enhanced membrane rigidity that counteracts the acute effect of the substance. More alcohol is therefore required to obtain its results; the consequence is tolerance. When the depressant effect of alcohol on nerve activity is removed by withdrawal of the drug, the central nervous system undergoes a phase of overactivity that endures until the neuroadaptive change declines. The phase of rebound hyperexcitability is manifested as an abstinence syndrome. A concurrent though less important mechanism exists for tolerance: alcohol induces an increase of the enzymes in the liver that promote its metabolism.

A detailed description of alcohol misuse and dependence, and of its many organic, psychological and social sequelae, forms a project too large for inclusion here. Paradoxically the medical complications arise in part from the relative impotence of alcohol as a psychoactive agent. Unlike the majority of drugs that affect the mind, copious and therefore potentially damaging amounts of alcohol are required to produce its desired psychoactive effect. The ill effects that are usually described are listed in table 2.1.

Table 2.1   Consequences of alcohol misuse and dependence

Medical	Psychological	Social

Injuries
  Death from acute poisoning (from alcohol
  alone or in conjunction with other
  sedatives)
Nervous system
  Peripheral neuritis
  Pressure damage to individual nerves
  ('Saturday night palsy')
  Global brain damage
  Wernicke's encephalopathy
  Korsakoff's psychosis
  Degeneration of the corpus callosum
  (Marchiafava's disease)
  Degeneration of the pons (central pontine
  myelosis)
  Degeneration of the cerebellum
Respiratory tract
  Infections
  Carcinoma of the larynx
Gastrointestinal tract
  Carcinoma of the oropharynx
  Carcinoma of the oesophagus
  Gastritis
  Enteritis
  Nutritional deficiencies
  Carcinoma of the rectum
  Pancreatitis, acute and chronic
  Fatty liver
  Hepatitis
  Cirrhosis
The blood
  Anaemias
  Macrocytosis
  Leucopenia
  Thrombocytopenia
  Rebound thrombocytosis
Cardiovascular system
  Hypertension
  Stroke
  Alcoholic heart muscle disease
  Arrhythmias
Muscles
  Myopathy, acute and chronic
Endocrine system
  Impotence
  Male infertility
  Cushingoid syndrome
Bones
  Osteoporosis
  Avascular necrosis of femoral head
	Anxiety
	Depression
	Morbid sexual
	  jealousy
		Impaired
		  interpersonal
		  relationships
		Separation,
		  divorce
		Crime
		Occupational
		  decline

Medical	Psychological	Social
Kidneys		
Nephropathy		
Metabolism		
Hypoglycaemia		
Glucose intolerance		
Exacerbation of acute porphyria		
Exacerbation of cutaneous hepatic		
porphyria		
Exacerbation of gout		
Fetus		
Fetal alcohol effects		

Benzodiazepines

This class of sedative–hypnotic is the category most widely prescribed for minor emotional problems. Awareness of the dependence-producing liability of benzodiazepines is leading doctors and patients towards their avoidance in favour of non-drug alternatives or towards their employment for short periods of two to four weeks. Several of the benzodiazepines are transformed, mostly in the liver, to metabolites that are also active. As with barbiturates the liability of particular benzodiazepines to produce craving and dependence is said to depend on the duration of activity of the drugs and on their active metabolism. The presumption is that the substances with shorter half-lives in the plasma and so with briefer activity provoke withdrawal symptoms more rapidly and frequently during repeated administration. Benzodiazepines with relatively short half-lives, usually of 6–12 hours, and with inactive glucuronidated metabolites, include oxazepam (Serax), lorazepam (Ativan) and triazolam (Halcion). Yet the dependence potential relies heavily on potency. Lorazepam (Ativan), with its high potency, is the benzodiazepine compound most likely to produce severe dependence.

There are specific benzodiazepine binding sites within the brain that are associated with the receptor sites for the neuroinhibitor substance gamma-aminobutyric acid (GABA). Occupancy by benzodiazepines of their particular recognition sites promotes the depressant effects of GABA on brain functions and so induces sedation and sleep.

Abrupt suspension of the regular intake of a benzodiazepine can provoke a severe abstinence syndrome with anxiety, tremor, convulsions and delirium. The features resemble those induced by rapid withdrawal of alcohol or barbiturates except that fits are less likely to follow cessation of alcohol. Indeed, a common cause of fits in severe problem drinkers is discontinuance of a benzodiazepine that has been unwisely prescribed over a long period. Cross-dependence exists between individual benzodiazepines and between them and alcohol. The latter feature allows therapeutic usage of a short course of a benzodiazepine in decreasing dosage to alleviate the alcohol withdrawal syndrome.

There are patients who have been taking benzodiazepines on prescription over long periods. In such patients gradual withdrawal of benzodiazepines in a regimen that is phased over a term of weeks or months avoids the dramatic features described above but can lead to lengthy and distressing symptoms (Ashton, 1984). They include anxiety, panic attacks, phobias, depression and depersonalisation. Concentration and memory can be impaired; fatigue, drowsiness or insomnia may ensue. Palpitations, flushing, sweating and gastrointestinal complaints sometimes supervene. Pains, unusual tactile sensations or numbness, and sensitivity to sight, sounds, smell or taste are not uncommon. Muscle weakness or twitching and unsteadiness in standing or walking are other symptoms that can develop. The features are not attributable to recurrence of the original symptoms for which benzodiazepines were prescribed. They can commence while long-term medication continues, presumably because the advance of tolerance interferes with drug suppression of withdrawal symptoms. The condition may last for months, with full recovery taking up to a year or more.

An overdose of a benzodiazepine alone is unlikely to prove fatal. The combination of a high amount of a benzodiazepine with another cerebral depressant, such as alcohol, is hazardous, as is a benzodiazepine overdose in a person affected by physical illness. Benzodiazepines interfere with driving skills. Long-acting compounds such as nitrazepam (Mogadon), flurazepam (Dalmane), and flunitrazepam (Rohypnol), when taken for sleep, continue to exert a sedative action on brain function the following morning.

The majority of people who take benzodiazepines receive the medication on prescription. Illicit drug users may also consume benzodiazepines, usually intermittently, for a number of reasons. The psychotropic effect can be perceived as exhilarating and may be enhanced by the injection of a crushed tablet or the contents of a capsule; misusers of other drugs may seek through benzodiazepines temporary relief of psychological distress; although opioids and benzodiazepines are not cross-dependent, the latter can be taken to blunt opioid withdrawal symptoms.

Barbiturates

Reputedly named after a barmaid called Barbara from a Munich beer cellar, the barbiturates were the most commonly prescribed sedative during the middle years of the present century. They include amylobarbitone (Amytal) and its sodium salt; pentobarbitone (Nembutal) and its sodium compound; quinalbarbitone (Seconal) and its sodium derivatives; and butobarbitone (Soneryl; Butisol). Tuinal contains the sodium salts of amylobarbitone and quinalbarbitone. Phenobarbitone, which is commonly used for epilepsy, is a long-acting barbiturate that rarely attracts misuse and dependence.

It appears that barbiturates exert part of their depressant action in the central nervous system by occupancy of recognition sites that are located near the receptors for the neuroinhibitory agent gamma-aminobutyric acid. In this respect barbiturates resemble benzodiazepines, but differences exist between the effects of the two drug categories, especially in the lethality of high doses of the former.

Barbiturates induce dependence with a withdrawal syndrome after abrupt cessation that is similar to, but perhaps more severe than, that which follows rapid termination of benzodiazepines. Overdose of barbiturates may be life-threatening even in the absence of alcohol, of other drugs or physical illness. For these reasons the prescribing preference of doctors has moved from barbiturates to benzodiazepines. During the 1970s barbiturate misuse became popular among illicit drug takers in London who often injected preparations manufactured for oral consumption. Overdoses, tissue damage around injection sites, and social deterioration were prominent features until the custom declined in popularity.

Other sedatives

Chlormethiazole (Heminevrin) is a sedative and anticonvulsant that effectively suppresses alcohol withdrawal features. The proneness of the compound to misuse and dependence has generally led to its replacement for this purpose by regimes consisting of a short course of a benzodiazepine drug.

Methaqualone (Quaalude, Revonal, Sopor) has been used as a sedative and hypnotic. The drug underwent a misuse vogue in the 1970s. It is now infrequently employed for non-medical purposes except as a furtive addition to powders containing, or allegedly containing, heroin.

Compounds derived from the chloral molecule are sometimes prescribed as sedatives or hypnotics and are vulnerable to misuse. Chloral hydrate, dichloralphenazone (Welldorm) and ethchlorvynol (Placidyl) are examples.

Glutethimide (Doriden) and meprobamate (Equanil, Miltown) are sedative hypnotics which can provoke misuse but are now rarely prescribed.

Antihistamines are taken legitimately to counter allergies, travel sickness and other forms of nausea and vomiting. They tend to possess a sedative side-effect which occasionally leads to their misuse, alone or in conjunction with other drugs. Diphenhydramine (Benadryl) has been marketed in combination with methaqualone as a proprietary preparation (Mandrax) that was formerly widely misused; in Britain misuse of the composition ceased almost overnight when legal regulations to control the possession of methaqualone were introduced. Cyclizine (Marzine), another antihistamine, and the opioid dipipanone are the active constituents of the compound Diconal whose misuse in Britain was also quickly curtailed by legal restrictions on prescribing of dipipanone. Cyclizine and other sedatives are sometimes injected simultaneously with oral methadone in the hope of obtaining rapid euphoria.

Stimulants

Caffeine

The most commonly taken stimulant is caffeine, present in tea, coffee, cocoa, chocolate and cola-flavoured drinks. Caffeine exerts a mildly activating effect on the brain and mental processes. Allegations that caffeine is a major source of harm to other organs are offered from time to time, and refuted. A high level of consumption, in the order of six or more cups of coffee a day, is associated with caffeinism. The syndrome involves anxiety, tremor, palpitations, irritability and headache; lethargy and depression have been also described. Withdrawal of caffeine is reported to produce headache and emotional uneasiness (Griffiths *et al.*, 1986). Consumption of caffeine is so widespread that evidence of harm would be obvious if the practice were often injurious.

Amphetamine-like drugs

Substances within this category have a stimulant action on the central nervous system and a peripheral effect that activates the sympathetic system. Their central stimulant action can lead to misuse and dependence. Several drugs in the group suppress appetite; their prescription for this purpose has induced dependence among patients. Amphetamine (Benzedrine) and its analogues dextroamphetamine (Dexedrine) and methylamphetamine (Methedrine) exert their central activity by release of the neurotransmitter agents noradrenaline and dopamine, by inhibition of neuronal re-uptake of the agents and perhaps by a direct agonistic effect on the receptor sites for the two neurotransmitters.

There are a number of drugs which possess similar central stimulant and peripheral sympathomimetic actions. Their chemical structures resemble that of amphetamine. Misuse of phenmetrazine (Preludin), diethylpropion (Apisate, Tenuate), methylphenidate (Ritalin), phentermine (Duromine) and phenylpropanolamine has been described.

Tranylcypromine (Parnate) is a monoamine oxidase inhibitor that is employed for the treatment of depression. Unlike other inhibitors of monoamine oxidase the drug has a chemical structure allied to amphetamine and is subject to misuse.

Various plants contain ephedrine, whose structure and activities also resemble those of amphetamine. Ephedrine is employed medically, mainly for the symptomatic relief of bronchospasm and nasal congestion. Ephedrine and its analogue pseudoephedrine are available in proprietary mixtures. In these forms the two drugs, and ephedrine in other preparations, are occasionally associated with misuse or dependence.

Tolerance develops to amphetamine and allied compounds, as does physical dependence. Sudden termination of prolonged use is followed by several days of lassitude and low mood. The physical nature of the symptoms is demonstrated by an objective withdrawal feature. During chronic amphetamine intake the electroencephalogram shows suppression of rapid eye movement (REM) sleep; drug withdrawal temporarily provokes a rebound excess of REM sleep. The condition, although possessing a physical basis, does not require medication.

Amphetamines are taken by mouth, by sniffing or by intravenous injection. Since doctors became reluctant to prescribe amphetamines the drugs have been manufactured in illegal laboratories. Much amphetamine usage is of the casual or recreational type which does not as a rule bring drug takers to the attention of the medical services, though the risk of infections from shared syringes and needles is always a possibility. Those who develop dependence on an amphetamine can take the drug daily over a period of months or years. A pattern that is more disruptive to the individual consists of an extremely rapid repetition of intake that lasts until supplies and drug user are exhausted. This type of sequence resembles 'runs' of intense cocaine administration.

Acute toxicity from amphetamine-like drugs leads to anxiety, restlessness, hallucinations, violence to self or others, and hypertension. Convulsions, coma and death may ensue. Chronic intoxication is associated with a psychosis, of which paranoid delusions, hallucinations (auditory, visual or tactile), overactivity, repetitive behaviour and aggression are features. Although thought disorder is not prominent, the state resembles schizophrenia. Amphetamine psychosis usually remits within days or weeks of drug cessation.

On rare occasions amphetamine usage can lead to bleeding inside the skull that is subarachnoid or intracerebral in origin. Another complication is occlusion of the cerebral vessels, with angiographic appearance of 'beading' and focal signs of damage to nervous tissue.

Khat

The preparation consists of leaves of the evergreen plant *Catha edulis* which is grown in the Yemen countries and nearby regions of Africa. Khat is chewed for its stimulant effects. Over 20 compounds are present In the plant, several of which are similar in chemical structure to amphetamine. The main component is cathinone, whose effects parallel those of amphetamine.

Khat consumption generally takes place as a group activity, conducted after work. The mild euphoria and promotion of conversation that accompany its use might be considered to offer harmless recreational benefit, but khat intake can lead to psychological dependence, headaches, anorexia and constipation. Impaired working ability, nutritional deficiency and reduced resistance to infection can develop. Paralytic ileus of the bowel has been noted.

The potency and therefore the price of khat decline within hours of removal of leaves from the plant. Perhaps for this reason the preparation is rarely encountered outside its area of growth. There is, however, some export by air to other countries for consumption by immigrants who acquired a liking for khat in their native countries. Overindulgence when a supply arrives can elicit a transient amphetamine-like psychosis.

The social and economic disadvantage of khat have compelled governments to adopt measures against its production and consumption (Drake, 1988).

Cocaine

The shrub *Erythroxylon coca* is the source of the stimulant drug cocaine. The plant is native to Andean regions of Bolivia and Peru where for centuries its leaves have been chewed by peasants to relieve fatigue and hunger. During the 1970s the expanded illicit market for cocaine led to extensive planting of coca bushes not only in Bolivia and Peru, but also in other countries of South America.

Cocaine, in the form of its hydrochloride salt, had already become available to doctors towards the end of the nineteenth century. Its local anaesthetic properties were a boon to ophthalmic and dental patients for decades. More regrettably a German doctor, dependent on morphine, noticed that cocaine counteracted the somnolence induced by the opioid. For a period Sigmund Freud advocated and prescribed cocaine as an alleged remedy for morphine dependence and for depression.

Cocaine preparations can be swallowed, injected, sniffed or smoked. Cocaine hydrochloride is the active compound in both pharmaceutical and street cocaine. The simultaneous injection of this salt and of an opioid, usually heroin, is known as 'speedballing'. Coca paste is a crude extract of coca leaf which contains high concentrations of cocaine hydrochloride and cocaine sulphate. Smoking coca paste produces a quick euphoria similar to that from intravenous injection, and this practice spread through South America and elsewhere from the early 1970s.

Cocaine freebase, in which cocaine is freed from hydrochloride or sulphate salts, was developed in the United States in the mid 1970s. When freebase is smoked, the cocaine is rapidly absorbed through the lungs and passes by a short route of blood circulation to the brain. The effects of smoking freebase are felt some 8 seconds after inhalation. 'Crack', or rock cocaine, consists of small crystal-like pellets of freebase that are ready for immediate smoking without further chemical processing. The terms derive respectively from the cracking sound of the material when heated and from its appearance.

Cocaine appears to exert its stimulant effect on the nervous system through an increase in activity of the transmitter agents dopamine and noradrenaline. Following intravenous injection, inhalation or sniffing, there is a feeling of intense pleasure and excitement. The 'rush', as it is called, lasts for some seconds and is followed by a less vivid state of enjoyment and exhilaration. The euphoric condition subsides within 30 minutes; it may be replaced by anxiety, tremulousness, depression, irritability, insomnia and the craving for more cocaine. Repeated intoxication can produce hallucinations in several sensory modalities. Voices call out the user's name; lights sparkle in the periphery of vision ('snow lights'); insects are felt in the skin ('cocaine bugs', 'formication') so that the body surface may be damaged from scratching. A paranoid state can develop in which the drug taker imagines pursuers or victimisers. Acting on these delusions, or more simply from irascible oversensitivity, the cocaine user may be violent.

Tolerance develops to cocaine. Metabolic or dispositional changes are insufficient to account for the substantial degree of tolerance that can develop, and adaptive changes in the nervous system, as yet inadequately understood, are undoubtedly influential. The drug itself is quickly transformed by esterase enzymes in the liver and plasma to water-soluble products that are excreted in the urine, chiefly as benzoylecgonine and ecgonine methyl ester. Depending on the method employed for analysis, cocaine metabolites are detectable in the urine for a period of 2 to 6 days after consumption.

It has been a matter of uncertainty whether the anhedonia that follows the pleasurable state induced by cocaine is a psychological reaction to the loss of enjoyment or represents a physical disturbance, perhaps an abstinence syndrome. The disagreeable features are not provoked by the sporadic, occasional use of cocaine, and their development in regular heavy users within less than an hour of drug intake is unusual for a withdrawal syndrome. Yet their consistent pattern, their relief by further drug consumption and their gradual abatement during an abstinent period of weeks suggest a physical basis of some kind.

It is arguable that although increased neuronal release by cocaine of the transmitter substances dopamine and noradrenaline contributes to the gratification and excitement of its administration, the process eventually depletes the brain of these transmitters. The depletion, combined with the short half-life (1 hour) of cocaine, may help to account for the quick succession of pleasure and displeasure that arises and for the rapid repetition of cocaine intake which ensues (Washton and Gold, 1987). If this explanation is correct, then the onset of displeasure could not be viewed as a withdrawal feature consequent on a neuroadaptive reaction to the acute actions of the drug.

The rapid alternation of euphoria and dysphoria, combined with impairment of judgement and self-control, can lead to 'runs' lasting for days in which cocaine administration is frequently repeated until supplies are consumed. Other substances, such as alcohol or opioids, may then be taken to excess to counteract subjective distress.

The somatic ill effects of cocaine are local and general. Skin ulcers around injection sites are attributable to the action of the drug in constricting nearby blood vessels rather than to infection. Similarly the nasal discharges and the perforations of the nasal septum that follow repeated cocaine sniffing are due to alternations of constriction and reactive congestion of blood vessels within the nose. As with other drugs that are injected illicitly, generalised infections or infections of specific organs such as the heart can follow the use of contaminated material or equipment. Persons who misuse cocaine or other drugs by routes that do not involve injections are at risk of systemic infection such as AIDS or hepatitis if they resort to female or male prostitution to fund their supply (see chapter 8).

Acute fatalities can follow cocaine administration (Arif, 1987). Their number is increasing in North America because of the spread of smoking practices that favour the rapid intake of high amounts of cocaine. Two common patterns are described. The most frequent involves the onset of convulsions and respiratory failure. The second pattern arises from stimulant effects on the cardiovascular system that singly or in combination can be quickly lethal; they comprise hypertension, tachycardia, abnormal heart rhythms, angina, myocardial infarction and bleeding into the brain. There is a further fatal route in which delirium develops, with clouding of consciousness, delusions, paranoid thoughts, and sudden death without convulsions. Perhaps, as with certain rapid deaths from sniffing volatile inhalants, the coalescence of overactivity and a toxic effect on the heart explains the latter fatalities.

Cocaine can precipitate a psychosis of a less dramatic nature that takes days or weeks to subside. In this respect the disorder resembles the psychosis induced by amphetamines. Withdrawal of cocaine after long-term usage can be succeeded by a prolonged mood of depression; the precipitation of a lengthy depressive disorder by abstention occurs with other psychoactive substances, notably the benzodiazepines.

Cannabis

The substance is derived from a shrub variously known as *Cannabis sativa*, *Cannabis indica* or Indian hemp. The flowering tops of the plant contain the greatest concentrations of its psychoactive constituents. Over 60 agents, known as cannabinoids, are distinctive to the plant. The leading psychoactive compound is the laevo isomer of Δ^9 tetrahydrocannabinol (Δ^9THC).

Cannabis is distributed in three forms: as a herbal product, as a resin and as an oil. In this order the materials possess progressively larger quantities of Δ^9THC and other cannabinoids. World-wide there are over a hundred terms for cannabis and its preparations.

Cannabis products can be taken by mouth, but are commonly smoked to achieve a more rapid and more powerful psychoactive effect. The initial effects consist of mild euphoria and relaxation, with an early vivacity and loquacity that soon tend towards a contented languor. Sensations appear more vivid and enjoyable; speech becomes long-winded, interrupted by breaks in the chain of thought, and fails to reach its end-point. Inattention, introspection and reduced sensitivity to the moods of companions can develop. Time appears to pass more slowly. Larger doses of cannabis, especially in naive users, may induce tremulousness, depersonalisation, hallucinations and paranoid ideas. Repetition or 'flashback' of the mental results of cannabis can recur at intervals unassociated with recent drug consumption. Cannabis can also precipitate recurrences of LSD experiences in persons who have taken the hallucinogen.

The immediate somatic changes include reddening of the conjunctivae, dry mouth and fast pulse. Hypertension is found as a temporary result, although the blood pressure can drop below normal on sitting up or standing.

The blood level of Δ^9THC falls quickly in the first 30 minutes after smoking, then more slowly, with a plasma half-life of about 19 hours. Its metabolites, some of which are psychoactive, are removed more slowly; their half-life is around 50 hours. Twenty-five to thirty per cent of Δ^9THC and its products remain in the body after a week; they are especially retained in lipid tissue and therefore remain within the nervous system. The possible ill effects of prolonged storage in the brain and elsewhere are unknown, although the accumulation could play a role in the psychotic reactions and personality abnormalities associated with high intake of cannabis.

Cannabis is the most extensively used illicit drug. The majority of those who take it are not harmed, but adverse consequences undoubtedly occur. In the United States there is an over-representation of cannabis smokers among drivers implicated in fatal accidents, and studies in volunteers in experimental conditions indicate that driving performance is impaired. Contrary to a popular misconception, dependence can develop. As well as other hazards, dependence exposes users to legal risks from drug-seeking behaviour if they participate in illicit distribution of the drug to finance and ensure their own supply. The abstinence features include restlessness, irritability, insomnia, anorexia and weight loss (Jones *et al.*, 1975).

Heavy cannabis intake can generate an acute psychotic illness that shows schizophreniform and hypomanic aspects, but subsides within a relatively brief interval of a few hours to seven days. An increasing body of reports describes a more prolonged though still time-limited psychosis which resembles schizophrenia in those who take cannabis regularly. There remain doubts whether extensive consumption of the drug is a cause or an accompaniment of the more enduring psychotic states. The close temporal association of cannabis intake followed by the onset of prolonged psychosis make it likely that the drug can act to precipitate a protracted psychotic condition. It is known that cannabis exacerbates schizophrenia in patients whose clinical state has been controlled by neuroleptics.

A group of features known as the 'amotivational syndrome' is shown by some chronic cannabis users. Lack of drive, deficient concentration and indifference to accepted social values are prominent. The features resemble the acute effects of cannabis so may indicate a long-term effect of the drug. On the other hand the characteristics could reflect the personalities of those who choose a life-style that embodies regular cannabis consumption. The issue is undecided.

Cerebral damage from frequent cannabis intake has been suspected, but examination of the brain by computed tomography and by blood flow measurements does not reveal cerebral atrophy (Ashton, 1987).

Harm to the lungs can follow repeated smoking of cannabis, with wheezing and sputum production and with forced expiratory volume decreased relative to forced vital capacity. Cannabis is generally smoked in a mixture with tobacco, but among males the detrimental effect of the mixture on pulmonary function is greater than from tobacco alone. The drug exerts a mild suppressant effect on the immune system.

Cannabis reduces the number and motility of spermatozoa; it is unclear whether the drug diminishes male fertility. There are conflicting reports on the effect of cannabis on the male sex hormone. The effects on female sex hormones and reproduction are not known. There are suggestions that cannabis may damage chromosomes; Δ^9THC crosses the placenta (and also enters breast milk). However, neither genetic defects nor intrauterine damage have been noted.

Cannabinoids, including the synthetic compounds nabilone and levonantradol, have been utilised in therapy. The preparations relieve nausea from anticancer drugs, reduce spasticity, are anticonvulsant, and lower eye pressure in glaucoma. Their possible immunosuppressive activity poses at least a theoretical risk during antiemetic use for cancer chemotherapy. In general the psychoactive and cardiovascular effects of cannabinoids have limited their therapeutic usefulness.

Hallucinogens

A hallucination may be defined as a perception that originates from a process within the brain and not from an actual sensory event. Drugs that produce hallucinations exert other important effects: illusions (altered perceptions of sensations), delusions (false beliefs incompatible with the subject's background and not amenable to reason) and mood alterations. There are over a hundred plants, including many fungi, that contain hallucinogens. Among native peoples, especially in South America, preparations of the plants have been deliberately consumed for their psychotropic effects. There are also hallucinogenic compounds of a synthetic nature.

LSD

LSD or lysergic acid diethylamide is the most widely known drug in this category. It is a laboratory derivative of the alkaloids found in the ergot fungus *Claviceps purpurea*, and a liquid preparation of it may be absorbed on to other materials, such as blotting paper; the drug is also distributed in small flat strips known as 'microdots'.

The effects of LSD develop gradually, to reach a height after 2 to 4 hours. Illusions are often prominent. Colours may appear vividly; objects are sharply outlined and can seem to approach or recede or, whilst stationary, to expand or contract. Hallucinations, if they arise, are usually visual. Synaesthesiae can occur, in which a sensation in one modality evokes perceptions in another; sounds may be seen and colours heard. The body image can be disturbed so that the body, or a part of it, appears to enlarge or shrink.

Mood changes are intense, various and labile. Euphoria, ecstasy or excitement can pivot to depression, anxiety or fear. A 'bad trip', in which the predominant mood becomes dysphoric, is a frequent and unpredictable occurrence that can follow a succession of pleasant LSD experiences; the dysphoria is often linked to disturbing hallucinations. A depressed mood can arise as an acute effect of the drug or follow during the subsequent day; in the latter case the low mood endures for a day or two.

The author has given LSD to patients. This took place at a time when the drug had a vogue as an aid to psychotherapy. Therapists and patients believed that under its influence events of psychodynamic importance would be relived. The patients experienced the predicted effect. Later the drug came to achieve cult status among intellectuals, who considered that with its help they would achieve profound religious or mystical insights. The two examples illustrate how expectations of the effects of a drug help to determine its results.

The LSD experience begins to decline some 12 hours after taking the drug. Occasionally features induced by LSD recur days, weeks or months after drug ingestion. Flashbacks' of this nature (also known as the 'Hyde effect' from the fictional character described by Robert Louis Stevenson), usually occur without an obvious precipitant, though they can be evoked by another drug such as cannabis. Extreme instances of LSD consumption in which the user takes the drug repetitively over a phase of a few days or weeks are uncommon; perhaps not surprisingly the practice can induce a psychosis which mimics schizophrenia, but subsides within weeks. Withdrawal symptoms and signs do not occur with LSD although tolerance rapidly develops. When used in treatment it was quite usual for the initial dose level of 50 μg to be raised after half a dozen administrations to amounts between 400 and 800 μg.

The mood changes, with accompanying hallucinations when present, have brought about injuries and deaths. The tragedies follow elation and overconfidence, panicky conduct to avoid a fearful experience, or depression with suicidal thinking.

The somatic consequences of LSD are mainly those of increased activity of the sympathetic nervous system. They comprise dilatation of the pupils, tremor, fast pulse and a rise of blood pressure and temperature. Nausea, dizziness and muscle weakness can also supervene.

The mechanism of action of LSD is not quite clear. A portion of its molecule resembles the neurotransmitter serotonin (5-hydroxytryptamine, 5-HT). It has been proposed that LSD, and the drugs mescaline and psilocin, produce their psychotomimetic effects through an agonistic action on the presynaptic 5-HT receptors.

Mescaline

The mescal cactus, found in Mexico and neighbouring areas of the United States, contains the hallucinogenic agent, mescaline. The cactus has been chewed by Indians in slices or buttons which are referred to as 'peyote' or 'peyotl'. The practice has been copied by Caucasians.

Psilocybin: psilocin

These twin substances are the active components of *Psilocybe semilanceata* (Europe) and *P. mexicana* (N. America). The somewhat forbidding name refers to the 'magic mushroom', which grows in a diversity of climates and regions. Its growing season is the same as for common edible mushrooms, namely late summer and autumn. The psychedelic result requires ingestion of a handful or more of the mushrooms, whose potency is enhanced by heating. In the United Kingdom it is an offence to possess the mushrooms if they have been so treated.

The effects of psilocybin and psilocin, including their transience, resemble those of other hallucinogens. Users are sometimes brought to hospital because of acute dysphoria, but are ordinarily fit for discharge by the following day.

Other hallucinogens

Amanita muscaria is a vividly coloured fungus that is found, albeit sparsely, in many regions. The plant was formerly consumed by Siberian shamans to induce trances, as well as by Viking warriors. Its psychoactive properties are attributed to its ingredient bufotenine.

Mace and nutmeg possess myristicin as a psychotropic compound. Its effects, which take several hours to develop, resemble those of atropine. They include excitement, hallucinations, dry mouth, fast pulse and dilated pupils.

There are many other agents that can produce results similar to LSD. The substances are chiefly of historical import, though it remains possible that changing fashions of drug experimentation could lead to their reappearance. Hallucinogenic drugs that have been so misused include dimethyltryptamine (DMT) and 2,5-dimethoxyl-4-methylamphetamine (DOM, 'STP').

Atropine-like drugs

Although they are not usually classified as hallucinogens, it is convenient to consider atropine and allied drugs at this point because the mental changes that form the basis for their misuse bear similarities to those induced by hallucinogens. Atropine and its sister alkaloid hyoscine are found in the solanaceous group of plants that contains *Atropa belladonna* (deadly nightshade), *Hyoscyamus niger* (henbane) and *Datura stramonium* (Jimson weed).

The cerebral and peripheral results of the preparations follow principally from their antagonistic effect on the activity of the neurotransmitter acetylcholine. Mental stimulation, agitation, hallucinations and clouding of consciousness can be succeeded by somnolence and coma. Widened pupils (hence the term 'belladonna'), facial flushing, dry mouth and a fast pulse are present.

Atropine compounds are usually taken by mouth, though there has been a vogue of smoking herbal medicines containing the substances. Atropine-like drugs are used to treat parkinsonism, as are synthetic anticholinergic preparations such as benzhexol (trihexyphenidyl, Artane). The artificial compounds have also been misused for their psychotropic effects, and, because they produce a mild sense of well-being, schizophrenics who have been prescribed the preparations to counter parkinsonism induced by neuroleptics are sometimes reluctant to cease using them.

Phencyclidine

In addition to hallucinatory effects the drug has stimulant and sedative properties. Phencyclidine was employed as a general anaesthetic, but the practice was discounted because hallucinations developed in patients after recovery from anaesthesia. The compound can be taken orally, sniffed or smoked, or injected intravenously. Prolonged states of anxiety, depression or psychosis can arise. Deaths follow from violent behaviour, from accidents or from direct toxicity that leads to coma and convulsions. Fortunately, a cult for phencyclidine in North America proved short-lived and the drug did not establish itself elsewhere.

Volatile inhalants

There are numerous volatile fluids that produce vapours which are inhaled for their psychoactive effects. The general anaesthetics ether, chloroform and trichlorethylene (trilene) have been misused for this purpose. Anaesthetists are vulnerable to anaesthetic misuse as an occupational hazard. Trichlorethylene, when formerly employed as a solvent in industry and in clothes cleaning, posed a similar risk for employees. Other volatile substances which are currently misused by inhalation are commercially marketed. They appear as agents which keep commodities like adhesives in a semifluid state and also constitute aerosol propellants.

The subject of volatile inhalants is therefore broader than its best known activity of glue sniffing. The products which are subject to misuse cover lighter fuel, other gas fuels, cleaning agents, paint thinners, aerosol sprays and even petrol. Their active constituents include toluene, trichlorethane and butane.

The inhalants cause an intoxicated state in which the mood can swing from hilarity to irritability. Lack of judgement and disinhibition occur. Hallucinations, usually visual in nature, may appear. The effects last only for about 30 minutes, so frequent sniffing takes place to renew the desired results. Abstinence features are not prominent.

Inhalation of volatile agents usually takes place as a group pastime among youngsters in their early or middle teens. Most of the subjects outgrow the activity within months, but harm occurs to a minority. Friction with parents and impaired performance at school can develop. More tragic and dramatic are sudden deaths. During the years 1981 to 1985 there were 385 fatalities in the United Kingdom from misuse of volatile substances (Anderson *et al.*, 1986). More than half the deaths resulted from direct toxicity. Fatal cardiac arrhythmia can be elicited by volatile inhalants, particularly in the presence of sympathetic nervous system stimulation. The latter may develop in the course of physical activity provoked by intoxication, or from autoeroticism. Inhalants are sometimes taken on a solitary basis to facilitate autoerotic behaviour; a number of deaths ensue from the combination. The remaining fatalities are attributable to injury while intoxicated, to inhalation of vomit, or to an inhaling method that involves placing a plastic bag over the head. About a third of the United Kingdom deaths have been in persons aged 20 years or more; the greater part take place during solitary rather than group inhalation.

There are several organic complications which are severe though fortunately rare. The list includes encephalopathy, cerebellar impairment, peripheral neuritis and status epilepticus. Liver and kidney damage can also arise.

A minority of inhalers do not cease the activity and develop a psychological dependence. Their inhaling practice is then pursued as a solitary pastime. The consequence is a failure of the personality to mature adequately, with emotional and social maladjustment.

Simple analgesics

Aspirin and paracetamol are well known drugs employed for the relief of painful and inflammatory disorders. When taken in high dosage they have an intoxicating result which can provoke their misuse and dependence. Young people may take aspirin on a sporadic basis for its mental effect, but those who overuse aspirin or paracetamol are usually older people, often females, with neurotic or domestic troubles who rely on the preparations over long periods.

Dependence of a psychological nature can develop on either compound. High intake of aspirin produces the symptoms of salicylism, with nausea, dizziness and deafness. Subjects then resort to their usual remedy for discomfort in the form of more aspirin. There are no withdrawal features, and drug cessation quickly leads to an improvement in well-being.

A serious complication is a form of kidney disease known as analgesic nephropathy. Patients may honestly deny taking drugs if they believe the products are safe and not worthy of mention. Direct questioning is therefore needed if the diagnosis is suspected.

Myths concerning the alleged powers of simple analgesics as panaceas for symptoms based on emotional distress, and traditions concerning their acceptability as the appropriate remedy, formerly contributed to analgesic misuse. Following the decline of these social factors the misuse of analgesics has become less common.

Other non-steroidal anti-inflammatory drugs have not been implicated as leading to misuse or dependence.

References

Anderson H.R., Bloor K., Macnair R.S. and Ramsey J. (1986) Recent trends in mortality associated with abuse of volatile substances in the UK. *Br. Med. J.*, **293**, 1472–1473.

Arif A. (ed.) (1987) *Adverse Health Consequences of Cocaine Abuse* (Geneva: World Health Organization).

Ashton H. (1984) Benzodiazepine withdrawal: an unfinished story. *Br. Med. J.*, **288**, 1135–1140.

Ashton H. (1987) Cannabis: dangers and possible uses. *Br. Med. J.*, **294**, 141–142.

Drake P.H. (1988) Khat chewing in the Near East. *Lancet*, **i**, 532–533.

Griffiths R.R., Bigelow G.E. and Liebson I.A. (1986) Human coffee drinking, reinforcing and physical dependence producing effects of caffeine. *J. Pharmacol. Exp. Ther.* **239**, 416–425.

Jones, R.T., Benowitz N. and Rackman J. (1975) Clinical studies of cannabis tolerance and dependence. *Ann. N.Y. Acad. Sci.*, **282**, 221–239.

Washton A.M. and Gold M.S. (eds) (1987) *Cocaine: A Clinician's Handbook* (New York: Guilford Press).

Bibliography

Jaffe J.H. (1985) Drug addiction and drug abuse. In *The Pharmacological Basis of Therapeutics*, 7th edn eds Gilman A.G., Goodman L.S., Ball T.W. and Nurrad F. (New York: Macmillan), pp. 532–581.

Madden J.S. (1984) *A Guide to Alcohol and Drug Dependence*, 2nd edn, (Bristol: John Wright).

WHO Expert Committee on Drug Dependence (1987) Twenty-third Report. *Tech. Rep. Ser.* No. 741. (Geneva: World Health Organization).

3

Extent and Pattern of Drug Abuse and Dependence

S. Das Gupta

Synopsis

This chapter looks at the attempts that have been made in the UK to estimate the prevalence of drug abuse. All the studies emphasise that epidemiology is an inexact science, particularly in an area such as drug misuse where the activity is illegal and has a stigma attached to it. However, there is ample evidence that, after a period of relative stability in the early seventies, the eighties have seen a rapid escalation of drug abuse. An attempt has been made to examine the illicit drug problem in the context of both socially accepted drug use and the use of medically prescribed drugs, by the community as a whole. After a broad review of the official statistics and of general and localised surveys, the pattern and extent of the current use of drugs are described. The chapter ends by describing the demographic characteristics of drug abusers and the problems they present.

Introduction

Of all topics in mental health epidemiology, drug abuse comes closest to resembling an infectious disease. There is a host and an agent, and the transmission is from person to person. The rate also varies substantially in both time and space. Of course, this does not necessarily mean that drug abuse is a disease, and one important difference is that the abuser is a willing victim.

Epidemiology has many definitions. In simple terms it means the study of a disorder in relation to the population in which it occurs, and its variations among different groups and over different times. One of its basic aims is to study the prevalence and incidence of illness as well as its social and demographic characteristics.

The incidence denotes the number of new cases of the condition in a specified period, but there are considerable difficulties in estimating the incidence of drug abuse. Attempts have been made in the USA to estimate the trends in incidence from the reported year of first use by people attending for treatment. In Britain some studies have tried to chart initiation to heroin use, and Home Office figures do give the number of new cases notified during each year thus providing figures for 'treated' incidence as opposed to 'true' incidence which relates to the time when people start to use heroin or first become dependent.

The prevalence of a condition is defined as the number of individuals or cases who manifest the condition under study. In simple terms it is concerned with head counting. It is expressed as a rate, e.g. the number per 100 or per 1000 population, and it is usually estimated over a defined period, e.g. a week, 30 days or a year. Some large-scale studies of drug abuse in the general population have estimated 'lifetime prevalence'. When the prevalence is estimated at a specific time, it is called point prevalence. The prevalence of drug problems can exhibit rapid fluctuations according to the availability of drugs, their price, or personal decisions to stop, etc.; because of these factors period prevalence estimation is a more appropriate measure.

There are considerable problems in assessing the prevalence of drug abuse in a community. Drug abuse is an illegal act and considerable social stigma is attached to it. Even if great efforts are made to maintain anonymity and confidentiality, many people will still try to conceal their drug use. It is well known that only a small proportion of drug abusers are known to agencies.

The second problem comes from the difficulties of defining a case and of adhering to a universal set of definitions since various terms such as drug use, drug misuse, dependence and addiction are in current use. In defining a case one has to decide what one is assessing: whether it is just the drug use itself or the problems that are created by drug use. The growth of substance abuse in the past decade has revealed that not all drug users use drugs compulsively nor do all have social, medical or legal problems.

Drug abuse is not a static disorder. The number of drugs abused is constantly increasing as the fashion changes. The prevalence figures for particular drugs are likely to change from period to period reflecting the fashions as well as the opportunities related to drug use.

Pattison et al. (1982), Hartnoll et al. (1985) and Ghodse (1987) have critically reviewed the various methods of estimating the prevalence of drug abuse. There are two categories of methods, direct and indirect. Direct methods try to estimate the actual number of drug takers, by relying on surveys of self-reported drug abuse and on official notification figures. The indirect methods use various mortality and morbidity data such as drug-related deaths, hepatitis B statistics, non-fatal drug emergencies and enforcement statistics (e.g. arrests and convictions for drug-related offences, the quantity of drug seizures) to indicate trends in drug abuse rather than the actual number of drug takers.

Enforcement statistics

The Home Office Statistical Bulletin (1988) publishes three sets of figures each year in relation to the enforcement of drug laws. They are the number of seizures of controlled drugs, the quantities of drugs seized, and the number of persons dealt with for offences involving controlled drugs. There are 16 tables which give a breakdown of seizures and offenders by drug types, as well as by age and sex of offender. The latest figures published in 1988 represent the results of enforcement activities in the previous year, i.e. 1987. The tables also contain the figures, where these are available, of the previous ten years for ready comparison, which show that after increasing continuously since the mid 1970s, the number of seizures of controlled drugs has remained more or less the same in the years 1985, 1986 and 1987. In 1987 the number of seizures was about 30 650. A particular feature within this was the substantial decline in the figures relating to heroin: heroin seizures continued the decline first noticed in 1986 and were down by another 27% in 1987. Offenders dealt with for offences involving heroin were also down as were the new addicts notified as addicted to heroin. Nevertheless heroin remained the drug involved in most seizures and drug offences among Class A drugs.

The statistics also showed that:

- The vast majority of seizures and drug offences involved Class B drugs, and cannabis was the drug involved most frequently.
- A substantial number of seizures and offences involve amphetamines with the quantity of amphetamines seized increasing again in 1987.
- A sizeable number of drug offences involve LSD although the numbers have been decreasing since 1984.
- The quantity of cocaine seized in 1987 was over 400 kg, four times more than in the previous year, and was the highest on record.
- The number of both male and female offenders (29 700) went up in 1987 from the fall in 1986, but still was smaller than 1985. There was a welcome decline, however, in the under-17 age group. The mean age of drug offenders (26 years) was much the same as in the previous year. The most common offence was unlawful possession, which constituted about 84% of the total offences.
- Eighty-six percent of the seizures were made directly from people and of that figure about 44% were from people either in the 'street' or 'open spaces', reflecting the street availability of drugs. However, enforcement statistics are affected by changes in the amount, direction and effectiveness of the enforcement effort, and therefore changes in yearly data may not necessarily indicate changes in prevalence. None the less, taken with other official statistics, they are a good indicator of trends in the prevalence of drug abuse.

Notification figures

Since 1968 all medical practitioners have had a statutory duty to notify to the Chief Medical Officer at the Home Office the name, address, sex and date of birth of any person they attend whom they consider to be, or have reasonable grounds to suspect of being, addicted to heroin, cocaine, methadone and eleven other notifiable drugs—all of which are classifed as Class A drugs. An addict is defined as a person who, as a result of repeated administration, has become so dependent upon a drug that he has an overpowering drive for its administration to be continued. The Home Office maintains an index based on these notifications, and the figures are published yearly. A supplementary table contains details notified from each police-force area.

These statistics, provided in eight tables, show the number of addicts notified and the number recorded as receiving notifiable drugs. The figures are broken down further to provide information about specific drugs of addiction, the age and sex of the addict, as well as the drug prescribed in treatment and the source of notification. The bulletin also gives figures for the previous ten years for ready comparison. It shows that the number of addicts notified fell for the first time in 1986 after many years of growth. Altogether 8135 addicts were notified during 1986 of whom 5325 were new addicts (i.e. first notifications) and 2810 were renotifications. The figures for 1987 which are available now show a further fall of about 400. There were 4593 new notifications and 3100 who were renotifications. The number of addicts notified has increased since the late 1960s, but the period of fastest growth occurred in the years between 1980 and 1985 when the number increased at the rate of 30% per annum. The fall between 1985 and 1987 was due to a fall in the number of new addict notifications to heroin.

Among addicts notified for the first time in 1987, 89% were reported to be addicted to heroin either alone or with other drugs, and the next most common drug was methadone with about 14%. Addicts reported to be dependent on cocaine, either alone or in combination with other drugs, constituted about 10% of new notifications. Just under 27% of notified addicts were females. The average age of new addicts was 26 years. The number of new addicts under 21 years of age (1050) was less than it was in 1986, which itself was less than that in 1985. About half the addicts were first notified by general practitioners in 1987 and about a sixth by prison medical officers.

The first thing to remember about the addict index is that it does not cover all drugs. Only people who are dependent on notifiable drugs such as opiates and cocaine are included. Secondly the figures represent only those addicts who have come to medical attention because of some medical or legal problem. Thus there is no doubt that it underestimates the actual number of addicts because a good proportion of drug users do not come into contact with doctors. Furthermore, Ghodse's (1977) study of a London casualty department showed that, in at least 77% of events among patients clearly identified by medical staff of the casualty department as addicted to narcotic drugs, notification was not made. A recent study by Strang and Shah (1985) in the North West of England also confirmed this.

Although the degree of under-reporting is likely to vary from one area to another and from time to time, there is a feeling that, because of increased awareness, notification by doctors has improved and loss to the system may be less than previously. However, it is fair to say that notifications indicate trends rather than actual prevalence and that notification does not indicate initial use since there is always a time lag between initial use and notification.

Surveys of self-reported drug abuse in the general population

National studies

In the UK there have been three relevant studies using a national sample. The one whose method is logically the most sound was carried out in 1981 and looked at self-reported cannabis use (Mott, 1985). A representative sample of the population in Great Britain over the age of 16 was interviewed face to face, and in this population 5% reported having used cannabis at some time (7% of males and 4% of females) although only 2% admitted to having used it during the previous 14 months. Of males of the 20- to 34-year age group in England and Wales 16–18% reported having ever used cannabis with 5–8% doing so during the previous year. The percentage of females reported ever using was half that reported by men.

The major aim of the study was to elicit information about crime, and the information about cannabis was obtained in this context. Thus the reliability of the responses is in doubt, and it would be misleading to interpret the data as indicative of prevalence. It can, however, form a baseline against which other national or local surveys can be compared.

Two other earlier studies are worth mentioning. The first was commissioned by the Office of Population Censuses and Surveys (OPCS) and was conducted by an independent research organisation in England and Wales in 1969 (OPCS, 1973). The survey was intended to assess public attitudes to the use of six controlled drugs—'pep pills', cannabis, LSD, heroin, cocaine and amphetamines—and subjects were asked whether they had ever used any of the drugs and also whether they had ever known anyone taking any of the controlled drugs. The selected sample was 1968 people in England and Wales between the ages of 16 and 19. They obtained a response rate of 80% with about 5% admitting to 'ever using' illicit drugs of whom 4% had taken 'pep pills', 2% cannabis and less than 0.5% heroin, cocaine and LSD. There was no breakdown according to their age or sex.

Another survey was commissioned by the BBC in 1973 (Midweek, 1973) but the sample was even smaller. Subjects were asked whether they had ever used drugs for non-medical purposes. There was a 73% response rate and from these figures a national estimate was made. According to the calculations, 3.8 million people had ever used cannabis, 1.3 million had used amphetamines and 659 000 had taken LSD.

In the United States, the National Institute of Drug Abuse has conducted regular household surveys of self-reported drug use. No such surveys are done in the UK, even though other household surveys do occur, because of the particular problems of obtaining information about illicit drug use. The respondents are likely to understate their consumption and the heavy users may be very difficult to contact. To be reliable, surveys of an infrequent behaviour have to cover a very large sample and this is very expensive and time consuming.

Studies in defined geographical areas

There have been a number of studies which have tried simple enumeration to estimate the prevalence of drug abuse, usually of opiates, in local communities.

One of the earliest studies was done in Crawley, a new town about 35 miles from London with a population of approximately 62 000, 41% of whom were under 20 years of age (De Alarcon and Rathod, 1968). The study covered the age group 15–20. The first survey was carried out in 1967 and then the same survey was continued until 1970, although less thoroughly than the initial survey. A case register of opiate abusers was made with information from probation offices, police, referrals for treatment, survey of hepatitis cases in the age group between 15 and 25, survey of admissions to the casualty department for overdose of amphetamines and/or barbiturates, and information from patients under treatment about new users known to them. Fifty confirmed users plus 48 probable users were identified and this rose to 102 confirmed users and 37 suspects by 1970. The survey calculated a prevalence rate of 8.5 per 1000 population aged 15–20 in 1967, or 14.75 per 1000 when only the males were considered.

Several stages of the epidemic were demonstrated: in the first stage, from 1962–1965, a small number of individuals from Crawley had experimented with heroin whilst living in other towns. In the second stage they then formed a nucleus of heroin users in Crawley and in the third stage, from 1966 to 1967, the population was swelled by a large number who were initiated and reinforced into drug use. The incidence, which was 1.1 per thousand in 1965 in the age group 14–19, rose to 6.5 per thousand in 1967. They were able to trace two users who had initiated the majority of this drug use. The initiation was on a 'convivial basis' with individuals known to each other through truanting together, going to the same social club, etc.

Another survey in a provincial town (Kosviner *et al.*, 1968) used a social network method. In 1967 the researchers made initial contact with four heroin users, and through the network of their friends other heroin users were traced. They also checked all available sources such as medical and psychiatric hospitals, local general practitioners, medical officers of health, the police and probation services. They identified 37 heroin users in a population of 100 000. The researchers continued the survey until 1970 and therefore they had the opportunity to follow up some of the original cohorts as well as to read the changing nature of drug misuse in the community.

Another study during that period was that of Plant (1975) in Cheltenham. He used a well-known social network method called snowballing and participant observation. Snowballing is a technique by which the researchers get introduced to an expanding network of people through the people they contacted initially. Participant observation is a method in which the data are collected through identifying with the daily life of the people to gain an insider's view of the group. Between 1970 and 1972 Plant contacted 200 drug users all of whom had used cannabis, and over this period a picture of their lifestyle and their characteristics was drawn: 60% of the group were between 19 and 22 years of age, 77% used LSD and 54% had used amphetamines. Of the 30 persons (15%) who had injected drugs at some time, only three (1.5%) did so regularly. These injectors appeared as an extreme and 'deviant' group in comparison with non-injectors. However, Plant made it clear that his study was not a comprehensive survey of the total drug users in the town under study.

There were a number of other studies during that period looking at various geographical areas. One of the authors of the Crawley study also did a survey in Oxford along with other workers in 1969 (Arroyave *et al.*, 1973). The prevalence of heroin and methadone users was 5.9 per thousand in the 15–29 age group. The study is of interest since it has been repeated recently by Pevelar *et al.* (1988) using similar methods.

More recently, Hartnoll *et al.* (1985) studied prevalence of drug use in two districts in London (Camden and Islington) between 1977 and 1983. In order to assess more accurately the extent of opioid dependence they chose three approaches: the use of routine statistics, surveys of agencies who have contact with drug users, and fieldwork among drug users. Regular opioid users, in their definition, were those who used opioid drugs daily, or at least six days a week for at least one month in a specified period. They recognised that intensive case finding is not possible in large metropolitan areas, and therefore used different, indirect methods based on different assumptions and derived from different data in the hope that collectively they would provide a more valid estimate than could any single technique alone.

They arrived at a 'best estimate' figure for annual period prevalence for three age groups: 12 per 1000 of the 16- to 24-year-old population, 25 per 1000 of the 25- to 34-year-old, and 5 per 1000 of 35- to 44-year-old. They also found that the prevalence of regular opioid users during 1982–1983 was at least five times the total number of addicts reported in Home Office figures. However, a study in Glasgow in 1981 suggested that under-reporting might be even more significant and that only one in ten was notified (Ditton and Speirits, 1981).

The rise in the incidence of opiate use in recent times has stimulated a string of surveys in various parts of the country, basically using multi-agency enumeration methods. Surveys have been conducted in South Tyneside (Pearson et al., 1985), Bristol (Parker et al., 1988), Brighton (Levy, 1985), Glasgow (Haw, 1985), the Wirral (Parker et al., 1987) and Oxford (Pevelar et al., 1988), but comparison is difficult since there are differences in respect of case definition, drug definition, agencies used, time period and methods employed. It does, however, indicate that there is widespread variation in the prevalence of opioid users. The incidence appears to be highest in London, the Wirral and Glasgow. The Wirral study showed an annual prevalence rate of 3.9 per thousand with most cases concentrated between the ages 16 and 24 years old where the rate was 18.2 per 1000. This survey, carried out in 1984–1985, indicated a rapidity and depth of spread unknown in the United Kingdom before. The Glasgow study used routine statistics between 1980 and 1983 and did a prospective study involving four agencies in two areas of Glasgow with fieldwork during the first three months of 1984. The annual prevalence rate was calculated at four known opioid users per 1000 of population. However, the South Tyneside study completed during a six-month period in 1981 estimated the annual prevalence rate as 1.2 known opioid users per thousand population, and recent evidence suggests that Tyneside and other north-eastern communities in the UK continue to have a relatively low prevalence compared with north-western towns and cities. The prevalence in Bristol and Brighton is also lower.

The recent study in Oxford (Pevelar et al., 1988) is interesting in that it replicated the study that was done in 1969 in the same city. The study covered the period 1 April 1984 to 31 March 1985, and, as in the previous study, information from various agencies was supplemented by extensive fieldwork studies. The 12-month period prevalence rate was 3.7 per 1000 in the age range 15–49 years, and this finding suggested that the prevalence of heroin misuse in Oxford in 1984–1985 was not different from that of 1969.

Glanz and his colleagues carried out a survey in 1985 of a 5% random sample of general practitioners in England and Wales (Glanz and Taylor, 1986). The GPs were asked to report how many different patients they had seen for problems associated with misuse of heroin and other opiate drugs over a four-week period. From the results of the survey they calculated that 30 000–44 000 new cases of opiate misuse were likely to present to general practitioners in a year, but they felt that this was a cautious estimate.

Special populations

Studies in schoolchildren

A number of studies in various localities have tried to assess the extent of drug abuse among the schoolchild population over different periods of time.

Plant *et al.* (1984) conducted a study of schoolchildren in five schools in Lothian in south-east Scotland during 1979 and 1980 and followed them up later in 1983. They were primarily looking at alcohol use among teenagers, but also included questions like, 'Have you ever used drugs for kicks or out of curiosity?', and gave a list of drugs in the questionnaire. They found that among 1036 schoolchildren aged between 15 and 16, 15.2% of boys and 10.7% of girls had used drugs at some time; 7% had used cannabis, 5% tranquillisers and 2.5% amphetamines. Only 1% admitted to ever using heroin. When 92.4% of the study group were re-interviewed in 1983, they found that the proportion of drug users had increased to 37% of boys and 23.2% of girls.

In general the surveys show that the number of 'ever used' increases with age and that more males than females are likely to have ever used. There is also some evidence of geographical variation in different parts of the country. The local studies in the south of England arrived at a figure of 19% who admitted to drug use with 14% admitting to cannabis use, 12% solvents and 4% admitting to using other drugs, mainly amphetamines. Less than 1% admitted to using heroin (Pritchard *et al.*, 1986). This is similar to results obtained in a survey conducted in England and Wales when 17% claimed use of cannabis, 6% solvents and 2% admitted to using heroin at some time (Williams, 1986).

The use of illicit drugs is sometimes associated with a history of early smoking of tobacco, drinking alcohol, mixing with older children, having more sexual experience than other children, etc., and the term precocity has been used to describe this association. For example, Plant *et al.* (1984) found that young people who were heavy drinkers at 15–16 were more likely to have used illegal drugs in later years.

A survey carried out in 1987 by the Schools Health Education Unit based at Exeter University recently reported a much lower use of illicit drugs among schoolchildren. It covered more than 18 000 pupils aged between 11 and 16 years, and although it was done in schools which volunteered to take part in the study, the sample was thought to be fairly representative. It found that cannabis had been taken by less than 1 in 25 of fifth-year pupils. Only 2.6% of boys and 2.1% of girls in the fifth year reported using solvents and less than 1% in all ages had used heroin. However, there was evidence that drugs were more easily available in some areas than others (Balding, 1987).

A survey in 1986 among 3333 adolescents in state comprehensive schools in London selected on a geographical basis showed a much higher incidence (Swadi, 1988). More than 20% of 11- to 16-year-olds had used solvents or illegal drugs at least once, about 8.4% indulged in repeated use and 5% used hard drugs (stimulants, hallucinogenic drugs, tranquillisers, cocaine, heroin). Heroin was the least used substance (1.7%). The survey did not find any significant sex difference but the prevalence of substance abuse showed a sharp increase by the age of 14. The author suggested that a prevention programme should be targeted to younger pupils and that the educational programme should encompass the whole range of drugs both licit and illicit.

Surveys of students in higher education

All the studies of drug abuse by students in higher education in this country were done before 1980 so that information about any recent changes is lacking. There is evidence from earlier studies that, apart from geographical variation, there may also be time trends in that studies done earlier showed a lower prevalence. On the other hand, researchers could not find evidence of change in the proportion of users in new students between 1970 and 1978.

Somekh (1976), in his study of six London colleges between 1971 and 1972, found that about 34% of his sample admitted to ever using illicit drugs; 32% of the total sample admitted to cannabis use, 9% to amphetamines, 8% to LSD, and 1% to opiates. Over half of the sample only used cannabis. There was no evidence of an increase in the drop-out rate from colleges, nor any effect on exam achievements, nor increased medical problems in relation to drug use.

Kosviner *et al.* (1973), who studied the incidence of cannabis use by students in higher education, found that about 1–3% were using cannabis four times a week. They felt that those who used less frequently were more similar to non-users but that the more frequent or heavier users demonstrated attributes which differentiated them from ordinary non-users. They also found that students in social sciences, arts and medicine were more likely to have used illicit drugs than students in physical science and engineering. There is also evidence that variation exists in different colleges in the same area.

Drug abuse in the medical profession

The prevalence of drug abuse by members of the medical profession is thought to be higher than that of the general population. They are regarded as especially vulnerable because of their knowledge of drugs and their access to them and also because of occupational stress, but the actual prevalence of drug abuse among the medical profession in this country has never been established.

In one study of 192 doctors treated at two London hospitals between 1954 and 1964, 17% were diagnosed as being addicted to drugs (A'Brook *et al.*, 1967). More recently, Stimson *et al.* (1984) identified in the Home Office index 89 doctors who came to notice between 1970 and 1983, of whom about 12% were females. They found that about six doctors came to the attention of the Home Office every year although they felt that this was an underestimate because of the way they came to notice not through treatment but through police investigation. They found that doctor addicts came to attention much later in life than other addicts, and calculated that the onset of medical addiction is usually when the client is in the mid-thirties; the drug of use was more likely to be a synthetic opiate than street heroin.

Patterns of drug taking

There are three kinds of drug use: experimental, recreational or dependent. Although large numbers of people use drugs at some time, in most cases such use is limited to occasional use or use for a limited period only. Those who use one particular drug regularly may also use other drugs. Stimson and Oppenheimer (1982), in their study of opiate addicts attending clinics and receiving a prescription for heroin, found that only 16% said they restricted themselves to the drugs that the clinics prescribed, and it was apparent that, although heroin was the preferred drug, the cohort was also using a wide range of other drugs in addition.

Often people combine two drugs with different pharmacological characteristics to heighten the effects. Users of intravenous heroin sometimes take amphetamines or cocaine along with it so that the depressant effect of heroin can be overcome by the stimulant effect of the latter and vice versa. One of the early favourites was a drug called 'purple hearts' because of the shape of the tablets, which combined amphetamine with a small dose of barbiturate. Opiate users often take hypnotics to help them to sleep at night or to avoid withdrawal symptoms and sometimes to get a 'kick'. Some abusers have a much more chaotic pattern of drug taking. They will use any available drugs either simultaneously or one after another, and this kind of multiple drug abuse or polydrug abuse is not uncommon among urban drug abusers. The Advisory Council on the Misuse of Drugs noted in 1982:

> most drug misusers are not now solely dependent on one drug. The same person may be using a number of drugs and may be dependent on more than one of them. Opioid users will very often misuse barbiturates, amphetamines, hallucinogens, tranquillisers and alcohol. During the 1970's a more clearly defined group of multiple drug misusers emerged—individuals not necessarily dependent on any one drug but psychologically dependent on drug misuse

It also appears that there are stages of progression in the use of licit and illicit drugs in adolescence and through young adulthood. Most of the people who use heroin have used alcohol, cannabis, amphetamines and other substances as well at various stages, and are liable to continue to use those drugs although less frequently.

Extent of abuse of specific drugs

Cannabis

Cannabis is the commonest illicit drug of abuse. The Home Office figure for offences in relation to 'possession of cannabis' in 1986 (16 446) was about four times that for possession of all other drugs combined (4361) (Home Office, 1987).

There have been a number of surveys of cannabis use in secondary-school pupils and college and university students. In addition there have been several national sample surveys. As expected the surveys suggest that the young are much more likely to use cannabis and that more males have used it than females. The British crime survey (Hugh and Mayhew, 1983) shows that the age group between 20 and 34 contained the highest proportion, 16–18% saying they had ever used cannabis with 5–8% saying that they had done so during the previous year. A survey of 15- to 24-year-olds in Great Britain in 1982 found 17% admitting to cannabis use with 4% admitting to current use—figures which are very similar to those found in the British Crime Survey. A study in 1969 estimated that about 3.8 million people have 'ever used' cannabis, and the Legalise Cannabis Campaign estimates that about two million people used cannabis daily; however, this is considered to be an overestimate. The British Crime Survey also found that in the England and Wales sample a higher proportion of informants living in inner city areas admitted to cannabis use compared with those living in country areas. Mott, in her review of studies conducted between 1968 and 1972, found that the studies indicated that about a third of students, about 15% of non-students of similar age, and around 10% of school pupils have used cannabis (Mott, 1976).

Studies of cannabis users in the past have found an association with hedonism and with certain political, religious and social attitudes involving the concept of bohemianism. However, it is now used by a much wider group of people, rather than being confined to any particular group. Cannabis is usually smoked along with tobacco by making 'joints', although it can be eaten as well. Quite often it is taken in a social setting in a recreational way although there is a minority who use cannabis regularly. Most use it without encountering any problems.

In a survey in Bristol by Parker *et al.* (1988), only 9% out of 759 problem drug abusers had problems with cannabis. 'Those having problems were typical vulnerable teenagers or young adults whose cannabis use contributed to psychoses, not obtaining work, not coping at school, or difficulties with parents.'

Amphetamines

Amphetamines were one of the commonest drugs of abuse in the 1950s and 1960s when they used to be prescribed quite freely by doctors. In the 1960s amphetamines constituted about 2.5% of all prescriptions issued in the National Health Service, and most illicit amphetamines were pharmaceutical drugs. Recent surveys have shown that it is still the second most common drug of abuse next to cannabis, but that it is now illicitly manufactured in small laboratories or imported from Holland, which is the main source of supply. Like all other drugs, we do not know the actual extent of its abuse. The 1982 survey mentioned earlier found that 5% of the 16- to 34-year-olds polled admitted to using amphetamines. The Home Office figures for the number of seizures of amphetamines in 1986 was 2950, which is roughly the same as the number of heroin seizures (2746). The quantity of amphetamines seized has increased consistently and trebled between 1983 and 1986. In some parts of the country amphetamine abuse is much more prevalent than opiate abuse, and in a survey in West Suffolk it was calculated that 1% of the 15–44 age group were using amphetamines.

The illicit amphetamine is basically amphetamine sulphate of varying purity. It is relatively cheap, at about £10 to £12 per gram. It can be sniffed or taken orally, but injection has become more common. Epidemics of infectious hepatitis through injecting amphetamines have been reported in different parts of the UK.

Opiates

Heroin

In 1986, 91% of new addicts notified to the Home Office were addicted to heroin and most of the surveys carried out recently show that the vast majority of problem drug abusers who contact various agencies are heroin abusers. The number of heroin addicts notified to the Home Office in 1987 was about 6812. Mention has already been made of the work of Hartnoll and colleagues in London (1985) and of Ditton and Speirits (1981) in Glasgow who suggest that there are at least five to ten heroin abusers for every one user known to the Home Office. These are the hidden users who do not come into contact with agencies.

Most of the heroin available in the illicit market is imported from Pakistan. The price has been remarkably stable at about £60 to £100 per gram for some time, and at street level it is available in bags sold at £5 to £10 containing heroin of varying purities.

In the 1960s and 1970s heroin almost always used to be injected but in the late 1970s and early 1980s sniffing, smoking heroin mixed with tobacco, and 'chasing' became comparatively commoner and in some areas over half the new heroin users are reported to be 'chasing the dragon'. In 'chasing the dragon', heroin is heated in tin foil and the fumes are inhaled. This is possible because of the availability of South-East Asian heroin of sufficient purity.

The illicit heroin market is like a pyramid. At the bottom are the users who are many, and at the top are the importers. The profit is enormous since the difference between the money paid to the farmer who produces opium and the price that addicts pay is astronomical. Wagstaff and Maynard (1986) guesstimated that the total expenditure on heroin in the UK in 1984 was between £111.7 million and £237.8 million, representing about 3–6% of the total expenditure on tobacco and between 1 and 2% of the total expenditure on alcohol.

The distribution of heroin abusers is not uniform throughout the country. Liverpool and Glasgow may have the same prevalence rate as London, whereas it is lower in the North East, Bristol and Brighton. Within the same city, heroin abuse is commoner in depressed areas, and there is a higher than average unemployment rate among heroin abusers.

Methadone

Methadone is a synthetic opiate first manufactured in Germany during the war. It is the second most common drug of notification. In 1987, 14% of new notifications (630) claimed addiction to methadone. It is a longer acting drug which is absorbed satisfactorily when given by the oral route. Methadone mixture is the commonest drug prescribed by clinics for the treatment of opiate addiction. Of the 10 400 people recorded as receiving notifiable drugs in treatment of their addiction at 31 December 1987, over 9700 were receiving methadone.

Dipipanone

Dipipanone is another synthetic opiate which in 1982 became the second most common drug to which addiction was reported. However, since it was put in the same category as heroin and cocaine so that a licence from the Home Office is needed to be able to prescribe it, the number of people reported to be addicted to it has fallen significantly.

Dextromoramide

Under the brand name of Palfium, dextromoramide is also a sought-after drug in addict circles. The number of new notifications in 1987 was 189.

Dihydrocodeine

Dihydrocodeine is prepared from codeine, an alkaloid obtained from opium, and is a popular analgesic. As it is not a notifiable drug the extent of its oral use by addicts remains unknown.

Designer drugs

These are synthetic drugs, highly potent and manufactured illicitly. They have effects which are very similar to those of known drugs of abuse and dependence. They also sometimes have dangerous side-effects. Until recently their availability was limited to America only, but one drug, called 'Ecstasy', has now made its appearance on the streets of London on a limited scale.

Cocaine

As with all other drugs, little is known about the true extent of cocaine abuse in this country. There has been a fear that it might take over from heroin as the drug posing the biggest threat, following the American example where it is estimated that about 20 million people have used cocaine. Cocaine is one of the notifiable drugs, and the number of notifications gradually increased over the years until 1986. The number of new notifications in 1987 (677) was slightly less than that for 1986.

The enforcement statistics are, however, confusing. The Customs and Excise in 1987 seized over 400 kg of cocaine, which is way above the 101 kg seized in 1986, and for the first time the amount of cocaine confiscated exceeded that of heroin. The number of seizures made (720) was one of the

highest except for that in 1984 (900). The price and purity have remained
fairly stable. It is sold at £60 to £80 per gram, and the purity is 60-80%.
Although a number of reports of the availability of 'crack' have appeared,
one of which suggested that it had been manufactured in this country,
crack does not seem to be widely available yet. It seems that it is mainly
found in London and is more prevalent in the high-income bracket with a
slow spilling over into the provinces and perhaps down market as well. In
some parts of London cocaine is one of the recognised street drugs.

LSD

There was a time in the 1960s when the use of LSD achieved great
popularity and it emerged as the drug most closely associated with the
hippy culture. People were taking it to enhance their perceptual processes
as well as to increase their understanding of themselves. It was not
uncommon for people to take LSD daily, either on their own or in a group
setting. Subsequently it gained some notoriety when it was found that
Charles Manson committed hideous murders under the influence of this
drug. The incidence of its use in this country fell dramatically after
Operation Julie in 1977 when a policewoman acted as an undercover agent
and broke a manufacturing and distribution ring. As a result, in 1979 there
were only 216 seizures of LSD. There was a gradual increase between 1979
and 1984 followed by falls in 1985 and 1986. In 1987 the number of seizures
was about 300 and the quantity seized was less than in previous years.

Two national surveys, one in 1969 and one in 1973 (see p. 57),
indicated that about 1% of the population or about 650 000 had used LSD
at any one time. The 1982 National Opinion Poll survey among 15- to
21-year-olds suggested that about 3% had 'ever used' LSD.

Solvents

Solvents are not illicit drugs as such, but their abuse by young schoolchildren and adolescents generates a great deal of anxiety. Solvents are
inhaled and the usual practice is to pour the solvent into a plastic bag which
is then put over the head to enable the person to inhale the fumes. Mostly
it is a recreational activity but about a fifth of those who experiment go on
to regular use. There may be an enormous number who have experimented
with solvents, although it is a practice that tends to happen in epidemics
and then dies down to re-emerge again after some time. It occurs more
commonly between 10 and 17 years of age, and is more common among
boys than girls. In some schools about one in ten schoolchildren report
using solvents.

Psychotropic drugs

The use of illicit drugs cannot be understood properly unless it is seen against the perspective of the use of prescribed medicines with mood-altering effects and the use of recreational drugs by society as a whole. In addition, people who present with a drug problem are also likely to be using a number of psychotropic drugs in addition to whatever illicit drugs they are dependent on. Some of them receive a legitimate prescription from doctors, some obtain drugs from 'overspill' from others' prescriptions and some obtain them by breaking into pharmacies. In a survey among addicts attending St George's Hospital for three months in 1984–1985, 60% had benzodiazepines in their urine (Beary *et al.*, 1987).

The Department of Health routinely collects data based on an approximately one in 200 sample of all prescriptions dispensed at retail pharmacies, and these statistics are regularly published. They give an indication of the amount of psychotropic drugs being prescribed through Family Practitioner Committees. In 1975, when prescriptions for psychotropic drugs reached a peak, 47.5 million prescriptions were dispensed for antidepressants, tranquillisers, hypnotics and stimulants. Of these, 78% were for tranquillisers and hypnotics. Since then there has been a gradual but slow decline in the number of prescriptions for the latter two categories. There have also been changes in the pattern of psychotropic drug prescribing over the years. The number of prescriptions for barbiturate hypnotics, which was about 11.6 million in 1972, came down to 1.9 million in 1984 with a compensatory increase in the prescribing of benzodiazepine hypnotics. Benzodiazepines first became available in the United Kingdom at the start of the 1960s and since then there has been a phenomenal growth in their use. In 1979 there were 31 million prescriptions for benzodiazepine tranquillisers and hypnotics but this had fallen back to about 26 million by 1985. The reduction seems to be due to the reduced number of prescriptions for tranquillisers. There are various possible reasons for this including the introduction of a limited list of drugs in 1985 and an increased awareness of the dependence potential of benzodiazepines. In the 1980s there has also been a tendency for drugs with a shorter half-life, such as temazepam (Normison; Cerepax) and lorazepam (Ativan) to be prescribed increasingly.

In 1969 a survey was conducted by the Institute of Social Studies of the use of prescribed and over-the-counter medicines. People were interviewed about their use of medicines in the previous 24 hours and the last two weeks (Dunnell and Cartwright, 1972). In a sample of about 1400, 55% had taken some drug or medicine in the previous 24 hours, 11% of the sample had taken a psychotropic drug during the previous two weeks, and 40% of the sample were using medicines daily. There was also evidence that 34–48% of those who were taking psychotropic drugs were taking them over a long period having obtained several repeat prescriptions. In another survey carried out by the Institute for Social Studies in 1977, it was found that about 12% of adults had used psychoactive drugs in the previous fortnight and about 7% had first been prescribed that drug a year or more ago (Anderson, 1980). Murray (1972) has drawn attention to the use of minor analgesics (aspirin, paracetamol, etc.) in the general population. According to a poll in 1970, 9% of the population used minor analgesics weekly and nearly one million people took analgesics daily.

Long-term use of benzodiazepines

Studies of long-term benzodiazepine users have given us considerable understanding of so-called therapeutic addicts. It is known that a substantial proportion of those who are prescribed benzodiazepines receive them on a long-term basis. A recent MORI poll indicated that about 35% of clients who were taking benzodiazepines were taking them for periods in excess of four months, and it is accepted that about 30% of these long-term users will manifest severe physical withdrawal symptoms. From a considerable number of studies of long-term use, several factors emerge which are commonly related. Long-term users are more likely to be women (in one survey 75%) and over 40 years of age; they tend to experience high levels of emotional distress; and a large proportion have a diagnosis of depression. There is a strong association with physical illness. A previous history of psychotropic drug use is common.

Barbiturates

Barbiturates are extremely effective hypnotic drugs and they are also very cheap. Until the advent of benzodiazepines, barbiturates used to dominate the hypnotic/tranquilliser market so that at the beginning of the 1960s there used to be about 15 million Family Practitioner Service prescriptions for barbiturates each year. The increasing awareness of their dependence potential along with their use in parasuicide and suicide led to a concerted effort among medical practitioners to reduce their prescription. The final straw was the appearance of evidence of extensive barbiturate abuse by young drug abusers in the 1970s. In 1985 these substances were brought under the control of the Misuse of Drugs Act.

Alcohol

As in many other countries there has been a considerable increase in the level of consumption of alcohol in Britain since the Second World War; and there is general agreement that alcohol consumption has increased among females. A recent survey of adolescent drinking (Plant *et al.*, 1984), which looked at the drinking habits of 13- to 17-year-olds nationally, indicated that most young people had experienced a 'proper' drink by the age of 17 and that only 10% were abstainers. The same Scottish survey showed that among 15- to 16-year-olds about 15.1% of males and 9.5% of females had experienced at least one serious consequence of alcohol use. The consumption of alcohol per capita is highest among young people.

There are several indications of alcohol-related problems in the community. It is estimated that about 600 000–750 000 may have alcohol-related problems. About 10–27% of admissions to acute general medical facilities are due to alcohol-related disabilities, and about 14 500 patients are admitted each year to psychiatric hospitals with alcohol-related problems; of the latter about a third are first admissions. The number of people convicted for drunken driving is close to 100 000, and between 90 000 and 100 000 people are convicted each year for being drunk and disorderly in public places. Apart from all these, misuse of alcohol has been reported to be a major factor in football hooliganism, accidents, absenteeism and inefficiency at work.

There is no doubt that alcohol is a potent drug, and it has been suggested that if alcohol were to be introduced as a new drug today it would not be 'passed' by the Committee for the Safety of Medicines.

Demographic characteristics

Studies looking at the characteristics of problem drug abusers may be divided into two groups, those carried out in the 1960s and 1970s and those done in the 1980s. A review of the work done in the earlier period was made by Blumberg (1981).

Although one or two surveys have been unable to find much difference in the characteristics of drug users between earlier studies and recent ones, several others have found the population differing in a number of ways. The population in recent studies appears to be younger, more likely to be unemployed, single, and generally more socially deprived.

Social class

All the studies show that 90% of the problem drug abusers are born and brought up in this country and that minority groups are so far under-represented. The social class distribution of fathers of drug users, when studied in the 1960s and 1970s, was much the same as that of the general population with a slight over-representation of professionals and under-representation of unskilled people. Comparison of fathers' and addicts' occupational status indicated, as expected, a decline in the social situations of drug abusers. However, on the whole there was little evidence of drug abuse being associated with poverty and deprivation. There was, in some at least, an indication that the drug abuse was associated with rejection of middle class values.

A recent study carried out in 1984–1985 in London of a sample of drug takers at three different agencies confirms that they come from a variety of different social backgrounds although there was a preponderance of clients from social classes III, IV and V, 41% having one or both parents with problems with alcohol and drugs. Their educational achievement was low, 60% leaving school without any formal qualifications.

Social deprivation

In a study in the Wirral, carried out in 1984–1985, researchers plotted the area of residence of known users and worked out the rates of prevalence in relation to overall population as well as to young people between 16 and 24 years of age for each township. They then looked at the level of social deprivation using seven indicators: unemployment, council tenancies, overcrowding, households with three or more children, single parent households, unskilled employment and no access to a car. They found significant positive correlation between opiate use and each of the seven indicators of social deprivation (Parker *et al.*, 1987). There have recently been some studies, particularly from Scotland, which also suggest that a high rate of unemployment may be associated with a high rate of drug abuse in the area. These recent studies show a trend which contrasts with the findings of surveys in the 1960s and 1970s (Peck and Plant, 1986).

Age

Most illegal drug users are young. The average age of new addicts notified to the Home Office has remained steady at between 25 and 27 years. However, since 1980 the proportion of newly notified addicts under 21 years of age has been increasing both in absolute numbers and as a proportion of the total percentage. In the study in the Wirral mentioned earlier, over 92% of the known opioid users were between the ages of 16 and 30. One of the interesting findings of most studies is that the onset of non-medical psychoactive drug use usually takes place in a brief age span, between the early teens and mid-twenties. In the study in London by Sheehan and Oppenheimer (1988), 35% first used a psychoactive drug before the age of 14, and 91% by the age of 18.

Apart from adolescents, the other age group that seems to be prone to develop drug dependence is the middle aged, although they are more likely to be dependent on legally prescribed psychoactive drugs. The number of people over 50 notified to the Home Office is small; there were 42 in 1986, of whom 29 were male and 13 were female.

The extent of psychotropic drug use in the elderly is considerable: in a study of admissions to a geriatric unit, 18.7% of 1260 admissions were taking benzodiazepine hypnotics. It is also estimated that 40–45% of benzodiazepine prescription items are supplied to patients over the age of 65. Female consumption rates are about twice those of males. When it is considered that doctors sometimes prescribe tranquillisers for conditions other than anxiety or insomnia and that physical disorders and difficult social and domestic problems rate high on the list of reasons for prescribing long-term benzodiazepines, the high consumption of these drugs by the elderly is not very surprising.

Sex

Males are more likely to use illicit drugs than females. In 1986 about 70% of newly notified addicts were males and 30% females. The male/female ratio has been changing over the years. In the mid 1960s and 1970s the ratio fluctuated around 3:1. Recently the number of females using illicit drugs has been increasing. Hartnoll and colleagues (1985), in their study in London, found a male/female ratio of 1.8:1, but examining data for convictions the difference is even more pronounced. In 1987 about 87% of those convicted for drug offences were male.

Women and drugs

All studies indicate that women exceed men in their consumption of psychotropic drugs. The ratio of female to male is surprisingly consistent at about 2:1 over most parts of the world. There are obvious psychobiological differences between men and women as well as differences in social situations which may influence this differential incidence. Women also have specific problems in relation to premenstrual tension, pregnancy, unwanted pregnancy, abortion and the menopause, and the attitudes of doctors, who are predominantly male, may also be an important influence. It is recognised that women clearly do report more feelings of discomfort and more symptoms than men; they are also more likely to seek help earlier. The empirical evidence suggests that, contrary to popular opinion, women fulfilling numerous roles have lower morbidity, have fewer days sick, and take fewer sedatives and tranquillisers than women restricted to the traditional role of housewife.

It has been suggested that females who use illicit drugs have personality disturbances greater than their male counterparts. They are also suspected of having a less favourable prognosis. However, a study of the drug abusers who came to treatment in the London treatment agencies in 1984–1985 found the women to be very similar to the men in most of these respects, the main difference being that significantly more females were likely to have drug-using partners than male. Females also differed in their criminality in that they were more likely to be convicted at a later age than males; they are also likely to have fewer convictions during their drug use (Sheehan and Oppenheimer, 1988).

Problems related to drug use

The Advisory Council on the Misuse of Drugs has defined a problem drug user as a person who has physical, psychological, social or legal problems associated with drug use. Most of the recent studies involve multi-agency enumeration of problem drug abusers but the definition of problems can vary between observers. In addition, there is often a disparity between drug users and the agencies in the perception of problems, drug users having a tendency to minimise them. Longitudinal studies of adolescents clearly show that illicit drug use has an adverse effect on education, work history and physical health, and that criminal involvement is also increased.

A recent survey by Parker *et al.* (1988) in Bristol found that of 759 problem drug users over half had problems associated with opiates, 17% had problems with solvents, 13% with stimulants, 9% with cannabis and 3% with hallucinogens.

Social problems

Most studies suggest that the majority of drug users are single. They have a higher incidence of divorce or separation, indicating a greater degree of difficulties with relationships. They also have more problems with accommodation. In one of the recent surveys, 75% were unemployed and only 13% were in regular employment. Two-thirds of those who were unemployed were out of work for more than a year, and the majority (69%) were dependent on state benefits.

Stimson and Oppenheimer (1982), in their studies of opiate abusers in the late 1960s and early 1970s, used four variables—unemployment, irregular income, illegal activities and drug subcultural involvement—in an attempt to classify drug users. They found that they were a varied group but could be broadly classified into four groups. The 'stables', who were employed and had little involvement with the drug subculture, and the 'junkies', who were the most chaotic, were the two extremes while the 'two worlders' and the 'loners' were in between. The 'two worlders' were likely to be employed and to have a regular income, but their involvement with the drug subculture was quite extensive. The loners were neither employed nor did they have much involvement in the addict subculture. Their source of income was social security.

Medical problems

Some studies have looked at the range of medical problems encountered by drug users (Ghodse 1981). Not surprisingly, injectors reported having more problems than non-injectors, and Plant (1975), in his community survey of 200 drug users of whom only three were injectors, found very few who had suffered from physical harm; 12.5% of the sample reported having consulted a GP at some time due to problems with drug use.

Ghodse (1976) carried out a prospective study in 62 casualty departments of drug-related incidents over a period of one month in 1975. The drug dependence was carefully defined. The overwhelming majority (96%) of drug-related incidents were due to overdoses, and more than a quarter of them were taken by drug-dependent individuals. About 4% of incidents, 65 altogether, were due to complications related to drug use, e.g. infection due to injection, drug-induced psychosis, withdrawal reaction, etc. One in three patients presenting with a drug-related event under the age of 30 was dependent on drugs.

Of the sample of 150 drug misusers who attended three London agencies for the first time between 1984 and 1986, 11% reported experiencing skin infections and abscesses due to injection, 5% had infectious hepatitis, one person had septicaemia and 11% had overdosed, all within the previous four weeks. Enquiry about the lifetime experience of drug-related conditions revealed that 62% had experienced loss of weight of severe degree, 22% had had hepatitis, 16% had had an abscess, and 2% septicaemia (Sheehan and Oppenheimer, 1988).

Legal problems

It must be remembered that under present law the use of heroin and other drugs obtained illegally is itself a crime. In addition it is often suggested that some drug-dependent individuals have to resort to crime to obtain money for their drugs. However, drug abuse has a more complicated relationship with criminality, and 30–50% of young people attending treatment centres report a history of conviction before drug use with a subsequent conviction rate of 80–90% during drug use. Interestingly, once drug use starts, the rate of conviction does not differ between those who had a history of pre-drug conviction and those without. The recent study from London of 150 drug misusers seeking help for the first time revealed that 57% were currently involved with the law, 50% were on bail and 17%

were under police enquiry. During the period of drug use the total sample had 69 convictions per year between them. The self-reported criminal activity during the previous three months showed that 96% had been in illegal possession of drugs, 44% had obtained goods by false pretences, 41% had received stolen goods, 45% had stolen from a shop, and 50% had sold drugs.

Several studies indicate that, in general, stopping drug use also results in a decrease in criminal activity.

Conclusions

It is generally accepted that it is impossible to obtain accurate information about the number of people using illicit drugs. However, in spite of all their drawbacks, the official statistics obtained through the notification system, and the enforcement statistics obtained as a result of police and customs activities, remain the main source of information in the UK.

In recent times the Department of Health has encouraged the assessment and monitoring of the prevalence of drug misuse in all local health authority areas in England and Wales so that proper service provision can be made. It was also hoped that the impact of the efforts would be measured simultaneously.

Taking information from all sources together, a rough picture tends to emerge, certainly in relation to notifiable drugs (opioids and cocaine). In 1986 there were 14 800 addicts to notifiable drugs known to the Home Office. Multiplying that figure by a multiple of 5 or 10 will give us a figure of 74 000 to 148 000, which possibly is the best estimate of drug misusers using notifiable drugs. There is a wide variation in the prevalence of drug misusers in different localities, and also over time, and the use of a multiplier is likely to underestimate in some areas and to overestimate in others. In addition there is an unknown number who are using non-notifiable drugs such as amphetamine on a regular or occasional basis. In certain parts of the country amphetamines are the main drug of abuse by injection. There is no doubt that we have witnessed a rise in the incidence of drug abuse. It is not just the present rate of prevalence, but also the rate at which it is rising, that is worrying.

Evidence suggests that use of cannabis and other illicit drugs represents the later stages of drug-taking, which follows a well-defined sequence that starts with socially acceptable drugs such as alcohol and tobacco. Even in schoolchildren the number of pupils using alcohol and cigarettes is far greater than the number who experiment with solvents or illicit drugs at any one time.

The division between legal and illegal drug misuse is somewhat artificial. Psychotropic drugs and alcohol are as much a part of the drug scene as illegal drugs are for many young people. Similarly, many older people are prescribed and have been taking tranquillisers on a regular basis, not for any definable medical condition, but because they have got insoluble social or personal problems. Many alcoholics also misuse various drugs like chlormethiazole (Heminevrin) and benzodiazepines.

One of the major deficiencies in the study of the prevalence of drug misuse in the UK is the lack of regular national surveys of this subject. National household surveys are held in Britain regularly, and one way of rectifying the deficiency would be to include drug questionnaires in them and to ensure the anonymity of the responder. This would certainly give a much better picture about the use of drugs that are not notifiable at present.

There is ample evidence to show that young people who abuse illicit drugs tend to use legal drugs such as alcohol and cigarettes early and in greater quantities. There is also evidence that, if a person has not experimented with them by their late teens or early twenties, the chances of their using them later is greatly diminished. This has an important bearing on prevention strategies. The best campaign for preventing drug abuse may well be to concentrate on discouraging young people from starting drinking and smoking cigarettes at an early age.

References

A'Brook M.F., Hailstone J.D. and McLaughton I.E. (1967) Psychiatric illnesses in the medical profession. *Br. J. Psychiat.*, **113**, 1013–1023.

Advisory Council on the Misuse of Drugs (1982) *Treatment and Rehabilitation* (London: Department of Health and Social Security).

Anderson R. (1980) The use of repeatedly prescribed medicines. *J. Roy. Coll. Gen. Pract.*, **30**, 607–613.

Arroyave F., Little D., Litemendia F. and De Alarcon R. (1973) Misuse of heroin and methadone in the city of Oxford. *Br. J. Addiction*, **68**, 129–135.

Balding, J. (1987) *Schoolchildren and Drugs in 1987*. Schools Health Education Unit, Exeter (unpublished data).

Beary M.D., Christofides J., Fry D., Ghodse A.H., Smith E. and Smith V. (1987) The benzodiazepines as substance of abuse. *Practitioner*, **231**, 19–20.

Blumberg H.H. (1981) Characteristics of people coming to treatment. In *Drug Problems in Britain*, eds Edwards G. and Busch C. (London: Academic Press), pp. 76–115.

De Alarcon R. and Rathod N.H. (1968) Prevalence and early detection of heroin abuse. *Br. Med. J.*, **2**, 549–553.

Ditton J. and Speirits K. (1981) The rapid increase of heroin addiction in Glasgow during 1981. Background Paper 2, University of Glasgow.

Dunnell K. and Cartwright A. (1972) *Medicine Takers, Prescribers and Hoarders* (London: Routledge, Kegan and Paul).

Ghodse A.H. (1976) Drug problems dealt with by 62 London casualty departments. *Br. J. Prevent. Soc. Med.*, **30**, 251–256.

Ghodse A.H. (1977) Casualty departments and the monitoring of drug dependence. *Br. Med. J.*, **1**, 1381–1382.

Ghodse A. H. (1981) Morbidity and mortality. In *Drug Problems in Britain*, eds Edwards G. and Busch C. (London: Academic Press), pp. 171–215.

Ghodse A.H. (1987) Indicators of the extent of drug-related health problems. In *Psychoactive Drugs and Health Problems*, eds Idanpaan-Heikkila J., Ghodse A.H. and Khan I. (Helsinki: National Board of Health), pp. 28–51.

Glanz A. and Taylor C. (1986) Findings of a national survey of the role of general practitioners in the treatment of opiate abuse—extent of contact with opiate misusers. *Br. Med. J.*, **293**, 427–439.

Hartnoll R.L., Mitcheson M.C., Lewis R. and Bryer S. (1985) Estimating the prevalence of opioid dependence. *Lancet*, **1**, 203–205.

Haw S. (1985) *Drug Problems in Greater Glasgow* (Glasgow: SCODA).

Home Office Statistical Bulletin (1987) Statistics of the misuse of drugs, United Kingdom 1986.

Home Office Statistical Bulletin (1988) Statistics of the misuse of drugs, United Kingdom 1987.

Hugh M. and Mayhew P. (1983) The British Crime Survey. *Home Office Research Study, No. 76*. (London: HMSO).

Kosviner A., Mitchison M., Myers K., Ogborne A., Stimson G., Zacure J. and Edwards G. (1968) Heroin in use in a provincial town. *Lancet*, **1**, 1189–1192.

Kosviner A., Hawks D. and Webb M.G.T. (1973) Cannabis use amongst British university students. Prevalence rates and differences between students who have tried cannabis and who have never tried it. *Br. J. Addiction*, **69**, 35–60.

Levy B. (1985) Prevalence of abuse of substances in the Brighton health authority area, Brighton, Sussex (unpublished data).

Midweek (1973) *Survey of Drug Use in the United Kingdom* (London: Social Research Design Consultancy).

Mott J. (1976) The epidemiology of self reported drug misuse in the U.K. *Bull. Narcotics*, **28**, 43–54.

Mott J. (1985) Self reported cannabis use in Great Britain in 1981. *Br. J. Addiction*, **80**, 37–43.

Murray R.M. (1972) The use and abuse of analgesics. Scottish Med. J., **17**, 393–397.

Office of Population Censuses and Surveys (1973) *Public Attitudes on Drug Taking* (London: Home Office Research Unit).

Parker H., Newcombe R. and Bakx K. (1987) The new heroin users: prevalence and characteristics in Wirral, Merseyside. *Br. J. Addiction*, **8**, 147–157.

Parker J., Pool Y., Rawle R. and Gay M. (1988) Monitoring problem drug use in Bristol. *Br. J. Psychiat.*, **152**, 214–221.

Pattinson C.J., Barnes E.A. and Thorley A. (1982) Tyneside drug prevalence and indicators study. Newcastle Centre for Alcohol and Drug Studies (unpublished data).

Pearson G., Gillman M. and McIver S. (1985) Young people and heroin use in the north of England. Middlesex Polytechnic (unpublished data).

Peck D.F. and Plant M.A. (1986) Unemployment and illegal drug use: concordant evidence from prospective study and national trends. *Br. Med. J.*, **293**, 929–932.

Pevelar C., Green R. and Mandelbrote R. (1988) Prevalence of heroin misuse in Oxford City. *Br. J. Addiction*, **83**, 513–518.

Plant M.A. (1975) Drug takers in an English town. *Br. J. Criminol.*, **15**, 181–186.

Plant M.A., Peck D.F. and Stewart R. (1984) The correlates of alcohol related consequences, the illicit drug use among a cohort of Scottish teenagers. *Br. J. Addiction*, **79**, 197–200.

Pritchard C., Fielding M., Choudry N., Cox M. and Diamond I. (1986) Incidence of drug and solvent abuse in normal fourth and fifth year comprehensive school children; some social behavioural characteristics. *Br. J. Social Work*, **16**, 341–357.

Sheehan M. and Oppenheimer E. (1988) Who comes for treatment? Drug misusers at three London agencies. *Br. J. Addiction*, **83**, 311–320.

Somekh D. (1976) Prevalence of self reported drug use amongst London undergraduates. *Br. J. Addiction*, **71**, 79–88.

Stimson G.V. and Oppenheimer B. (1982) *Heroin Addiction, Treatment and Control in Britain* (London: Tavistock Publications).

Stimson G.V., Oppenheimer E. and Stimson C.A. (1984) Drug abuse in the medical profession—addict doctors and the Home Office. *Br. J. Addiction*, **79**, 395–402.

Strang J. and Shah A. (1985) Notification of drug addiction and the medical practitioner; an evaluation of the system. *Br. J. Psychiat.*, **147**, 195–197.

Swadi H. (1988) Drug and substance use among 3,333 London adolescents. *Br. J. Addiction*, **83**, 935–942.

Wagstaff A. and Maynard A. (1986) The consumption of illicit drugs in the UK. *Br. J. Addiction*, **81**, 691–696.

Bibliography

Ashton M. (1987) *Surveys and Statistics on Drug Taking in Britain* (London: ISDD Publication), April.

Ghodse A.H. (1987) Indicators of the extent of drug-related health problems. In *Psychoactive Drugs and Health Problems*, eds Idanpaan-Heikkila J., Ghodse A.H. and Khan I. (Helsinki: Government of Finland), pp. 28–51.

Mott J. (1976) The epidemiology of self reported drug misuse in the United Kingdom. *Bull. Narcotics*, **28**, 43–54.

Stimson G.C. (1981) Epidemiological research on drug use in general populations. In *Drug Problems in Britain—A Review of Ten Years*, eds Edwards G. and Busch C. (London: Academic Press), pp. 51–75.

4

Courses of Drug Use: The Concepts of Career and Natural History

John Strang, Michael Gossop and *Gerry Stimson*

Synopsis

What we see depends on where we are looking from. The natural history model of addiction starts with the end-point of the heroin addict and looks back through his or her career, seeking to make sense out of apparent chaos and to identify earlier stages so as to establish the natural process which led to the current situation. However, if the model is examined from the other end (i.e. the point of onset of use of drugs), then a radically different picture emerges in which the diversity of outcomes is a more striking characteristic than the orderly progression towards dependent use. Looked at from the viewpoint of the first-time experimenter, the natural history that leads to full-blown addiction is but one of many possible paths.

This chapter examines the concepts of career and natural history and suggests that they are distinct entities whose different contributions to our understanding become more evident when attention is paid to their separateness. The habit of referring to one or other of the concepts as if they were synonymous with the other should be avoided as it fails to exploit the full potential of understanding. Initial separate consideration of career and natural history should then be followed by consideration of the lines of intersection between the differing planes of the concepts, where study may be particularly interesting and instructive.

Introduction

Although researchers and drug workers have noted that not all drug users appear to be dependent users or regular users, the direct research evidence itself is paltry. This neglect is probably aggravated by the fact that most sources of information in the UK and elsewhere are based upon figures collected on drug users who come into contact with statutory services such as drug clinics, general practitioners or the prison service, and within this group it is likely that there would indeed be a high proportion of drug users who demonstrate a high level of problems related to their drug use and who have well established and/or high dose habits.

Is the choice of terminology really so important? Terminology represents much more than just the terms themselves: it represents the thinking behind the terms, and so the argument becomes much more than just a semantic debate. A colleague recently stood up at a meeting on the treatment of heroin addiction and began talking about his somewhat unorthodox treatment approach with some of the heroin 'fanciers' in his city. The challenge he was making to orthodox treatment approaches was as nothing compared with the challenge he was making to the concept of the heroin addict. If the attachment of the heroin user to his drug could be likened to the fondness of a pigeon fancier for his birds, then the whole context within which 'treatment' might be sought or delivered (or even be seen to exist) would require a fundamental re-examination.

More than ever before, there is now a need for a fuller understanding of the possible courses down which an individual and his or her drug use may travel. With the advent of HIV and its transmission through sexual and especially through shared-injection practices among some drug users, we are now in need of a more sophisticated understanding of the phenomenon of drug use and how it may change for an individual over time; and this improved understanding should inform us as we plan responses geared towards influencing in one way or another the course which that individual might follow. Somehow we need to make sense of various accounts of initial use of drugs such as 'I just wondered what it was like', of returning to drug use such as 'I wanted to see if heroin was as good as the first time', and of explanations of giving up such as 'I just decided I'd had enough'. Are these just illusions of choice—mere epiphenomena? If not, how can they be accommodated within a model for understanding the behaviour of drug use?

It is important to be clear that, quite apart from the different drugs themselves and routes of administration, the use of drugs may hold different meanings for each individual, and different meanings for the same individual at different points in time. The non-medical use of drugs has been described as being either experimental, recreational or compulsive. While it is unlikely that these terms refer to real categories, they are nevertheless useful markers in discussing the different possible personal meanings of drug use, and the terms appear to have real relevance in discussions with drug users themselves. Use of drugs experimentally or recreationally is often seen by the drug user themselves as positive (i.e. in pursuit of some positive effect) whereas the compulsive use of drugs is more likely to be associated with a wish to abolish some negative effect. Given that many drug users entering treatment give a history of prolonged periods of drug use during which they did not see this as a problem, it is surprising that so little attention has been paid to the non-compulsive users of illicit drugs. Zinberg has drawn attention recently to opiate users who exercise considerable control over their drug use (Zinberg, 1984); and, in the UK, Blackwell (1983) has described various groups of casual drug users whose use or non-use of drugs, whose choice of drugs and whose pattern of drug use were influenced by a variety of factors including economic, social and personal considerations. It is important to note in this context that the term 'controlled' with regard to drug use is being used in a different way from its use with controlled drinking. According to both Zinberg (1984) and Blackwell (1983), an important feature of controlled opiate use may be the avoidance of daily use of the drug and of the development of tolerance, unlike the arguments that have been put forward in the alcohol field.

The issue of terminology and the way it influences our thinking is also evident within treatment services. In their day, pejorative terms such as 'dope fiend' were replaced by the more modern terms of 'drug addict' and more recently 'drug dependent' which in the UK endorsed the view that use of drugs was a medical disorder and not a moral disorder or vicious indulgence. In the early 1980s, the Advisory Council on the Misuse of Drugs (1982) introduced the term 'the problem drug taker' referring to 'any person who experiences social, psychological, physical or legal problems related to intoxication and/or regular excessive consumption and/or dependence as a consequence of his own use of drugs'. As with choice of models for understanding the course of drug use, the choice of terms for the drug taker has a marked influence on how the drug worker, drug taker and society make sense of the whole scenario. Certainly, the widespread embracing of the term 'the problem drug taker' in the UK was accompanied by a greater recognition of the volitional nature of the behaviour and of the social context within which the behaviour occurred. This was often in contrast to the relationship that may have existed between drug taker and drug worker when guided by the prior terminology of the drug addict or drug dependent (defined as 'a psychic, and sometimes also physical, state resulting from the interaction between living organism and a drug, characterised by behavioural and other responses that always include a compulsion to take the drug on a continuous or periodic basis in order to experience its psychic effects, and sometimes to avoid the discomfort of abstinence'). Sadly, there is a tendency to move between one term and another with scant regard for the different origins and significance of the terms, and a corresponding lack of appreciation of the influence the terminology may have upon subsequent outcome.

The next part of the chapter includes a more detailed examination of the concepts of career and of natural history. The implications of these two concepts have recently been examined in the drug field by Thorley (1981) and in the alcohol field by Edwards (1984). Both commentators conclude that the evidence is heavily against a simple medical concept of natural history in which there is insufficient regard paid to the powerful non-biological influences that may exist such as cultural context, peer-group influence and various other cultural and social factors. However, as Edwards points out, we should bear in mind that these two ideas are not necessarily competing: the real challenge may be to determine how they may be brought together. Edwards' article is a particularly lucid charting of these troubled waters which not only identifies in passing the deficiencies of each of the concepts of career and natural history, but also emphasises the value of their separateness and draws attention to the need for a meaningful synthesis between these two types of understanding which lie on planes at an angle to each other so that the interplay and intersections are likely to be particularly enlightening.

The concept of career

'Junk is not a kick—it's a way of life' (Burroughs, 1953).

The concept of the drug-using career evokes an altogether different set of associations from those triggered by the concept of natural history. Ideas such as contingency (external factors which can influence the course of drug taking) and voluntarism (that people exercise choices in their behaviour) generally have a higher profile with the career concept. This concept of a drug-using 'career' is largely derived from interactionist studies influenced by the Chicago school of sociology under Everett Hughes. The passage through life could be seen as a career, during which an individual may enter and leave various activities. Many writers in this genre have likened a deviant career to an 'occupation' and have described such unusual 'occupations' as cheque forging and prostitution as well as drug and alcohol use.

A detailed description of the heroin user's life on the streets in New York was conducted in the late 1960s by Preble and Casey (1969) in which they gave a full description of the different roles which might be occupied in the extended drug-using network—not only roles within use of the drug, but also within its importation and distribution and in the criminal activities which raised funds for its purchase. The original paper by Preble and Casey captures much of the same quality as William Burroughs' 'Junkie'—a sense of the ups and downs, but above all of great involvement in the lifestyle.

The concept of a 'deviant career' has been developed to describe such movement in and out of various roles over time. Pearson and his colleagues (1987) point out that, just as there is no typical heroin user, so there is no typical heroin user's career; but nevertheless they find it useful to describe four different levels of involvement with drugs:

(1) the non-user;
(2) initial offer/experimentation;

(3) (a) occasional/recreational use, and
    (b) the grey area of transitional use;
(4) addictive use.

Pearson describes such levels of involvement as statuses, with movement
between them being effected through transition points and with each status
being associated with different possible exit routes towards abstinence.
Various studies (e.g. Chapple *et al.*, 1972; Robertson *et al.*, 1986; Parker *et
al.*, 1988) find evidence of individuals moving in and out of drug use during
their career, which Parker refers to as the incidence and outcidence which
together result in the prevalence of the behaviour within a community. The
idea of career has also been extended to 'illness careers' in which illness is
considered as a social phenomenon as well as a biological disturbance. This
approach underlies Stimson and Oppenheimer's organisation of their
follow-up data into stages of a hypothetical addict career including routes
into addiction, how people become patients, how they organise their lives
while using drugs, and how they stop using drugs (Stimson and
Oppenheimer, 1982).

The concept of natural history

> We admitted that we were powerless over our addiction, and that our lives had
> become unmanageable
>
> (Narcotics Anonymous, first step.)

Just as there are attractions to reliance on the career concept, so it is with
natural history. 'Epidemics' occur, the condition can be passed on from
one individual to the next, and the disadvantaged or vulnerable appear to
be particularly susceptible to 'infection'. The second Brain Report in the
UK (ICDA, 1965), which eventually led to the establishment of the first
special drug treatment centres, referred to heroin addiction as a socially
infectious condition. Sociologists (e.g. Parker *et al.*, 1988) and
epidemiologists (e.g. Hunt and Chambers, 1976) have found value in using
the concept of the epidemic, although accompanying their use of this term
with understandable disclaimers and apologies. However, when we choose
to look more carefully at the concept of natural history, we find that it is
used in different ways by different authors. Are we to take it as a term that
describes the natural history of the whole behaviour as would appear to be
the case with the early writings from Winick (1962) with his concept that
drug addicts would inevitably 'mature out' over time (and the later recent
revivals of this concept in the UK); or are we to regard natural history as a
much more tightly defined concept (as proposed by Edwards, 1984) which
refers to 'the sequential development of designated biological processes
within the individual'? Thus it shares with the more sociological concepts
the longitudinal perspective and the sequential nature of the levels of

involvement of models such as Pearson's. Edwards cautions against mistakenly equating the study of personal biological evolution with a narrowly biological explanation of the entire sequence of events. The idea of a natural history of reactivity to drugs would embrace such phenomena as the metabolic and neuro-adaptational changes (tolerance) and the possibility that there might be genetic moulding of initial and subsequent responses to use of drugs.

Proponents of the natural history model often hold the view that there is a largely inevitable progression of the 'disease' until death or some other resolution occurs. Thus Winick (1962) put forward his early psychodynamically influenced model of 'maturing out' which held that young people used opiates as a maladaptive coping mechanism at a particular stage in their lives, and that they would spontaneously cease to use opiates once these problems became resolved in the transition to adulthood. Progressive deterioration to a personal 'rock bottom' is a popular view in Alcoholics Anonymous and Narcotics Anonymous, where a 'disease' model of addiction is publicly embraced and is a central part of the philosophy. However, in its application, the AA/NA concept of a disease model stands out in stark contrast to the usual understanding of a disease model, in that the self-help movement places great emphasis on personal responsibility and self-efficacy *specifically because* they believe that they suffer from a lifelong disease from which compensatory changes such as total abstinence and following the 12 steps are their only means of avoiding disease progression.

Brickman and his colleagues (1982) have identified four models which may specify helping and coping behaviour. The four models are defined according to their high or low attribution of responsibility for the problem and attribution of responsibility for the solution. Thus, in the 'moral model', there are high levels of attribution of responsibility to the individual for both the problem and the solution; whereas with the 'medical model' there is generally a low level of attribution to the individual of responsibility for the solution (and usually for the problem also). In this regard, the 12 steps/NA model is interesting in that, despite apparently embracing a strong medical model, it nevertheless places great responsibility on the individual for self-help and self-change.

Two of the most determined criticisms against the natural history model are that it diminishes personal control/direction and hence responsibility for change, and that it also places intervention in the hands of doctors. The drug taker and family may feel *as if* they are incapable of intervening constructively, and there may sometimes be value to drug taker and family in holding this view: value either because it temporarily legitimises the behaviour that would otherwise be classed as deviant and relieves them from feeling guilty; or value because it may provide a framework for response as in the case of work with NA. Eiser and Gossop (1979) have examined the attitudes of drug users admitted to an in-patient drug dependence unit and found differences in the extent to which such individuals saw themselves as either 'hooked' or 'sick', and that drug users varied in their responses according to the extent of prior contact with drug treatment services.

The need for synthesis of these two concepts has been emphasised by Edwards and others. All too often, champions of one view or another will borrow from one or other models according to whether or not it supports their pre-formed view. Rather there should be an examination of the implications of the issue from various different standpoints so as to gain a better three-dimensional grasp of the sequential nature of the drug-taking behaviour.

In the next section an examination is made of some of the particular features which appear to be significant characteristics of the course of drug use over time.

The variability of the course

A striking early observation is that the drug user does not progress in a predictable and orderly manner through a series of stages of drug-taking behaviour. The drug user who experiments may cease to use once his curiosity is satisfied; and the occasional recreational user may not progress to daily use (see discussion of chippers (i.e. people who inject occasionally), for example (Zinberg, 1984)).

Having recognised that occasional opiate use may occur, it then becomes necessary to consider whether it is always possible for such a drug user to resume occasional use even after periods during which they have been addicted. The popularly held view among treatment agencies and many drug addicts themselves is that, once they have become firmly addicted, they are no longer able to move back to that stage of drug taking when they could take it or leave it. The behaviour appears to have become an all or nothing phenomenon. However, despite this widely held view, there are studies which present some evidence to the contrary including the Vietnam study, after which Robins *et al.* (1974) reported that 'contrary to conventional belief, the occasional use of narcotics without becoming addicted appears possible even for men who have previously been dependent on narcotics'. Also, what might be happening by way of biological adaptation to the 'stable addict' who neither abstains nor deteriorates and whose daily dose of drugs remains constant over years or decades? And what of the drug addict who gives up drug taking for a new love? Somehow our understanding of the changing nature of drug use over time must accommodate such diverse developments. The most incorrect and unnatural use of the concept of natural history is to lend credibility to the view of inevitability—a professional version of the 'slippery slope' theory. Such a view fails to acknowledge the rich range of alternatives available at each point in the course of an individual's drug use, and also fails to recognise the ability of the individual to exercise influence over the probabilities of which options come to pass. The power of non-biological influences appears considerable. Not only do such factors appear to be major influences on the onset of drug use as in the whole 1960s phenomenon in the western world and in smaller epidemics (e.g. Robertson's description of the Edinburgh epidemic and Parker's description of the Mersey epidemic, both in the early 1980s), but such factors appear to be powerful influences on the movement out of drug using as well. One of the most striking examples in recent times is a study of drug use by American soldiers during and after their period of serving in the Vietnam war (Robins *et al.*, 1974). Forty-three per cent of the 451 general sample of enlisted men in the US Army going to Vietnam in 1971 used opiates while in Vietnam. However, on follow-up back in the US one year later, only 9.5% had used any narcotics. Of 91 men who reported that they had been addicted while in Vietnam, only two reported continuing that addiction on their return to the US. Robins *et al.* (1975) have subsequently suggested that the impact of prior predispositions to deviance may become manifest in settings with greater opportunities to express deviant behaviour, and she cites the Vietnam experience as a particularly vivid example. She also observes that in the 'post-epidemic' years there was a decline in the number of drug initiations for this cohort followed by a gradual return to pre-Vietnam levels, and she suggests that there may be a temporary 'immunity' for those who survive exposure to such high-risk situations.

Recent findings in the UK provide further evidence that progression down the slippery slope is by no means inevitable. Gossop *et al.* (1988) have reported on the characteristics of heroin addicts who take their drug by smoking ('chasing the dragon'), many of whom have continued with this less efficient route of administration for many years and have developed regular high dose habits without progressing on to injecting. This apparent robustness of the behaviour of heroin smoking differs from the findings of Robins and her colleagues with the Vietnam sample, in which those who continued to use heroin on their return to the US usually changed from their Vietnam pattern of smoking or sniffing to a US pattern of injecting (Robins *et al.*, 1974).

Natural patterns of cessation and recovery

One of the early descriptions came from Winick (1962) with his hypothesis that age and length of addiction were related to a spontaneous 'maturing out' process. Many subsequent studies have failed to support his simple hypothesis, and it may be more productive to consider the factors (including age and duration of drug use) which may influence the timing of cessation. More recently Anglin *et al.* (1986) have provided evidence from a large follow-up study suggesting that a natural process of maturing out may exist but that it may be conditional on addiction-related or contextual factors such as property-crime and drug dealing which slow down the rate of any such maturing out.

Stimson and Oppenheimer (1982) have reported on the progress over a decade of heroin addicts recruited to the study from London out-patient drug dependence units soon after their inception in 1968. Of the 128 subjects, 40 were drug free on follow-up and had travelled down a variety of paths to reach this drug-free state; 21 had received out-patient treatment (17 slowly withdrawing their dose of drugs over months or years and 44 stopping abruptly or unexpectedly); 12 had received in-patient detoxification (of whom 10 had two or more such in-patient detoxifications); six in prison; and one in a therapeutic community. Drug-free status on follow-up was frequently associated with achievement of employment and giving up old addict friends, and for many it had involved a geographical move. Eight of these 40 drug-free subjects had continued to use opiates occasionally for a few months, and for two of them this continued for several years. During the first year 13 drank alcohol heavily although only one appears to have experienced longer term problems with use of alcohol. In his study of the process of recovery of this same group, Wille (1981) identifies two basic patterns: (i) a planned, internally motivated, voluntary way of becoming abstinent, and (ii) an external, enforced way.

Schasre (1966) has examined the factors associated with spontaneous remission from heroin use in 40 subjects and identified the following factors: negative experience with peers, pressure from partner, increased awareness of the stigma of addiction, geographical move or the disappearance of a drug dealer.

Waldorf and Biernacki (1979) have reviewed the literature on the natural recovery from opiate addiction, and in a series of studies in San Francisco have identified certain themes which occur frequently. They suggest that the process of natural recovery concerns an alteration in the person's identity, with the replacement of an addict identity with some more ordinary identity. Biernacki (1983) later proposes that for those who are particularly deeply immersed in the world of drug use it may be necessary to create a new emergent identity to facilitate natural recovery rather than relying on some pre-existing ordinary identity. Similarly, Jorquez (1983) suggested that becoming abstinent and maintaining abstinence comprise two concurrent processes: extrication, involving the severing of social ties and dependencies to the drug world; and accommodation, involving the adjustment to the new ordinary lifestyle.

Evidence for stages of dependence and orderly progression

Separate from the above consideration over whether or not progression takes place, there is also the related issue of whether any such progression follows a predetermined course such as would be seen with most diseases. It is at this stage that some of the confusion becomes most apparent. Some individuals may find it convenient to consider early points of contact with drug use (e.g. experimentation and early recreational use) as if they were a prodrome of a later clinically manifest illness, but we must be careful not to slip from 'as if' statements into actual statements and thus reify the metaphor. There may be value in regarding the spread of a wave of popularity for Space Invaders through a school as spreading like an epidemic through a close group of friends, through a class, then between classes and finally spilling out into the extended community: it may be useful to regard a fascination with Space Invaders as if it were a disease but it would clearly be mistaken to regard the analogy as reality. On the other hand, we may wish to look at neurochemical changes or altered psychophysiological responses to examine their degree of reversibility and to gauge whether they might alter the likelihood or nature of any subsequent drug use. In these latter examples, it may be more fruitful to look for evidence of critical thresholds and stages of general and neuroadaptational changes which might subsequently influence the course of drug use for that individual. Edwards (1984) explores some of the possibilities within the alcohol field but finds rather surprisingly that there has been little human research on this topic. Issues such as the speed of reinstatement of tolerance and other adaptational changes are clearly of direct significance to the course of drug use for those individuals who are not drug-naive; but we are still ill-equipped to deal with straightforward questions such as whether altered biological responses may influence the likelihood that a drug user will follow one course or another.

Clinical studies within the drug field give information which appears to lend support to both the career concept and the natural history concept. When we examine studies of drug users which have paid attention to the changing patterns of drug use over time, we find evidence of considerable movement in and out of use from lighter to heavier use and vice versa. An early UK study of drug users living in the community was conducted by Hawks (1976) in Cambridge. He followed 37 heroin users identified during the first year of the study at which time he found that only 17 were regular daily users. When he followed up this original sample plus subsequent recruits, he found that there had been considerable variation in their patterns of use over time. Frequency of drug use had diminished over the three-year period so that by the end of the study only 11% were still regular users. A more recent study in Manchester (Strang *et al.*, 1987) found similar evidence of considerable changes in the pattern of drug use within individuals who were still using drugs at two-year follow-up. As with the Hawks study, Strang found that many of the changes that had occurred in the pattern of use of ongoing drug users were changes that were away from the popular conception of progression. Thus, 23 of the 55 ongoing drug users were injecting less frequently, and only two had increased the frequency of injecting.

Other studies have found evidence suggesting that the course of drug use changes according to the degree and duration of involvement. Chapple *et al.* (1972) adopted a simple three-stage chronological classification of early addict (stage 1), pre-chronic addict (stage 2) and chronic addict (stage 3), grouping them according to their length of involvement in the drug field and in receipt of prescriptions for opiates. Prognosis became progressively worse with progression through the stages. Gossop *et al.* (1989) have also reported on the apparent instability of occasional use among opiate addicts who have recently been involved in a detoxification programme. During the first two months after discharge, 25% were endeavouring to use drugs on an occasional non-daily basis; but by the final two months of the six-month follow-up period only 13 of the sample were still using in this way and the remainder had either become daily users (43%) or were abstinent (44%).

Recreational and controlled use

If the diversity of drug-taking behaviour and outcomes is so great among confirmed opiate addicts, the picture is even more diverse when we look at the broader population of drug takers including those who have stopped short of dependent use. Evidence from surveys into patterns of drug use in the community indicates that problematic/dependent use is a statistical rarity. For example Plant *et al.* (1985) conducted a survey on Scottish schoolchildren and found that overall levels of ever-used illicit drug use were high (37% of males and 23% of females) although the great majority of this group were not regular users. Opiate use was rare (1%) in this population of schoolchildren. Plant's follow-up survey of this sample also shows the considerable variations in patterns of use over time.

Qualitative data were collected by a market research company prior to the launch of the Government's anti-heroin media campaign in the mid-1980s, and these provide another unexpected source of information on recreational heroin users. The survey involved interviews with drug users both in and out of treatment, and identified drug users who did not regard themselves as dependent. This group was further subdivided into those 'verging on dependence' and those 'who seem able to control their drug use' (Andrew Irving Associates, 1985).

There clearly exist people who use drugs such as heroin for long periods of time while apparently avoiding the problems of dependence. A common clinical finding is that a heroin addict will have gone through an early period of months or years when the drug use was regarded as neither problematic nor dependent use. Various studies (e.g. Lindesmith, 1947; Chein *et al.*, 1964) have found evidence of long continued non-addictive users of heroin. Many of these may choose to remain out of contact with treatment services; but even among those who present for treatment, some may not be using regularly. O'Brien (1976) found that almost half of his sample of opiate addicts applying for methadone maintenance were actually using opiates on a less than daily basis (33% gave negative or weak positive responses to naloxone challenge and a further 12% were not tested because of other evidence that they were not daily users). Hartnoll *et al.* (1985) conducted snowballing interviews (see p. 59) on groups of heroin users, and concluded that there were two to three times more occasional users than regular users of heroin.

Zinberg (1984) located a group of controlled opiate users so that he might examine not only the drug but also the set and setting of drug use in order to identify factors that might stabilise or destabilise such use. Zinberg observed that it appears to be necessary for the recreational user to abide by certain rules in order to preserve the non-dependent nature of their use—rules such as membership of a knowledgeable network of non-daily users; restrictions on the frequency of use such as weekends-only use; a group of friends which includes non-users; and the coexistence of other important commitments including employment, family and recreational pursuits. A similar study in the UK (Blackwell, 1983) found that drug taking was often controlled as a result of financial considerations and the switching of resources from drugs to other articles of consumption. Blackwell identified a group of 'drifters' who moved into heroin use with no conscious attempt to control it, but who could take it or leave it according to economic, social or personal circumstances. These 'drifters' usually came from advantaged families, were articulate and educated and were mostly single.

Volition and attribution

Our understanding of the course of drug use must incorporate the explanations given by drug users for changes in their drug taking. When interviewed about such changes as stopping or reducing drug use, voluntaristic explanations are often given, identifying personal choice as one of the most powerful factors. Such cognitive–volitional factors may also play an important role in the return to drug use after becoming abstinent. In their investigation of what happens to opiate addicts after leaving treatment, Gossop *et al.* (1987) found that deliberate decision-making processes were commonly cited by subjects as a reason for returning to opiate use. In the alcohol field, Allsop and Saunders (1989) have also drawn attention to the fact that many relapses back to drinking occur in a similar way, and they have argued that 'any analysis of relapse should [recognise] the importance of an interaction of decision making, commitment and coping skills'.

Self-efficacy theory predicts that, if a treatment is to be successful, it

will exert an influence on the subject by enhancing the efficacy expectation—that particular individual's judgement on their own ability to execute
a certain behaviour pattern (Annis, 1986). Initiation, generalisation and
maintenance of various coping behaviours will be influenced by such
efficacy expectations; and their presence or absence will have a significant
influence on the drug takers' self-perceived and actual ability to implement
change in their drug-taking behaviour (for more detailed description see
chapter 6 on psychological treatments).

Flow within treatment

One area of considerable practical relevance to drug services and planners
is the extent to which the course of drug use may be influenced by a variety
of interventions including primary and secondary preventive health education, detoxification programmes, substitute prescribing, relapse prevention
strategies, and syringe exchange schemes among others. Treatment may be
seen as some intervention which corrects a disorder (natural history) and
then permits the resumption of normal function, or it may be seen as a
device which allows the drug taker to escape into recovery (career). It is
necessary to consider whether these interventions may be applicable at any
point in the course of drug use or whether they can only have an effective
impact at certain points. By definition this will be true for primary
prevention health education and also for other interventions such as
detoxification. Blackwell (1983) has described a model for the natural
history of opiate use which is based on her observations of drug users at
various stages of involvement with opiates and among whom much
movement constituted 'drifting' (a state of incomplete commitment to
opiate use). She proposes that drift challenge may occur as a result of
internal and/or external forces in which a challenge is posed to the present
drift status. Three possible courses can be identified down which the drug
taker may travel following such a challenge—towards loss of control,
towards the realisation that controls are necessary, and towards abstinence.

Prochaska and DiClemente (1983) have described a 'process of change'
in which they propose that change can be seen as comprising several stages.
Initially the individual may be 'pre-contemplator', but various influences
(positive or negative reinforcers) may bring about the move to 'contempla-
tor' at which stage the drug taker is conducting a cost–benefit analysis
looking at the present and alternative circumstances. Depending on the
result of this cost–benefit analysis, the individual may choose to move to
'action' to bring about a change in their circumstances, after which they
will need to conduct a further cost-benefit analysis as part of the 'maintenance' stage of the process in which the new set of circumstances is
examined. A particular advantage of this theoretical framework is that it
allows consideration of the possible impact of interventions at different

stages within the process. Thus the prescribing of substitute drugs may have an enabling effect for the drug taker seeking to implement an action such as detoxification while the same prescribing may inadvertently consolidate the precontemplative drug user in their ongoing drug-taking habit. Some interventions may promote flow while others might impede it or may divert the drug taker on to another course. Some might even cause movement back to an earlier level in the process of change.

The management of some of the long-term opiate addicts in the UK provides some interesting data with which we may consider the impact of treatment in the process of change. Stimson and colleagues at the Addiction Research Unit have described the characteristics and subsequent course of drug use of 128 opiate addicts recruited for the study from London drug clinics in 1968. An overlapping sample of long-term Canadian opiate addicts in London has been described by Zacune *et al.* (1971) who suggest that the maintenance prescribing of injectable drugs may have altered the course of their drug use (at least for some of them) so that they were less involved in criminal activities than in previous years and achieved a degree of social stability that had previously eluded them. However, it may also be the case that assurances of continued prescribing may have reduced the likelihood of an outcome to their drug use other than continued more stable use (outcomes such as abstinence, prison or death). If so, then we need to look at the potential influences of treatment on the course of drug use in ways that go beyond whether they merely act as possible escape routes to abstinence.

Edwards (1982) has described the basic work of treatment as 'nudging the movement along natural pathways of recovery' and states that such treatment is only likely to be effective in producing movement when '. . . its efforts are in alignment with the real possibilities for change within the individual, his family and social setting'. Thus treatment could be seen as a promoter of movement, intended to hasten movement down the present beneficial pathway or to realign the drug taker and his treatment on some new path. It also follows that if 'the nudge' is the key element of treatment, the direction, intensity and timing of this nudge must be varied according to individual client characteristics such as the present direction of movement, the extent to which the behaviour has become entrenched, and the existence of alternative pathways. As William Burroughs has put it, for many drug users the habit continues by virtue of the lack of attraction in any other directions, so that 'Junk wins by default' (Burroughs, 1953).

Evidence is emerging to indicate that drug users are able to reduce the intensity or damaging nature of their ongoing drug use with changes other than total abstinence; and it then becomes necessary to look at whether treatment and other interventions might alter the course of drug use even while it continues. This consideration has become more urgent since the recognition of the potential for HIV infection among injecting drug users;

and a new theme within drug treatment services has emerged with a more explicit harm reduction philosophy and a recognition of the benefit that may be accrued to individual and public health by the achievement of intermediate goals such as the move away from injecting or the cessation of sharing of injecting equipment.

Habit moderation and the malleability of behaviour

A growing body of evidence now exists indicating the considerable malleability of drug-taking behaviour among addicts and users who continue to use drugs. In the UK Hawks (1976) has reported that some of a cohort of opiate addicts had reduced the frequency of injecting; and more recently Strang *et al.* (1987) have reported on the frequency with which reductions in dose (45%) or frequency of injecting (42%) had occurred after a two-year interval with 55 on-going drug users. Ghodse *et al.* (1987) have reported on the marked change in reported needle sharing activity among drug addicts attending a London drug dependence unit.

Evidence from the evaluation of syringe-exchange schemes suggests that some drug injectors are helped away from high-risk behaviours—such as sharing syringes—and that they also make positive changes in their sexual behaviour away from HIV-high-risk activity (Stimson *et al.*, 1988). The changes are small, but are consistently in the direction of less risk-laden behaviour. In the last few years, several studies have found evidence of changes in the nature of the ongoing drug use such as the increased frequency of use of bleach in equipment cleaning from 5% to 50% in San Francisco (Newmeyer, 1988), and Jackson and Rotkiewicz (1987) found that HIV education and outreach work appeared to divert drug users into treatment programmes. Power (1988) looked at a sample of 81 regular drug users in London containing roughly equal numbers of those in contact and out of contact with services, and found that actual fear of the virus and its potentially fatal consequences was identified most commonly as the issue that prompted the considerable moves away from injecting. These represent interesting examples of diversions of the course that the drug use would otherwise have followed, and underlie the importance of careful study of the actual nature of the continued drug use rather than just noting whether abstinence has or has not been achieved.

One of the interesting observations to which insufficient attention has been paid is the benefit that may unexpectedly result from arrest and imprisonment. Vaillant (1975) describes a sub-set from his 20-year follow-up comprising 34 addicts who had 'committed felonies so serious that they warranted sentences long enough to include prison and at least a year of parole'. Surprisingly, 24 of these 34 addicts were successful in remaining abstinent in the community for a year or more, leading Vaillant to conclude that 'the efforts of the law to punish these addicts resulted, without meaning to, in the addicts' unexpected rehabilitation' (Vaillant, 1975). In the UK, Blackwell (1983) has reported on the unexpected benefit for that small proportion of her cohort who had been imprisoned, and she suggests that 'enforced abstinence can be a sufficient, but not necessary, condition of recovery'.

Gossop *et al.* (1988) have reported on the apparent robustness of heroin smoking ('chasing the dragon') as a behaviour while observing that many such heroin chasers continued with this route of administration without beginning to inject. This may provide further evidence of the extent of control exercised by drug users over the course of their continued drug use as opposed to the popular view that they are relentlessly driven by the monkey on their back.

References

Advisory Council on the Misuse of Drugs (1982) *Treatment and Rehabilitation* (London: Her Majesty's Stationery Office).
Advisory Council on the Misuse of Drugs (1988) *AIDS and Drug Misuse: Part I* (London: Her Majesty's Stationery Office).
Allsop S. and Saunders W. (1989) Relapse and alcohol problems. In *Relapse and Addictive Behaviour*, ed. Gossop M. (London: Routledge), 11–40.
Andrew Irving Associates (1985) *Heroin Misuse Publicity Campaign: a Qualitative Study Designed to Guide the Effective Targetting and Development of a Mass Media Campaign* (London: Andrew Irving Associates).
Anglin M.D., Brecht M.L., Woodward J.A. and Bonett, D.G. (1986) An empirical study of maturing out: conditional factors. *Int. J. Addictions*, **21**(2), 233–246.
Annis H.M. (1986) A relapse prevention model for treatment of alcoholics. In *Treating Addictive Behaviours: Processes of Change*, eds Miller W.E. and Heather N. (New York: Plenum Press), pp. 407–434.
Biernacki P. (1983) *Pathways from Heroin Addiction: Recovery Without Treatment* (Philadelphia: Temple University Press).
Blackwell J.S. (1983) Drifting, controlling and overcoming: opiate users who avoid becoming chronically dependent. *J. Drug Issues*, **13**(2), 219–235.
Brickman P., Rabinowitz V.C., Karuza J. Jr, Coates D., Cohn E. and Kidder L. (1982) Models of helping and coping. *Amer. Psychol.*, **37**(4), 368–384.
Burroughs W. (1953) *Junkie* (originally Ace Books, and subsequently (1966) London: New English Library).
Chapple, P.A.L., Somekh D.E. and Taylor M.E. (1972) Follow-up of cases of opiate addiction from the time of notification to the Home Office. *Br. Med. J.* **2**, 680–683.
Chein I., Gerard D.L., Lee R.S. and Rosenfeld E. (1964) *Narcotics, Delinquency and Social Policy—the Road to H* (New York: Basic Books).
Edwards G. (1982). *The Treatment of Drinking Problems: A Guide for the Helping Professions* (London: Grant McIntyre).
Edwards G. (1984) Drinking in longitudinal perspective: career and natural history. *Br. J. Addiction*, **79**, 175–184.

Eiser J.R. and Gossop M. (1979) 'Hooked' or 'sick': addicts' perceptions of their addiction. *Addictive Behav.*, **4**, 185–191.

Ghodse A.H., Tregenza G. and Li M. (1987) Effect of fear of AIDS on sharing of injection equipment among drug abusers. *Br. Med. J.*, **295**, 698–699.

Gossop M., Green L., Phillips G. and Bradley B. (1987) What happens to opiate addicts immediately after treatment: a prospective follow up study. *Br. Med. J.*, **294**, 1377–1380.

Gossop M., Griffiths P. and Strang J. (1988) Chasing the dragon: characteristics of heroin chasers. *Br. J. Addiction.*, **83**, 1159–1162.

Gossop M., Green L., Phillips G. and Bradley B. (1989) Lapse, relapse and survival among opiate addicts after treatment: a prospective follow-up study. *Br. J. Psychiat.*, **154**, 348–353.

Hartnoll R.L., Mitcheson M.C., Lewis R.G. and Bryer S. (1985) Estimating the prevalence of opioid dependence. *Lancet*, **i**, 203–205.

Hawks D. (1976) Heroin users in a provincial town and their follow-up over a three year period. In *Drugs and Drug Dependence*, eds Edwards G., Russell M.A.H., Hawks D. and MacCafferty M. (London: Saxon House), 73–86.

Hunt L.G. and Chambers C.D. (1976) *The Heroin Epidemic: A Study of Heroin Use in the United States* (New York: Spectrum).

ICDA (Interdepartmental Committee on Drug Addiction, Brain Committee) (1965) *Drug Addiction—Second Report* (London: Her Majesty's Stationery Office).

Jackson J. and Rotkiewicz L. (1987) A coupon program. Presented at the IIIrd International Conference on AIDS, Washington, DC.

Jorquez J.S. (1983) The retirement phase of heroin using careers. *J. Drug Issues*, **13**(3), 343–365.

Lindesmith A.R. (1947) *Opiate Addiction* (Texas: Principa Press of Trinity University).

Newmeyer J.A. (1988) Why bleach? Development of a strategy to combat HIV contagion among San Franciscan drug users. In *Needle Sharing among Intravenous Drug Abusers: National and International Perspectives*, eds Battjes R.J. and Pickens R.W. (Rockville, MD: National Institute on Drug Abuse), 151–159.

O'Brien, C.P. (1976) Experimental analysis of conditioning factors in human narcotic addiction. *Pharmacol. Rev.*, **27**, 533–543.

Parker H., Bakx K. and Newcombe R. (1988) *Living with Heroin: the Impact of a Drugs 'Epidemic' on an English Community* (Milton Keynes: Open University Press).

Pearson G., Gilman M. and McIver S. (1987) Becoming a heroin user and heroin using careers. In *Drug Use and Misuse: A Reader*, eds Heller T., Gott M. and Jeffery C. (Open University; Chichester: John Wiley).

Plant M.A., Peck D.F. and Samuel E. (1985) *Alcohol, Drugs and School Leavers* (London: Tavistock).

Power R. (1988) The influence of AIDS upon patterns of intravenous use: syringe and needle sharing among illicit drug users in Britain. In *Needle Sharing among Intravenous Drug Abusers: National and International Perspectives*, eds Battjes R.J. and Pickens, R.W. (Rockville: National Institute on Drug Abuse), pp. 75–88.

Preble, E. and Casey, J.J. (1969) Taking care of business—the heroin user's life on the street. *Int. J. Addictions*, **4**(1), 1–24.

Prochaska J.O. and DiClemente C.C. (1983) Stages and processes of self-change of smoking: towards an integrative model of change. *J. Consult. Clin. Psychol.*, **51**(3), 390–395.

Robertson J.R., Bucknall A.B., Welsby P., Roberts J.J.K., Inglis J.M., Peutherer J.F. and Brettle R.P. (1986) Epidemic of AIDS related virus (HTLV-III/LAV): infection among intravenous drug abusers. *Br. Med. J.*, **292**, 527–529.

Robins L.N., Davis D.H. and Goodwin D.W. (1974) Drug users in Vietnam: a follow-up on return to U.S.A. *Amer. J. Epidemiol.*, **99**, 235–249.

Robins L.N., Helzer J.E. and Davis D.H. (1975) Narcotic use in South East Asia and afterwards. *Arch. Gen. Psychiat.*, **32**, 955–961.

Schasre R. (1966) Cessation patterns among neophyte heroin users. *Int. J. Addictions*, **1**, 23–32.

Schur E.M. (1966) *Narcotic Addiction in Britain and America: The Impact of Public Policy* (London: Associated Book Publishers).

Stimson G.V. and Oppenheimer E. (1982) *Heroin Addiction: Treatment and Control in Britain* (London: Tavistock).

Stimson G.V., Aldritt L., Dolan K. and Donoghoe M. (1988) Syringe exchange schemes for drug users in England and Scotland. *Br. Med. J.*, **296**, 1717–1719.

Strang J., Heathcote S. and Watson P. (1987) Habit moderation in injecting drug addicts. *Health Trends*, **19**, 16–18.

Thorley A. (1981) Longitudinal studies of drug dependence. In *Drug Problems in Britain: A Review of Ten Years*, eds Edwards G. and Busch C. (London: Academic Press), pp. 117–169.

Vaillant G. (1975) The place of coercion in addiction treatment. In *Drug Dependence—Treatment and Treatment Evaluation*, eds Bastrom H., Larsson T. and Ljungstedt N. (Stockholm: Almqvist and Wiksell), 81–89.

Waldorf D. and Biernacki P. (1979) Natural recovery from heroin addiction: a review of the literature. *J. Drug Issues*, **9**, 281–289.

Wille, R. (1981) Ten year follow-up of a representative sample of London heroin addicts: clinic attendance, abstinence and morality. *Br. J. Addiction*, **76**, 259–266.

Winick C. (1962) Maturing out of narcotic addiction Bull. Narcotics, **142**, 1–7.

Zacune, J., Mitcheson M. and Malone S. (1971) A comparison of Canadian narcotic addicts in Great Britain and Canada. *Bull. Narcotics*, **23**, 41.

Zinberg N. (1984) *Drug, Set and Setting: The Basis for Controlled Intoxicant Use* (New Haven: Yale University Press).

Bibliography

Edwards G. (1984) Drinking in longitudinal perspective: career and natural history. *Br. J. Addiction*, **79**, 175–184.

Stimson G.V. (1973) *Heroin and Behaviour* (Shannon: Irish University Press).

Waldorf D. and Biernacki P. (1979) Natural recovery from heroin addiction: a review of the literature. *J. Drug Issues*, **9**, 281–289.

5

Clinical Management

Judith R. Morgan

Synopsis

It is tempting to think of the clinical management of people with drug problems in terms of specific actions, particularly of prescribing drugs. We are conditioned, as a society, to think in terms of medical treatment being some sort of action by 'the doctor' on 'the patient'. While such a medical model can have its uses, particularly in minimising paralysing guilt over actions committed under the influence of drugs, the ultimate goal of any treatment and rehabilitation must be to enable the drug user to regain responsibility for the areas of life which have become out of control. Prescribing drugs, admission to hospital etc. may be part of this, but their role in relation to the whole process needs to be carefully weighed, particularly when faced with a person anxious for immediate answers to urgent problems but who, in reality, has long-standing difficulties which may take considerable time and effort to begin to tackle.

In attempting to manage a patient with a drug problem, it is important to consider the individual rather than the stereotype. Individuals need careful assessment and need to be involved with any decision about treatment. This latter does not necessarily include drug treatment, and any prescription for drugs must be considered as part of an overall treatment plan. Treatment may be long term but can be considered in terms of shorter-term achievable goals which must be reviewed at regular intervals. Many patients can be treated in a general practice setting, but more complex problems should receive specialist intervention.

This chapter will deal with the management of the medical problems arising from the excessive use and abuse of drugs described in chapter 2. However, it must be borne in mind that any medical treatment should be regarded as an adjunct (and sometimes only a minor adjunct) to ongoing counselling and rehabilitation.

Treatment of overdosage and acute toxic reactions

People who take mind-altering drugs recreationally do so for their psychic effects. In the case of many such substances, the desired effect only occurs at doses above what would normally be considered therapeutic, and in fact intoxication may well be the desired effect. Because of the pharmacological characteristics of the particular drugs used and/or the behavioural characteristics of the drug-using population, overdosage and acute toxic reactions are not at all uncommon among drug users. Reasons for a particular episode of overdose are often complex and not easily determined. However, the following should be borne in mind when faced with a person who has taken such an overdose:

(1) *Loss of tolerance.* When a drug user is withdrawn from the drug, tolerance to its effects is rapidly lost. If the user attempts to return to a previously tolerated dose level, serious overdosage may occur. This is a particular danger with drugs causing respiratory depression such as opiates and sedatives, particularly barbiturates.

(2) *A drug-dependent person seeking greater effect.* Because of tolerance to the effects of drugs, a drug-dependent person will not get the same desired effect when taking the drug as an occasional user. Such a person may well still desire this effect and may take larger doses to achieve it. These larger doses may bring them into toxic levels. This is a particular danger for barbiturate users because tolerance is limited and may develop to the desired (by the user) effects but not to the toxic effects, so that a person may become dependent on a dosage level dangerously close to the lethal. For stimulant users also, a person may habitually be taking an amount where a small extra quantity will produce a toxic reaction.

(3) *Risk-taking behaviour.* Many drug users enjoy the thrill of doing something which is dangerous. Gambling with death may be part of this thrill. A person with very low self-esteem may also see an overdose as a way of proving whether or not significant others, or the world in general, care for them.

(4) *'Automatic' behaviour.* Even a person taking normal, therapeutic doses of sedative drugs may, under the effect of the drug, forget that they have taken their dose and repeat it. This can lead to serious overdosage. For a person taking sedative drugs for their mind-altering effect, this problem can be compounded when, on recovering from a sleepy state, they may feel slightly unwell, although still intoxicated, and interpret this as drug withdrawal. Some such intoxicated patients have convinced unwary doctors that their state is due to drug withdrawal.

(5) *Intentional overdose—suicide and parasuicide.* Many drug takers take their drug to anaesthetise themselves from emotional scars and relationship problems. In addition, the drug taking itself may exacerbate low self-esteem and alienate family and friends. It should not, therefore, be surprising that deliberate self-harm is not uncommon among drug-using populations.

Therefore, in addition to any medical treatment of overdoses, attention must be paid to the context of the reasons for the overdose, and appropriate management instituted. Many drug-using patients admitted to hospital following overdoses discharge themselves prematurely. While this may be unavoidable in some instances, it is sometimes the result of unsympathetic treatment. An admission to hospital can provide an opportunity for a drug user to assess his life and consider future options.

Medical treatment of overdosage and acute toxic reactions

Volatile substances

Management of intoxication due to solvents is like the management of intoxication generally: difficult! If possible, the substance should be removed from the person who should be allowed as much fresh air as possible. They should be prevented from indulging in behaviour dangerous to themselves or others, although physical restraint can be self-defeating.

Unconsciousness due to solvent abuse should be treated seriously. Any substance or plastic bags should be removed and the patient positioned on his side. On admission to hospital, the standard routine for the management of the unconscious patient should be initiated. Inhalation of vomit is a possibility and intubation may be necessary. Cardiac monitoring may reveal arrhythmias requiring treatment, and for some solvents liver damage may be a possible complication and should be investigated.

Coma may persist for several days, during which supportive treatment will be necessary.

Cannabis

Any physical problems resulting from cannabis overdosage are likely to be overshadowed by the psychological. In the UK cannabis is usually smoked, and since the supervening euphoria and blunting of consciousness prevent further inhalation of the drug, acute physical effects of overdosage are rare. Loss of consciousness is not complete and patients retain their cough reflex. Longer term physical effects are dealt with in chapter 2.

The psychological effects of cannabis to be covered here include acute panic reactions, acute and chronic intoxication and 'cannabis psychosis' (so-called). The treatment of acute panic reactions is mainly of reassurance. They usually occur in inexperienced users or those on the fringe of the drug-using culture. Rarely, mild sedation may be indicated.

As with other drugs, the treatment of intoxication is centred around removal of the substance and keeping the user safe. The chief problem with cannabis intoxication is the length of time the drug remains in the body. For those whose chronic intoxication causes behavioural problems, 'treatment' has to centre around counselling but it is frequently difficult to achieve a drug-free state. It is probable that some cases of so-called cannabis psychosis are in fact cases of chronic intoxication (Ghodse, 1986). Admission to hospital may be indicated but persuading the user to reduce or cease his intake is often problematic. Cases of true psychosis should be treated along conventional lines.

Hallucinogens

Acute toxic reactions and psychological sequelae to LSD use are of more importance than the physical effects which are not, in themselves, life threatening. However, the use of other hallucinogens, particularly those deriving from fungi, can result in serious physical effects, although the chief danger is in misidentification of the mushroom! *Amanita muscaria* (fly agaric) can produce serious effects in overdose: delirium, convulsions, coma and heart failure. Treatment consists of a stomach wash-out in the early stages, and of circulatory support and symptomatic treatment if fits supervene. For treatment of poisoning with other varieties of fungi, readers are referred to standard texts.

Users of LSD and the other hallucinogens may have dysphoric and indeed frightening experiences, commonly referred to as a 'bad trip'. Most such episodes are dealt with outside of a medical context by simple reassurance and so-called 'talking down'. Indeed this management may well be the treatment of choice for those few cases which come to medical attention. The addition of a minor tranquilliser or mild sedative may be necessary on occasion. Some such reactions may be prolonged for over 48 hours, depending partly on the dose consumed, and may require hospitalisation. Rarely, some individuals may be precipitated into a psychotic illness indistinguishable from schizophrenia. This should be treated along conventional lines.

Stimulants

Hyperactivity, irritability and incipient or actual psychosis may interfere with the assessment and treatment of any physical effect of stimulant overdosage. These can be treated by sedation and/or anti-psychotic medication, which is sometimes required in high doses. Barbiturate medication may be useful if hypertension, hyperthermia or convulsions are present, combined with general supportive measures. Amphetamine excretion may be encouraged by acid diuresis.

Amphetamine psychosis and other similar stimulant psychoses are acute toxic reactions to the drug, and recovery occurs when the substance is eliminated from the body. In many instances no specific treatment will be necessary, other than ensuring that the person is safe. However, if hyperactivity or delusions are persistent, or place the person at risk of harm to self or others, admission to hospital and drug treatment with sedatives and anti-psychotic drugs may be necessary.

If psychotic symptoms persist after urine tests for the presence of the drug become negative, the disorder will need to be treated along conventional lines for schizophrenic psychosis. Helping such a person to maintain a drug-free state may be rendered more difficult by their inability to respond to conventional counselling, as well as the paucity of rehabilitation facilities for drug users with associated mental illness.

Sedatives and tranquillisers

The frequency of barbiturate overdosage has fortunately reduced with the advent of the much safer benzodiazepine sedatives. The latter, in overdosage, cause unconsciousness, which is sometimes prolonged, but seldom death unless complicated by pre-existing respiratory disease or if they are taken in association with other drugs. However, unconscious patients always need careful nursing and supportive measures in hospital. Barbiturates and some other non-benzodiazepine sedatives (particularly methaqualone) taken in overdosage can rapidly cause death. Coma is accompanied by respiratory depression, hypotension and hypothermia. The passage of an endotracheal tube and close monitoring of respiratory function are usually required with assisted respiration where necessary. Circulatory support by intravenous infusion and body heat conservation by wrapping in blankets may be necessary. Forced alkaline diuresis may be considered in severe barbiturate poisoning. A high urine output should in any case be maintained.

Opiates

As with other drugs leading to coma, overdosage with opiates carries with it the risk of inhalation of vomit. Vomiting is, however, a specific side-effect of opiate drugs and, combined with the powerful respiratory depressant effect, makes suffocation a very real danger in opiate overdosage. Thus, protection of the airway must have high priority when treating patients unconscious as a result of opiate overdosage.

A fortunate difference from other drug overdoses discussed so far is the availability of specific antagonists for opiate overdosage. Naloxone 400 µg injected subcutaneously, intramuscularly or intravenously and repeated once or twice at intervals of 2–3 minutes if respiratory function does not improve can be life saving. In the case of overdoses of long-acting opiates such as methadone, further lapses into unconsciousness may occur and require further administration of naloxone.

Specific mention should be made here of combined preparations of opiate-related drugs such as dextropropoxyphene with paracetamol (Distalgesic, Cosalgesic). Abuse and overdosage of these preparations are increasingly common, and death, unfortunately, not rare. Administration of opiate antagonists may need to be combined with specific treatment for the paracetamol component to prevent liver damage. Readers are referred to standard texts on the treatment of overdosage (see British National Formulary 1988, pp. 38–44).

Drug withdrawal

Patients and doctors have appeared to conspire to give detoxification a mystique which has sometimes served to deter non-medical helpers from becoming involved. Drug users themselves sometimes have an emotional need to purvey an atmosphere of unhelpability which can justify their remaining on drugs and which deskills others, and doctors have unfortunately sometimes been guilty of perpetuating this medical mystique. This has also extended within the profession, with drug detoxification being seen as the province of the specialist. This is not to deny the role of the specialist in cases of difficult drug combinations, complicating mental illness or personality disorder, pregnancy, etc., but case selection, as in other branches of medicine, is important in deciding which patients can be dealt with by generalists. The role of the doctor in some cases will be to reassure the drug user or relative that withdrawal can safely be accomplished by merely stopping the drug. Many families of young, intermittent users of heroin or even those with some degree of physical dependence on its use have been able to successfully withdraw 'their' patient by treating them as if suffering from a mild dose of 'flu.

It is, of course, not at all easy to stop using something which has brought comfort and pleasure, sometimes for a large portion of a person's life. In the early stages of withdrawal, and sometimes for a prolonged period, this comfort and pleasure will be exchanged for a feeling of dysphoria mingled with what can only be described as a bereavement. Pharmacological treatment of such states can be at best only a temporary expedient and, at worst, can hinder positive developments. Doctors, with limited time at their disposal, may not be in the best position to counsel individuals when first seeking help, but anxious patients, and perhaps even more particularly, relatives will often not take kindly to being advised to consult yet another agency. However, if the doctor has some knowledge of the local drugs advisory agency or community drug team and can ring them up, it will be possible to create an impression of a collaborative effort. This will convey to the patient the message that 'Giving up drugs requires hard work and is not easy but we can work together on this'. In this instance, a referral to a counselling agency can be seen as part of the overall plan. Treatment contracts, in which any prescriptions are made contingent on attendance for counselling, can be part of this (see below).

It can be useful for the doctor to consider the following working model for the management of a patient seeking help for a drug problem (table 5.1).

The initial requirement in the model is that the person attend in a condition in which he can be communicated with. This means placing on the person the responsibility of not being intoxicated. Many hours of time have been wasted attempting to counsel intoxicated people. Unfortunately, however, some 'wasted' time may be necessary in persuading stoned and talkative patients to 'come back tomorrow'. There may also be a temptation not to wish to see them again, but a promise of an early appointment can ease the situation and begin to define the boundaries of a productive counselling relationship.

It is important to realise that a patient may be intoxicated because of a medical illness. People accustomed to self-medicate for physical or emotional disease may well overmedicate when really ill. It is important, therefore, that those presenting to doctors or to accident and emergency departments in a state of intoxication be medically assessed before being told to come back when 'straight'. It is not unknown for serious and life-threatening conditions to be missed in these circumstances. The author has personally seen cases where septicaemia and spinal osteomyelitis have been overlooked, and the person sent away from more than one hospital! Furthermore, a person presenting with intoxication may have taken a dangerous overdose of drugs and may need to be observed to see whether the level of consciousness is deteriorating.

Rarely, people who are habitually intoxicated, particularly on sedative drugs, may interpret any condition which is not intoxication as withdrawal. Such people may need admission to hospital before any long-term work with them can begin.

Drug withdrawal states may also interfere with the ability of a person to co-operate actively in the process of assessment and planning of management. Unfortunately, drug prescriptions in these circumstances may pre-empt other important stages, e.g. consultation with other agencies, the taking of an adequate history, etc., and may dictate a treatment approach (i.e. out-patient prescription for drugs) which is inappropriate for the person's needs. It is probably unwise to prescribe addictive drugs to a newly presenting person in withdrawal unless:

(a) the condition is life-threatening (as sedative withdrawal can be), or
(b) the prescriber is experienced in treating addictive problems.

Certainly the doctor should make clear that any prescription is only in

Table 5.1 A working model for doctors and others collaborating in the management of persons seeking help for a drug problem

A. *Identifying the problem*
  1. Require that the person attend 'straight' (but NB and beware medical problems in intoxicated people)
  2. History (a) present drug use, frequency, dosage
              (b) chronological progression of use
              (c) previous treatment
  3. Social status (a) accommodation
                   (b) financial
  4. Legal status (a) pending court cases
                  (b) involvement of probation service
  5. Physical examination (a) drug specific, e.g. injection sites
                          (b) general health
  6. Pathological tests (a) urine testing for presence of drugs
                        (b) testing for specific health problems, e.g. hepatitis, HIV
  7. Notification to Home Office if relevant
  8. What is the person's expectation of 'help'?

B. *Review*
  1. Is immediate action required:
     medical intervention?
     social help?
     legal help?
  2. Plan of further management:
     further information needed
     counselling
     specific medical intervention—detoxification
                                    —other

C. *Further management*
  1. Advice to 'patient'/family
  2. Counselling of 'patient' and/or family
     (a) initial—to determine degree of dependence, family or emotional factors contributing to drug use, motivation for treatment
     (b) ongoing—individual counselling, family or marital therapy, self-help groups
  3. Detoxification
     (a) drug-free
     (b) symptomatic treatment
     (c) in-patient detoxification
     (d) out-patient detoxification
  4. Rehabilitation
     (a) residential
     (b) self-help groups
     (c) 'community'
  5. Possibility of long- or short-term drug maintenance

order that a longer term plan can be made, and only small quantities of any addictive drug (one or at the most two days' supply) should be given at this stage, with a further appointment given to drive the message home. This further appointment could well be with a non-medical advisory agency with more time available to consider the options. Symptomatic treatment with non-addictive drugs may be a possibility (see below).

Increasing stress is being laid on the need to 'attract' drug users to treatment in order to prevent the spread of HIV infection (Department of Health and Social Security, 1988). Prescriptions for drugs can attract drug users into contact with treatment agencies where they can receive counselling about intravenous drug use, safer sex, etc. Certainly the assessment procedure need not always be lengthy, and may in some cases be carried out in a single interview. However, care must be taken that people taking drugs in a non-addictive manner are not further handicapped by becoming addicted to powerful drugs by medical intervention. It is here that the person's expectation of help is of importance. Some cases are relatively straightforward. A young person, perhaps brought by parents, giving a relatively short (6 months to 2 years) history of daily heroin use and requesting help with detoxification will not require intensive investigation and counselling before initiating a short community detoxification programme, although it would be wise to confirm the presence of drugs by a urine test. An older person with extensive involvement with opiates and perhaps several attempts to become drug-free and requesting lifetime 'maintenance' on his drug will require much more investigation and consultation with previous treatment agencies before any prescription can be issued, and should probably be referred to a specialist clinic. A person with multiple drug problems and seeking his next 'fix' may need to be told that the general practitioner will treat his medical problems but will not prescribe any mind-altering substance. Some such people may appreciate the boundaries thus offered and be able to be engaged in the beginning of a counselling relationship. Many doctors are unwilling to take drug-using patients on to their practice list because they fear the demands for drugs. It is perfectly possible for the doctor to set such limits before agreeing to take them on.

Treatment contracts

A little must be said at this stage about management plans and treatment contracts before dealing specifically with detoxification. Many medical conditions seen in general and hospital practice are self-limiting, and a management plan is implicit in the immediate invervention—e.g. a course of antibiotics for a chest infection. Many common emotional and stress-related conditions seen in general practice are likewise self-limiting although the time course may be different. In short-term medical illnesses it is common for the patient to, as it were, hand over responsibility to the doctor who implicitly accepts the responsibility. However, increasingly this passive acceptance of the parental position of the doctor is being challenged and people are being urged to take more responsibility for their health. This comes both from vocal patients' groups who question the use of antibiotics and tranquillisers, some obstetric practices, and also the medical profession, who point to the contribution made to ill-health by smoking, stressful lifestyles, etc. In the field of drug use and misuse, it is not possible for the doctor to take total responsibility for treatment. If he or she allows the patient to hand over that responsibility, this can lead to situations where a patient can say that, unless the doctor prescribes more drugs, the patient will 'be forced' to commit crimes, etc. Careful delineation of boundaries as well as realistic assessment of starting doses in any reduction programme of drug treatment can pre-empt such situations.

Such delineations of boundaries may include the following:

(a) Starting dose of drug; amount to be reduced at each step; time interval between reductions.
(b) How frequently the patient is seen.
(c) Consequences of 'breaking the contract' by, for example, using other drugs.
(d) Whether the dose may be held steady or increased slightly at any point if the patient is experiencing difficulty.
(e) Regular attendance at a counselling agency.

Individual doctors will vary as to what limits they set and how much latitude they are prepared to allow around the limits. However, it is wise to define in one's own mind one's own limits, and where possible to be open with the patient as to what those limits are. It is then important to stick to these limits: too great a latitude will lead to anger on the part of the doctor if his or her normal treatment practice has been overstretched. However, a too rigid regimen will lead to an inability of the patient to comply. It may be wise for inexperienced practitioners to set quite strict limits to begin with and to refer on if difficulty occurs rather than become disillusioned by losing control of a situation.

If, for instance, attendance at a counselling agency is part of a treatment contract, it is important to have close liaison and to emphasise the importance of the attendance by stopping the drug prescription for non-attendance. Many counselling agencies have considerable experience of the treatment of people with drug-abuse problems, and they can often give useful advice about detoxification programmes. It is, however, important that the doctor retain responsibility for any drug prescriptions and set his or her own limits. Drug-using patients can be time consuming, and it is probably best not to treat too many people at the same time.

'Community' or in-patient detoxification?

Reference is made above to the co-operation between a general practitioner and a counselling agency/community drug team in the community detoxification of a person with a drug problem. This sort of co-operation can apply to any form of detoxification needing pharmacological intervention, analgesic or sedative/tranquilliser withdrawal being the most common. Cases most appropriately managed by this approach would be:

(a) young or relatively short-term (6 months to 2 years daily use) opiate users with few or no previous treatment attempts;
(b) people with good support from non-using relatives or friends;
(c) people dependent on prescribed drugs obtained from a single legitimate source.

It would follow that cases inappropriate for this type of community management would be:

(a) older, long-term opiate users with multiple attempts at treatment;
(b) people living in unstable accommodation (e.g. 'squats') or with other drug users;
(c) people dependent on drugs obtained from multiple sources, particularly those visiting several GPs under false names or as temporary patients unless local arrangements can be made to prevent this (not usually possible in larger conurbations).

Obviously, there will be a spectrum of cases falling between these extremes, and whether an individual patient will be referred to a specialist facility will depend on a variety of factors such as experience of the GP in treating drug problems, distance from a specialist facility, etc.

Specialist drug dependency clinics have the expertise and facilities to treat some of the more complicated patients within the community by out-patient detoxification, but travelling distances may inhibit this for some patients. Some drug problems are most appropriately treated by admission to hospital. Among these will be:

(a) patients dependent on large amounts of sedatives and tranquillisers, particularly if injected or obtained from multiple or illicit sources;
(b) patients living in chaotic social circumstances;
(c) those with serious medical or psychiatric complications of their drug abuse.

Other patients may wish for in-patient treatment, and some drug-using patients before the courts may be required by the court to be in an environment which renders them less likely to reoffend. In many cases, however, the non-availability of specialist beds inhibits choice. Some individuals may be able to be treated in general psychiatric beds, but the more complicated problems may require special units or at least nursing staff experienced in drug problems. A treatment contract for drug-using patients admitted to hospital is a useful tool. It can cover such aspects as

- action to be taken if illicit drugs or alcohol are consumed
- whether the patient may be searched
- whether visitors will be restricted to certain named individuals.

Detoxification from individual drugs

Volatile substances

Most misuse of volatile substances is experimental and of short duration. It is usually part of a spectrum of adolescent risk-taking behaviour and is best treated in that context. If the misuse continues, or when it occurs in older people, it may present similar problems to the misuse of other substances, with a lifestyle oriented around obtaining and using the substance. In such a situation, questions about detoxification and treatment may occur. For the young, there may be pressure for admission to hospital to remove them from the damaging effects of intoxication or the toxic effects of the solvent. It must be remembered, however, that admission to a specialised unit may expose a vulnerable young person to experienced users of a variety of drugs who may whet his appetite for other substances! Volatile substance misusers frequently experience craving for the 'high' of intoxication and some withdrawal symptomatology has also been described; this is rather vague and difficult to differentiate from a general feeling of dysphoria. No specific pharmacological intervention is required and management of the emotional sequelae to detoxification is considered under 'Maintenance of the drug-free state'. Many people who misuse volatile substances over a long period have a history of deprivation and may have considerable difficulty in social relationships. Brain damage as a toxic effect of the substance might compound such problems.

Cannabis

Individuals claiming to be dependent upon the use of cannabis are rare. Many people use cannabis on a regular basis but are able to stop with no physical or emotional sequelae. Even those claiming to be dependent on its use will experience no more on withdrawal than the anxiety common to those attempting to stop any tension-relieving habit. Some people experiencing discomfort or dysphoria as a result of personality disorder, or occasionally because of frank mental illness, have found that the distancing from reality afforded by cannabis use cushions them from the world. Unfortunately, it may also prevent the development of lifestyle changes, etc. 'Treatment' of such problems may need to be that of the underlying disorder but in general is covered under 'Maintenance of the drug-free state'.

Hallucinogens

Dependence upon hallucinogens is claimed even less commonly than on cannabis. LSD, in fact, is said to be 'anti-addictive' in that its use becomes less effective for several days after a trip although, notwithstanding this, some individuals do claim to be dependent on it. They usually have pre-existing histories of disturbance, either of mental illness or of severe or borderline personality disorder. Treatment is of the underlying disorder.

Stimulants

Amphetamines and amphetamine-like appetite suppressants

Withdrawal from these drugs leads to anxiety, depression and a general tiredness and apathy. This may be expressed in some individuals by a provocative aggression. The symptoms may last for some weeks and become indistinguishable from the general dysphoria associated with the withdrawal of any substance that produces dependence. In the initial stages, depression can be severe and suicidal and may require admission and treatment along conventional lines. In general, however, stimulant withdrawal does not require pharmacological intervention: there is no necessity for any prescription of reducing doses. However, for some patients who have become dependent on prescribed amphetamines or appetite suppressants and whose source of drugs is solely by prescription, a negotiated reduction of the prescribed dose may be the most expedient method of detoxification. For others, counselling and support in the community will enable them to stop their drug use. For many, particularly those using intravenous amphetamines or large amounts of stimulants, or those who are actually or incipiently psychotic, admission to hospital may be the best option. This will provide a safe environment where angry and depressed feelings can be expressed, and where access to drugs is restricted. Thus the individual is provided with a break in the cycle of craving–drug high–'come down', and can reassess his life and drug use. Occasionally, an underlying depressive or other mental illness may be discovered but more commonly the dysphoria will need to be managed along the lines discussed under 'Maintenance of the drug-free state'. Urine testing for the presence of amphetamine is an important adjunct to both in-patient and community management.

Cocaine

The management of cocaine misuse is, in most respects, similar to that of amphetamine. However, the intense drug 'high', followed quite rapidly by the 'come-down' and the very strong craving make the treatment of cocaine abuse particularly difficult. Mere detoxification by stopping the drug is not difficult but users are difficult to engage in treatment and frequently fail in follow-up counselling and therapy. Self-help groups and contracts involving family, friends or employers may be particularly helpful here.

Sedatives and tranquillisers

Withdrawal from sedatives and tranquillisers, in common with withdrawal from opiates, produces an observable physical syndrome. However, while all such states may be distressing to experience or observe, sedative withdrawal, like alcohol withdrawal but in contradistinction to opiate withdrawal, may cause serious and life-threatening complications such as epileptiform fits (Isbell *et al.*, 1950; Robinson and Sellers, 1982). A history of regular consumption of such drugs should therefore alert the doctor to the need for a detoxification programme. Many multiple drug misusers may seriously underestimate their use of such drugs, regarding them as of little consequence. The presence of benzodiazepines in a urine sample should prompt a careful and specific history of their consumption.

Although there is cross-tolerance between the various members of this group, it is usual to treat them separately for the purposes of detoxification.

Barbiturates

Patients on prescribed short-acting barbiturates in therapeutic (or even higher) doses may quite safely be withdrawn by a gradual reduction of their prescribed dose. It is probably not advisable to reduce at a faster rate than by 100 mg from the daily dose, weekly. For some people the rate of dose reduction may need to be slower than this. The patient should be told that their sleep will deteriorate initially but that after two weeks from their final dose they will probably be sleeping as well as they were when they took the drugs, and that thereafter sleeping will improve. For some patients with a particular fear of withdrawal, transferring to a safer benzodiazepine hypnotic may be an intermediate goal in a longer-term programme. However, this may merely compound the problem, not improving sleep and thereby increasing fear of ultimate withdrawal.

Patients obtaining barbiturates by illicit means (buying on the black market or by visiting multiple medical services) are more difficult to treat. Some may attempt to blackmail doctors to prescribe for them by stories of having had fits. Whether or not these stories are true, it is inadvisable to prescribe short-acting hypnotics to such patients at all. For most, admission to hospital is the only advisable option for treatment. However, it must be recognised that this is not always immediately available. If the doctor considers that there is a serious medical danger, it is possible to prescribe a long-acting barbiturate—phenobarbitone—in reducing doses (see below). It is particularly important that the boundaries of such a treatment contract be carefully delineated: such patients are frequently chaotic, and are skilled manipulators.

(a) Only one or at most two days' supply of the drug should be prescribed at a time, and the patient should be told to return at a specified date and time for further supplies.
(b) The dose should be inexorably reduced.
(c) Urine should be taken for testing for the presence of short-acting barbiturates and the patient told that their presence will terminate the contract.

As stated above, most such patients will probably require in-patient treatment in a specialised unit. On an in-patient basis, either phenobarbitone or short-acting barbiturates can be used in decreasing doses for detoxification. There are advantages and disadvantages to either. The use of short-acting barbiturates raises the possibility of intoxication in the early stages, with all its attendant problems. However, these drugs are rapidly eliminated, which means that the doctor can be certain (by negative urine samples) that detoxification has been achieved. The use of phenobarbitone produces less sedation in the early stages and a smoother detoxification, but it may be three weeks or longer after the final dose that the urine tests become negative for the drug.

Dosage of drugs can be determined as follows. If short-acting barbiturates are being used, 200 mg of pentobarbitone is given and the effect observed. If this does not produce undue sedation, a total daily dose of 800 mg in four divided doses is given daily and the total daily dose is then reduced by 100 mg daily. If phenobarbitone is being used, 30 mg should be given for each 100 mg of short-acting barbiturate taken, up to a maximum of 300 mg phenobarbitone daily.

Non-barbiturate hypnotics
Examples of non-barbiturate hypnotics include glutethimide (Doriden), methyprylone (Noludar), methaqualone (not now legally available in Great Britain but still occasionally illegally imported), chloral hydrate (as chloral mixture, or Noctec) and dichloralphenazone (Welldorm).

Most patients dependent on these drugs have been on regular prescriptions from their own GP. Withdrawal can usually be achieved as described

Table 5.2 Equivalent dosages of sedatives and tranquillisers (equivalent to 30 mg phenobarbitone). Adapted from *Guidelines of Good Clinical Practice in the Treatment of Drug Misuse*, DHSS, 1984

Barbiturates	
Phenobarbitone (standard)	30 mg
Amylobarbitone (Amytal)	100 mg
Butobarbitone (Soneryl; Butisol)	100 mg
Cyclobarbitone (Phanodorm)	200 mg
Heptabarbitone (Medomin)	200 mg
Pentobarbitone (Nembutal)	100 mg
Quinalbarbitone (Seconal)	100 mg
Quinalbarbitone + amylobarbitone (Tuinal)	50 mg + 50 mg
Non-barbiturate hypnotics	
Chloral hydrate (Noctec)	5 ml (500 mg)
Chlormethiazole (Heminevrin)	1 cap/1 tab/5 ml
Dichloralphenazone (Welldorm)	1300 mg
Glutethimide (Doriden)	250 mg
Methaqualone (Quaalude; Sopor)	250 mg
Methyprylone (Noludar)	200 mg
Benzodiazepines	
Chlordiazepoxide (Librium)	35 mg
Clobazam (Frisium)	10 mg
Clorazepate (Tranxene)	15 mg
Diazepam (Valium)	15 mg
Flunitrazepam (Rohypnol)	1 mg
Flurazepam (Dalmane)	30 mg
Ketazolam (Anxon)	30 mg
Lapiazolam (Dormanoct)	2 mg
Lorazepam (Ativan)	2 mg
Lametrazepam (Noctamid)	1 mg
Medazepam (Nobrium)	10 mg
Nitrazepam (Mogadon)	10 mg
Oxazepam (Serenid; Serax)	10 mg
Temazepam (Euhypnos, Normison; Cerepax)	30 mg
Triazolam (Halcion)	0.125 mg

under barbiturates by slow reduction of dose (usually by no more than one tablet nightly per week) accompanied by counselling and careful explanation. Patients need to be seen frequently: probably weekly but certainly as often as the reduction takes place.

Patients on larger doses, or those obtaining drugs illegally or by visiting multiple doctors, usually need admission to hospital, although the same advice as under 'Barbiturates' also pertains to these patients. The prescription of equivalent doses of phenobarbitone in reducing doses is possible. If admitted to hospital, the patient can be withdrawn either from the drug of addiction or from equivalent doses of phenobarbitone as described under 'Barbiturates'.

Chlormethiazole (Heminevrin)

This drug has been used to treat patients withdrawing from alcohol. However, problems such as overdosage, often in combination with alcohol, and dependence caused by its prescription on an out-patient basis have meant that its use should be confined to the in-patient withdrawal of patients with severe alcohol problems. Even in this situation, many practitioners prefer the use of benzodiazepines.

Most patients addicted to chlormethiazole are using large quantities, often obtained from several different doctors. Such patients are in the same position as those described under 'Barbiturates' and are often chronically intoxicated. Appropriate assessment and treatment are really only possible on an in-patient basis. If admission is not immediately possible, any treatment should be directed towards medical need only (i.e. prevention of fits), as with barbiturates. Equivalent doses of phenobarbitone can be prescribed for one or at the most two days at a time, and reduction of dosage applied as with barbiturates.

On admission to hospital, reduction can be accomplished either by gradual reduction of the dose of chlormethiazole (by reduction of one tablet/capsule daily or alternate days) or by transfer to equivalent doses of phenobarbitone and reduction as under 'Barbiturates'.

Benzodiazepines

The widespread use of benzodiazepine tranquillisers and sedatives for the relief of anxiety and insomnia, and to shield people from the effects of intractable problems of everyday life, has led to widespread dependence upon their use. This has resulted in mounting campaigns against them by the media and consumer groups. At times these campaigns have appeared not to recognise the intractable nature of some problems taken to doctors nor the concern felt for sufferers by their doctor, who prescribes in an attempt to take the edge off the patient's suffering. There have even been attempts to sue doctors for long-term prescriptions for tranquillisers, which appears to deny the role of the patient in searching for medical answers to non-medical problems. However, it must not be denied that doctors have not infrequently taken the easy way out by prescribing drugs for such problems and have not reviewed long-term prescriptions. Continued prescription of benzodiazepines for their sedative or tranquillising effects is subject to the law of diminishing returns, and at some point for most patients it becomes apparent that the problems of dependence upon the drug outweigh any benefit from taking it.

In addition, benzodiazepines are increasingly taking the place of, or adding to, the problems of barbiturate abuse among young multiple drug users, and indeed some young people are becoming dependent upon benzodiazepines alone, often in large quantities. These drugs are either obtained by visiting multiple general practitioners or bought 'on the streets'. Their availability on the illicit market is witnessed to by their cheapness.

Much has been written about the effects of benzodiazepine withdrawal. The severity of withdrawal symptoms will depend both upon the dosage and the length of time for which the person has been taking the drug. In all cases where a benzodiazepine has been taken regularly for more than a few weeks the dose should be gradually tapered off. This will reduce problems but the patient will need to be warned that he or she will possibly suffer anxiety or sleep problems as a specific withdrawal effect and that this is not necessarily a return of previous problems. For individuals taking higher than therapeutic doses (as defined by the British National Formulary) or for many months or years, the dangers of more severe withdrawal effects, e.g. fits or withdrawal psychoses, mean that special care must be taken. For the many withdrawal phenomena from these drugs, readers are referred to standard texts (e.g. Petursson and Lader, 1984).

All patients taking regular benzodiazepines should be encouraged to withdraw, and any patient being prescribed the drug should have the dangers of dependence explained. Longer term prescribing of these drugs should become the exception. However, many patients on long-term prescriptions may be reluctant to stop having the drug, either through the fear of withdrawal or continued need for a cushion from everyday problems. It will be a matter for individual judgement whether such patients should be coerced to withdraw. If a patient is chronically intoxicated or is experiencing problems of irritability as a result of the drug, it may be that a considerable amount of coercion is indicated!

Once a decision to attempt withdrawal has been made, the patient should be transferred from short- or medium-acting benzodiazepines to a long-acting drug such as diazepam or chlordiazepoxide in equivalent doses. Many problems described in the media as due to withdrawal from lorazepam (Ativan) have been due to the fact that this short-acting drug has been inappropriately prescribed in withdrawal schedules, resulting in rapidly altering blood levels of the drug and see-sawing symptoms. Such a transfer may be difficult for some patients who have become accustomed to the patterns of action of their drug. However, if the reasons for the transfer are explained and also the fact that while some discomfort may be inevitable it will not be excessive, the patient usually feels supported and able to continue. Once the transfer has been made, the reduction can proceed in decrements of 2 mg or 5 mg from the daily dose, probably at weekly intervals, although some patients may be able to reduce more rapidly and others may need a more cautious pace.

Patients need to be seen frequently—i.e. at weekly or two-weekly intervals, for counselling and reassurance. It is probably unwise to give more than a week's prescription of the drug unless the patient is very motivated and can be trusted not to exceed the prescribed dose. Some patients may be unable to handle even a week's prescription without the temptation to over-use.

Most patients benefit by other therapy during their withdrawal: either self-help groups or psychological treatment of anxiety or other symptoms. See under 'Maintenance of the drug-free state'.

Patients using large quantities of benzodiazepines, those with chaotic lifestyles, or those obtaining their drugs by deception from multiple doctors usually need admission to hospital for detoxification. Here, as with other sedatives, withdrawal can be accomplished at a more rapid rate than as an out-patient, since skilled nursing support is available. Harrison *et al.* (1984) have described detoxification from large quantities of benzodiazepines by the initial prescription of 40% of the original diazepam equivalent dosage, and daily tapering of 10%. This is based on the half-life of diazepam and its active metabolites. Unfortunately, many chaotic 'street addicts', with at best partial motivation, may not tolerate such a regimen and a more usual treatment programme will be to titrate dosage until the patient is slightly sedated, and then to withdraw by decrements of 10 mg, 5 mg or 2 mg (depending on initial dosage) daily or on alternate days.

Such patients require intensive support both during and after detoxification. A frequent hindrance to successful treatment is the ease with which they are able to obtain fresh supplies of the drug.

Use of anticonvulsants

Since withdrawal from sedatives and tranquillisers may be complicated by epileptiform fits, many practitioners will 'cover' the withdrawal by the prescription of anticonvulsant drugs. As described above, phenobarbitone alone may be used to withdraw patients from sedatives and tranquillisers: its long half-life in the body is useful in this context in preventing fits. If adequate doses of long-acting medication are used and the withdrawal schedule is suitably tapering, fits are unlikely to occur. However, patients may give inadequate information about their drug-taking, doctors may not believe their accounts, particularly if large doses are claimed, and for various other reasons the starting dosage may be too low and withdrawal too rapid. If there are serious questions about such matters or if there is a history of fits, withdrawal or otherwise, it may be appropriate to prescribe anticonvulsant doses of phenobarbitone or carbamazepine for the course of the drug withdrawal and for a few days (up to two weeks after diazepam) after it is completed. The anticonvulsant may then be tapered over a few days.

Opiates

Stories of the horrors of opiate withdrawal abound (e.g. Laurie, 1978). However, the fact remains that opiate withdrawal, while distressing to observe and even more distressing to experience, is not usually life-threatening, with the possible exception of those individuals with under-lying heart or kidney problems in whom dehydration could be dangerous. The pressure for medical intervention by worried users or their relatives may prevent useful intervention by non-medical counsellors and, even more important, may prevent the individual from discovering that he still has the power himself to stop the drug. It is not unusual for relatively recent users to recognise the onset of physical withdrawal symptoms and to stop taking the drug. Longer term users may also voluntarily undergo 'cold turkey' by isolating themselves from the drug or by entering residential rehabilitation units utilising this form of withdrawal. Thus, in considering detoxification from opiates, it is possible to consider a hierarchy of possible interventions (see Table 5.1).

Non-pharmacological: 'cold turkey'
For most young heroin users with a relatively short (6 months to a year) history of daily use and using relatively small amounts (probably no more than 0.25 g) of street heroin, this is a perfectly feasible method of withdrawal. It will usually be necessary to have the co-operation of the user although it is not unknown for parents to forcibly detain their youngster. A useful guideline for the helper is to treat the user as if suffering a dose of 'flu, thus indicating the level of care necessary. The user may be in bed, although this may not be absolutely necessary. They need to be kept warm and to have access to frequent hot baths. Plenty of fluids should be available. After about a week, the person will be over the worst of the physical effects and 'Maintenance of the drug-free state' will be the next need.

Symptomatic treatment
Some of the symptoms of opiate withdrawal are particularly distressing and may be treated as would such symptoms occurring in other contexts. This may enable medical practitioners who are unwilling to prescribe opiate-related drugs through fear or other reasons to treat their patients under-going withdrawal.

(1) Insomnia. This is an almost universal complaint of those undergoing withdrawal. It may be treated by benzodiazepine sedatives, prescribed for one or at the most two nights at a time, and preferably controlled by the carers. Because of possible problems in the prescription of benzodiazepines (oversedation, addiction), some practitioners may prefer the use of a sedative antidepressant such as amitriptyline or trimipramine, taken in adequate dosage in the evening.
(2) General aches and pains. The use of simple analgesics such as paracetamol or anti-inflammatory analgesics such as ibuprofen will at

least take the edge off the multiple aches and pains suffered by those withdrawing from opiates.

(3) Abdominal symptoms. Colicky abdominal pain is a common symptom in those withdrawing from opiates. This may be treated by antispasmodic drugs such as dicyclomine hydrochloride (Merbentyl), hyoscine (Buscopan) or mebeverine hydrochloride (Colofac). More severe symptoms of nausea, vomiting and diarrhoea may also be treated along conventional lines by the use of antiemetics and/or antidiarrhoeal drugs, although caution should be exercised when considering opiate-related drugs (e.g. diphenoxylate and loperamide).

Clonidine

Clonidine is also a symptomatic treatment for opiate withdrawal in that the person will undergo the normal withdrawal timespan but modified by the drug. It is considered separately because of its increased usage, and also because of the special precautions needed.

Clonidine is an α-2 adrenergic receptor agonist which appears to act by inhibiting the release of noradrenaline from the locus coeruleus of the brain. It is thought that the abrupt release of noradrenaline is responsible for many of the distressing symptoms of opiate withdrawal (Gold *et al.*, 1980). The major use of clonidine for many years has been in the treatment of hypertension, and hypotension can be a troublesome side-effect for some patients under treatment for opiate withdrawal. This effect may be potentiated by concomitant abuse of opiates or sedatives. This has therefore inhibited its use on an out-patient basis except in controlled situations where it is possible to check blood pressure regularly.

On an in-patient basis its main advantage over the use of methadone is the rapidity of the detoxification process, which takes about 7 days for heroin users although methadone users usually need 10–14 days. Some patients with heavy and longstanding opiate dependence still find the withdrawal symptoms excessive and may need methadone detoxification instead. Other patients for whom clonidine is unsuitable include those with excessive hypotensive or other reactions to its use, some with cardiac or renal problems, for whom hypotension may be dangerous, and all pregnant patients. The latter should always be treated with opiate-related drugs because of the danger of opiate withdrawal inducing miscarriage, premature birth or fetal brain damage (see chapter 10). In fact, it is always wise to enquire carefully about the possibility of pregnancy in female patients, and to carry out a pregnancy test if in doubt.

Clonidine is given in an average dosage of 0.1 mg four times daily with a maximum of 0.8 mg daily in divided doses. The dose is omitted if the diastolic blood pressure is below 55–60 mm. This is continued for 5–6 days (7–10 days for methadone users) and then tailed off. Further symptomatic treatment will often be necessary in addition.

Some practitioners have shortened the detoxification process even further by combining the use of clonidine for detoxification with the narcotic antagonist naltrexone (Chaney *et al.*, 1986; Kleber *et al.*, 1987). For the use of naltrexone in relapse prevention, see below.

Codeine and codeine-related drugs
Nothing relieves the symptoms of opiate withdrawal so well as an opiate or opiate-related drug. By analogy with the treatment described for sedative and tranquilliser withdrawal, it would seem that the most logical method of opiate detoxification would be to prescibe a drug with cross-tolerance with the abused opiate and progressively to reduce the dose. This method has indeed been the mainstay of treatment for opiate withdrawal for many years, the usual drug of choice being methadone (see below). Because of the mystique surrounding this drug, and also because of the practical problems of prescribing a controlled drug, many practitioners have preferred to use codeine or, more commonly, its stronger analogue, dihydrocodeine. However, these drugs are also widely abused and the fact that they are not officially controlled should not blind prescribers to the care needed in their prescription both generally and when attempting to detoxify addicts. Indeed dihydrocodeine is a drug which is frequently obtained by some patients by visiting multiple doctors. Both codeine (still available without prescription) and dihydrocodeine dependence in themselves are treatable by any of the methods outlined above.

Patients with either illicit opiate dependence or dependence upon codeine or its analogues should be assessed for the appropriateness of community detoxification (see under 'Community or in-patient detoxification?'). If this is decided upon, a treatment contract (see under 'Treatment contracts') should be agreed. Patients most suitable for detoxification using dihydrocodeine are those with a relatively short history of daily opiate use (6 months to 2 years) who have definitely had evidence of withdrawal symptoms. They may be those deemed to be unable to cope with the rigours of 'cold turkey' or symptomatic treatment alone. Patients dependent upon prescribed analgesics and obtaining their supplies from one source (their own GP) may also be suitable.

A daily dose of eight to twelve × 30-mg tablets of dihydrocodeine is suitable for most illicit users for whom this method is appropriate. If more is required, the prescriber would be advised to consider the use of methadone (p. 120) unless the patient is addicted to prescribed dihydrocodeine, when the dose should be that to which they are addicted.

Withdrawal should be by regular decrements of 1 tablet, the frequency of reduction being agreed beforehand and extending over 2–6 weeks for illicit opiate abusers, although longstanding users of prescribed drugs may need longer. The safeguards delineated under 'Treatment contracts' will need to be followed.

Some non-medical agencies have advised clients wishing to withdraw from illicit opiates who are unwilling to approach doctors, or who have had difficulties in obtaining medical detoxification help, to buy codeine linctus from a chemist and to use that to relieve symptoms. Some have gone further and have assisted clients by drawing up a withdrawal schedule using codeine linctus. While this may be helpful for some clients, care must be exercised that a further avenue of drug abuse is not opened up.

Methadone

Many opiate-dependent individuals find that codeine derivatives, while relieving withdrawal symptoms, leave something 'missing'. This is probably related to the euphoriant potential of opiates. If the aim of detoxification is to wean the patient, in stages, from dependence on an illicit and potentially damaging (particularly if injected) drug towards abstinence, it may be unhelpful for the initial stage to be too abrupt. Thus, the prescription of clean pharmaceutical opiates in reducing dose is a logical and humane form of treatment. Viewed this way, opiate prescription and reduction are very little different from the treatment of sedative and tranquilliser withdrawal already described. The actual drug to be used for the withdrawal could, in principle, be selected on the same criteria: i.e. short-acting drugs providing a shorter but symptomatically unpredictable withdrawal, and longer-acting drugs a longer but smoother one. In practice, the longer-acting synthetic opiate, methadone, is usually used for the same reason that diazepam is substituted for lorazepam. Some 'therapeutic addicts' who have become addicted in the course of analgesic prescription for a painful condition may be withdrawn on their usual drug but it may well be preferable to substitute methadone particularly for short-acting drugs such as heroin or dextromoramide (Palfium). Many opiate users have described the symptoms of methadone withdrawal as worse than those of heroin, and it is unlikely that they are all wrong. However, it is probable that this is merely a result of the longer timescale for the longer acting drug. Drug users, having grown accustomed to immediate answers, find long-drawn-out withdrawal difficult to tolerate. There is certainly some objective evidence of the length of time symptoms may last following methadone withdrawal (Gossop *et al.*, 1984). This may be an argument for the use of clonidine in withdrawal, and is certainly a factor to be taken into account when considering longer term methadone prescription (see below, 'Methadone maintenance).

Prior to beginning an out-patient methadone reduction scheme, it is usually wise to spell out a treatment contract (see 'Treatment contracts') with a patient and to make it clear that this will be adhered to.

Care must be exercised when establishing the starting dose of methadone, particularly when dealing with patients whose use has been mainly illicit. This is partly because drugs will have been taken for effect and not merely to relieve withdrawal symptoms and also because the strength of street drugs varies considerably. For in-patients, it is possible to titrate drug dosage against withdrawal signs so that when definite signs are observed 10–20 mg of methadone is given and then repeated at intervals of 1–2 hours until no more signs are observable, or the person is slightly intoxicated. When this sort of observation is not practicable, it is at least possible to give a test dose and to arrange to see the patient 1–2 hours later when gross over- or underdosage will be apparent.

The rate of reduction will vary according to the individual. On an in-patient basis, reduction may be relatively rapid: progressive daily or alternate day halving of the dose is possible but most units will have a slightly gentler regimen of perhaps 10-mg decrements (daily or alternate days) down to 40 or 50 mg and 5-mg decrements thereafter. This rate of reduction is possible on an out-patient basis for motivated patients and those with good support. Certainly for young people or those with a short history (6 months to 2 years) of daily use, a relatively rapid detoxification period of 3 to 6 weeks is desirable. Patients with less support, those with longer periods of drug use, or those with other problems may well need longer periods between reductions. If a planned withdrawal takes longer than 12 weeks, it should probably be considered as described under 'Methadone maintenance'.

While undergoing such a withdrawal, patients will need to be seen frequently, at least as frequently as the reductions, unless being seen by a counsellor or Community Drug Team member. Occasional lapses into illicit drug abuse may be expected and should not automatically lead to cessation of the contract (although see under 'Treatment contracts' for less experienced practitioners). Repeated lapses, persistent use of other drugs, and other failure to adhere to the treatment contract must lead to urgent reappraisal and discussion with the patient. Possible forms of action could be as follows:

(a) To restart the detoxification process. There may be some external factor which will warrant a return to a higher dosage and perhaps a renegotiation of the rate of reduction. Inexperienced practitioners should be aware, however, of the dangers of 'maintenance prescribing' by default. A decision on longer term prescribing must be a positive decision and not one reached by indecision at this stage.
(b) Admission for in-patient detoxification.
(c) Longer term so-called 'maintenance' prescription. This is considered below.
(d) Termination of the contract and cessation of prescription.

Acupuncture, electro-acupuncture and neuroelectric therapy
Acupuncture has been used in Chinese medicine for thousands of years for the treatment of a variety of ailments. Its more recent acceptance as an alternative therapy in western society has largely been based on its use for the relief of pain and has not generally implied acceptance of the traditional explanations of its efficacy. There has been some evidence that

one possible mode of action is by stimulation of the production of endorphins (Clement Jones *et al.*, 1980; Royal College of Psychiatrists, 1987). If this is the case, the use of acupuncture for the treatment of opiate addiction would be logical. Straightforward acupuncture (the application of needles to specified points in the body) and electro-acupuncture (electrical stimulation of the needles) have both been used in detoxification from opiates (Wen and Cheung 1973; Clement Jones *et al.*, 1979). Unfortunately, controlled and duplicated studies have not been forthcoming. A further modification of electro-acupuncture has been electrical stimulation of certain points without inserting needles. This treatment has been championed by Dr Meg Patterson in the form of neuroelectric therapy (NET) (Patterson, 1986). However, attempts at duplicating her results independently have not succeeded (Gossop *et al.*, 1984; but see for reply Patterson, 1985).

At present it would appear that acupuncture and related treatments should be regarded as possible adjuncts to other forms of therapy.

Maintenance of the drug-free state

It is perhaps a cliché to say that 'coming off is easier than staying off' but it is nevertheless true. Detoxification is often uncomfortable but the person has prepared himself for a period of discomfort and is able to withstand it; the day-by-day discipline of living life with its disappointments and stresses without something which has provided both a reward and a buffer is not at all easy. Many drug users are reluctant to contemplate this, particularly since it may imply a reassessment of lifestyle, and prefer to concentrate on what they regard as the purely physical problems of detoxification. It is important, however, for those involved in treatment to include this aspect in their counselling of drug users, probably from the first contact: it is not unknown for a person dependent on prescribed drugs for many years to make an impulse decision to 'come off' and to be precipitated into emotional and social chaos, perhaps complicated by alcohol abuse. It is understandable that a doctor prescribing drugs for a patient and aware of the problems caused both by the chemical dependency and by the dependent relationship should desire the patient to become independent. However, the doctor also needs to beware the temptation to ascribe all problems to the drug and to ignore the other needs.

A person giving up drug use suffers a loss of many things: at a basic level perhaps a comfort; a cushion against the outside world; a constant reliable companion when other relationships are fickle; something he can control when other parts of his life seem out of control. For a person who has obtained his drugs illegally, or even for one picking up a prescription daily, the ritual surrounding obtaining and using drugs provides a structure to life. At a time of high unemployment this is a not inconsiderable need. Therefore, to regard the loss of drugs as, in some sense, a bereavement is not an exaggeration, and a wise counsellor will recognise the need for grieving and its various manifestations, including anger, and idealisation of the object of the grief. Some form of counselling must therefore be available to anyone giving up drug use. Not all will avail themselves of this possibility, but, if its need has been considered from the first contact, it is more likely that the client/patient will at least recognise the need. For many organisations providing follow-up help and rehabilitation (whether residential or community), this will be an automatic part of the programme. These organisations are described in chapter 7.

Alternative ways of achieving a sense of satisfaction need also to be developed by the individual. For some these may come from relationships, employment, hobbies or a change of life philosophy (e.g. religious conversion). For others, a temporary bridge may be provided by involvement in a self-help group (e.g. Narcotics Anonymous) or by helping other drug users. This latter needs to be approached with caution.

New coping mechanisms for dealing with unpleasant emotions or anxiety-provoking situations will also need to be learned. This may involve specific forms of psychological intervention such as relapse prevention techniques or relaxation.

Residential rehabilitation may be appropriate for those whose lifestyle has become totally drug-centred, and therapeutic communities for those whose early life experience has been deprived or damaging. Marital and family therapy may also be necessary to help families to change patterns of interaction which may have developed to deal with a disruptive member but which may be counterproductive when the drug use has stopped.

Treatment and support of people with frank mental illness (particularly schizophrenia) or organic brain damage who also misuse drugs is particularly difficult. They may, paradoxically, be very suspicious of prescribed anti-psychotic medication and take it intermittently or not at all. If they require supportive accommodation, they may be excluded both from hostels for the mentally ill and those for ex-drug users. The staff of hostels for the mentally ill do not have the specific skills necessary for dealing with drug misusers, and hostels and therapeutic communities for drug users are often centred around intensive group therapy which may be damaging for psychotic patients. Even hospital admission may be problematic with acute psychiatric wards feeling ill-equipped to cope with drug users and specialist drug wards often being run along the lines of therapeutic communities.

Management of such individuals requires intensive interdisciplinary co-operation and may well involve drug treatment (both by conventional anti-psychotic drugs and methadone replacement), social intervention and support, caring nursing, and environmental manipulation. It certainly highlights the need for drug training for non-drug specialists, particularly doctors and nurses in general psychiatry.

The use of narcotic antagonists

As described above, narcotic antagonists can be used to reverse the effects of opiates taken in overdosage. These drugs act by preferentially occupying the opiate binder sites in the central nervous system, precipitating the opiate withdrawal state in an individual dependent on opiates. However, if used in a person who has been withdrawn from opiates, antagonists block opiate effects and could theoretically be used to break the cycle of craving leading to drug use and readdiction. For many years, the short duration of action of opiate antagonist drugs (3–4 hours for naloxone) prevented the development of this theory. However, with the advent of naltrexone, with a half-life of up to 96 hours, a pharmacological treatment for heroin abuse became a real possibility (Crabtree, 1984). It is obvious, however, that any treatment that involves taking medication regularly depends on patient compliance and that the use of naltrexone cannot therefore be regarded as a magic answer but as an adjunct to other strategies directed towards maintaining the drug-free state; it is particularly useful in preventing impulsive drug use which may lead to more serious relapse in an otherwise well motivated person.

Naltrexone is given in a dosage of 50 mg daily, or 350 mg per week in three divided doses (100 mg on Monday, 100 mg on Wednesday and 150 mg on Friday) (Crabtree, 1984). The patient should be detoxified first, and, if detoxified using opiates, should have been drug-free for two to five days. If clonidine has been used for detoxification, it is possible to start naltrexone after 24 hours (Chaney *et al.*, 1986; Kleber *et al.*, 1987). Most would regard the use of naltrexone as a bridge to provide some support over the period between ceasing the use of opiates and the development of longer term lifestyle changes. As such, the involvement of family or friends in the administration of the drug may be helpful, but, unless the user him- or herself is willing, family involvement may appear to be just another example of parental behaviour, to be rebelled against. Of course, narcotic antagonists do not have any action on stimulant or sedative abuse. Naltrexone is probably of most use for longer term users, whose preferred drug is an opiate, and who may have had previous experience of relapse triggered by an impulsive drug-taking episode but who are well motivated towards developing a drug-free lifestyle.

Methadone maintenance

Methadone maintenance as a treatment for heroin addiction was popularised in the United States in the 1960s by the work of Dole and Nyswander (1965; see also Dole *et al.*, 1968, and see p. 126). As practised in the United States and various other countries which have adopted the model, methadone maintenance has been just that: the replacement of illicit heroin use by a legal dose of oral methadone for an indefinite period. Dole and Nyswander themselves discouraged the withdrawal of methadone, and some workers have gone so far as to refer to methadone *patients* as 'ex-addicts'.

In recent years, some workers have tended to refer to any long-term prescribing as 'maintenance' prescribing. This has confused the picture. Prescribing of methadone and other opiates for the treatment of opiate dependence can range from a rapid withdrawal schedule to a lifetime prescription. 'Methadone maintenance' is a term best reserved for a prescription which is intended to be long term and in which there is no definite goal of reduction or abstinence, but of stabilisation of lifestyle. So defined, methadone maintenance is seen as a treatment strategy for a selected group of patients (see below) for whom it is the treatment of choice. Short-term holding prescriptions, or longer term reducing prescriptions, can then be placed appropriately in the spectrum of treatment possibilities, without being confused with drug maintenance.

In the earlier part of this chapter, the use of methadone for withdrawal from opiates was described. Reference was made to the length of time needed for withdrawal. Certainly, those patients whose lives have been totally disrupted by their drug use and attendant social circumstances are unlikely to be able to become abstinent on an out-patient basis within 12 weeks. If the person strongly wishes for abstinence and is able to consider residential rehabilitation, hospital admission should be considered. However, the question of longer term prescription or 'methadone maintenance' should be considered for others, but the treatment of this group should be carried out by doctors experienced in the treatment of drug problems.

Selection of patients

Patients suitable for longer term prescribing should be positively selected: shorter periods of out-patient detoxification should not be allowed to drift without reassessment and a positive decision.

In general, patients suitable for methadone maintenance are those who have a definite history of several years of dependency upon opiates. Typically, several attempts at abstinence will have been made. Ideally, experience will have shown that the patient has been able to at least start to stabilise his or her lifestyle while on prescription; perhaps stopping the use of illicit drugs. The changes possible for each individual vary; some are able to gain employment and others can cease reliance on criminality.

Assessment

The assessment necessary for this form of intervention needs to be more thorough than for a short-term out-patient detoxification: prescribing a short-term reduction prescription for someone who is not actually physically dependent is regrettable but not unredeemable; a long-term prescription in the same circumstances renders a self-reliant person dependent upon a drug and a doctor, and can be extremely handicapping of personality development (see below). It is usually necessary to see the person on several occasions, and to test the urine for the presence of drugs. Previous treatment agencies should be contacted and reports obtained.

The starting dosage must be carefully assessed. Dole and Nyswander advocated admission to hospital and gradual increase of the dose of methadone to achieve narcotic blockage (Dole *et al.*, 1968). However, this high-dosage approach has not shown significant advantages over lower dose regimens, in which an individual is rendered comfortable on a level of methadone which is sufficient to prevent withdrawal symptoms but does not lead to intoxication. This can be assessed by observation of the individual for a few hours in the clinic.

Ongoing treatment and supervision

The Dole and Nyswander model of methadone maintenance required daily attendance of the patient at the clinic to take the medication under supervision. The British model has, more commonly, required the patient to collect the medication daily from a pharmacy. Certainly daily dispensing of the drug is usually necessary at the start, although those patients who become stable may be able to earn the privilege of less than daily drug collection. The patient needs to be seen regularly by a counsellor (who can, but need not be, the prescribing doctor), and usually have a urine specimen tested for the presence of drugs on a regular basis. This latter will show that the patient is taking the prescribed drug, and also whether other drugs are being abused.

Review

All patients need regular review of progress and goals. Goals need to be continually updated so that a very chaotic patient may, for instance, have an initial goal of stabilisation of lifestyle, which may change to include accommodation, attendance at a day centre, employment, etc. as things improve, and may progress towards slow detoxification. Some units have fixed-term renewable contracts with their patients, with specific goals, so that all are aware that a review will take place at a specified time.

Problems

(1) *Continued drug abuse*
Some patients find methadone boring or continue to crave a drug high or episodes of intoxication and may use extra heroin or other drugs such as stimulants, benzodiazepines and alcohol. These may be discovered on testing the urine or may be apparent by the patient's attending the clinic in an intoxicated state. Isolated instances are common, particularly at the start of treatment, and can be dealt with in the course of counselling. Persistent abuse is more difficult and may need a reassessment of the goals of treatment. Some programmes have a system of penalties for the abuse of drugs; others may make supplementary doses of methadone contingent on 'clean' urine tests (Higgins *et al.*, 1986; Stitzer *et al.*, 1986). Some programmes have a low threshold stream in which the goal is merely to involve the user in a treatment programme. Movement towards any other goal would be at the instigation of the user.

Regular stimulant abuse may cause considerable problems since the individual will be more irritable and may also, without being strictly psychotic, become inaccessible to rational discussion.

Continued alcohol abuse which occurs in some long-standing metha- done-maintained patients will lead to the well known physical complica- tions of alcohol dependence. These may be exacerbated by pre-existing liver problems as a result of hepatitis. It may be more difficult for the patient to obtain treatment for alcohol-related problems because of his or her drug status.

(2) *Diversion of drugs*
The common situation in Great Britain of a patient collecting his or her prescription from a pharmacy for use at home renders the possibility of sale of the drugs to others a real possibility. This is a strong argument (albeit a non-clinical one) against the use of injectable drugs for a long-term prescription.

(3) *Continued 'patient' status*
A patient who is prescribed drugs is not only pharmacologically dependent on the substance but is also maintained in a dependent, child-like role. The doctor has duties to the state as well as to the patient, and is required to exercise control over prescriptions for opiate drugs. For some patients this position hampers personality development towards self-determination and maturity. This handicapping effect of prolonged prescription may only reveal itself after some time. For some individuals, however, the move from a self-reliant, streetwise person (albeit running a risk of legal, social and health problems) to a childlike dependent patient can be so rapid as to be alarming. The relationship between patient and doctor may become distorted and a situation similar to that between adolescent and parent may

develop with the patient having a lot of hostile feelings but unable to progress because of reliance on the prescription.

(4) *Hampered personality development*
In addition to the difficulties outlined above, the learning and personality growth which is prompted by facing and dealing with anxiety-provoking situations is slowed down by the artificial reduction of anxiety caused by the drug. Bereavement, for instance, may be handled by the drug user by increasing the drugs taken, thus suspending or retarding the necessary grief work. If the person later attempts drug withdrawal, the pain of many small bereavements may be very hard to cope with.

(5) *Increasing difficulty withdrawing*
The longer a person takes the drug, the more difficult it is to withdraw. This is both for emotional reasons such as that referred to in (4) above and the fact that alternative strategies for dealing with problems become harder, and also for purely physical reasons.

(6) *Health problems*
For those patients receiving regular prescriptions for injectable drugs, the repeated use of veins leads to fibrosis and, in some patients, the temptation to use deeper veins (e.g. femoral). This causes problems of venous drainage from the legs. Also, in spite of clean equipment, sterile procedures, etc., infections occur in some people. Long-standing suppression of painful stimuli may lead to a failure to recognise potentially treatable disease at an early stage.

Which drugs?

The above deals mainly with the use of oral methadone for the treatment of heroin addiction. There are benefits and problems which need to be weighed up individually in each case, but if other drugs, particularly injectable methadone or heroin, are used, the potential problems are increased and raise serious questions for the prescriber. This is not to say that there may not be a place for injectable drugs, but the situation will need to be continually reviewed. The Report of the Advisory Council on the Misuse of Drugs, *AIDS and Drug Misuse Part 1* (DHSS, 1988), suggests that long-term prescription of injectable drugs would be 'most exceptional' (para. 6.15 p. 52).

The prescription of amphetamines to long-term users has received scant consideration in the literature apart from suggestions that it is not helpful (DHSS, 1988). Further research must be awaited here.

The long-term prescription of benzodiazepines raises similar questions to that of oral methadone, but most observers agree that long-term prescription is undesirable.

References

British National Formulary No. 16 (1988) (London: British Medical Association and Royal Pharmaceutical Society of Great Britain).

Chaney D.S., Heninger J.R. and Kleber H.D. (1986) The combined use of clonidine and naltrexone as a rapid, safe and effective treatment of abrupt withdrawal from methadone. *Amer. J. Psychiat.*, **143**, 831–837.

Clement-Jones V., McLoughlin L., Lowry P.J., Besser G.M., Rees L.H. and Wen H.L. (1979) Acupuncture in heroin addicts: changes in metenkephalin and beta-endorphin in blood and cerebrospinal fluid. *Lancet*, **ii**, 382–383.

Clement-Jones V., Tomlin S., Rees L.H., McLoughlin L., Besser G.M. and Wen H.L. (1980) Increased β-endorphin but not met-enkephalin levels in human cerebrospinal fluid after acupuncture for recurrent pain. *Lancet*, **ii**, 946–949.

Crabtree B.L. (1984) Review of naltrexone, a long-acting opiate antagonist. *Clin. Pharm.*, **3**, 273–280.

Department of Health and Social Security (1984) *Guidelines of Good Clinical Practice in the Treatment of Drug Misuse*. Report of the Medical Working Group on Drug Dependence (London: HMSO).

Department of Health and Social Security (1988) *AIDS and Drug Misuse Part 1*. Report by the Advisory Council on the Misuse of Drugs (London: HMSO).

Dole V.P. and Nyswander M.E. (1965) A medical treatment for diacetylmorphine (heroin) addiction. *J. Amer. Med. Assoc.*, **193**, 646–650.

Dole V.P., Nyswander M.E. and Warner A. (1968) Successful treatment of 750 criminal addicts. *J. Amer. Med. Assoc.*, **206**, 2708–2711.

Ghodse A.H. (1986) Cannabis psychosis. *Br. J. Addiction*, **81**, 473–478.

Gold M.S., Pottash A.C., Sweeney D.R. and Kleber H.D. (1980) Opiate withdrawal using clonidine: a safe, effective, and rapid non-opiate treatment. *J. Amer. Med. Assoc.*, **243**, 343–346.

Gossop M., Bradley B., Strang J. and Connell P.H. (1984) The clinical effectiveness of electrostimulation vs oral methadone in managing opiate withdrawal. *Br. J. Psychiat.*, **144**, 203–205.

Harrison M., Busto U., Naranjo C.A., Kaplan H.L. and Sellers, E.M. (1984) Diazepam tapering in detoxification for high-dose benzodiazepam abuse. *Clin. Pharmacol. Ther.*, **36**, 527–533.

Higgins S.T., Stitzer M.L., Bigelow G F. and Liebson I.A. (1986) Contingent methadone delivery: effects on illicit opiate use. *Drug Alcohol Depend.*, **17**, 311–322.

Isbell H., Altschul S., Kornetsky C.H., Eisenman A.J., Flanary H.G. and Fraser H.F. (1950) Chronic barbiturate intoxication, an experimental study. *Arch. Neurol. Psychiat.*, **64**, 1–28.

Kleber H.D., Topazian M., Gaspari J., Riordan C.E. and Kosten T. (1987) Clonidine and naltrexone in the outpatient treatment of heroin withdrawal. *Amer. J. Drug Alcohol Abuse*, **13**, 1–17.

Laurie P. (1978) *Drugs, Medical, Psychological and Social Facts* (Harmondsworth: Penguin).

Patterson M.A. (1985) Electrostimulation and opiate withdrawal [letter]. *Br. J. Psychiat.*, **146**, 213.

Patterson M.A. (1986) *Hooked? NET The New Approach to Drug Cure* (London: Faber & Faber).

Petursson H. and Lader M.H. (1984) *Dependence on Tranquillisers* (New York: Oxford University Press).

Robinson G.M. and Sellers E.M. (1982) Diazepam withdrawal seizures. *Can. Med. Assoc. J.*, **126**, 944–945.

Royal College of Psychiatrists (1987) *Drug Scenes* (Gaskell: London).

Stitzer M.L., Bickel W.K., Bigelow G.E. and Liebson I.A. (1986) Effect of methadone dose contingencies on urinalysis test results of polydrug-abusing methadone-maintenance patients. *Drug Alcohol Depend.*, **18**, 341–348.

Wen H.L. and Cheung S.Y. (1973) Treatment of drug addiction by acupuncture and electrical stimulation. *Asian J. Med*, **9**, 138–141.

Bibliography

Ministry of Health and Scottish Home and Health Department (1965) *Drug Addiction*, Second Report of the Interdepartmental Committee (London: HMSO).

Strang J., Ghodse H. and Johns A. (1987) Responding flexibly but not gullibly to drug addiction. *Br. Med. J.*, **295**, 1364.

Department of Health and Social Security (1982) *Treatment and Rehabilitation*. Report of the Advisory Council on the Misuse of Drugs (London: HMSO).

6

Psychological Treatments

Michael Gossop and *John Strang*

Synopsis

Drug dependence is not a single entity. The people who run into problems with their drug taking are not a single, unitary group. The problems that drug takers may develop are not all the same. The differences that exist between individual cases are considerable and, in order to be effective, any treatment intervention must reflect those differences. The sort of treatment that may be appropriate for a 35-year-old intravenous heroin addict with a history of dependence stretching back for 15 years or more may be quite unsuitable for a 16-year-old schoolboy who has been caught by his teacher sniffing glue in the playground. Similarly, the 50-year-old who has become seriously addicted to benzodiazepines prescribed by her family doctor may require a different type of treatment intervention to the 25-year-old who has become a compulsive user of cocaine.

For these reasons, this chapter will not advocate any specific type (or types) of treatment as being in some sense the answer to the question of how best to treat such diverse problems. Instead, it will look more broadly at what a psychological treatment intervention might sensibly attempt, and try to outline some recent treatment approaches that are being used. It is beyond the scope of this chapter to attempt any comprehensive review of all available treatment options, and the reader should be cautioned that there may be many other approaches not mentioned here which may be equally promising and worthy of discussion.

Problem definition and treatment goals

A recent editorial posed the question 'What is the most effective way to treat opiate addiction?' (Gossop, 1987). This apparently simple question should carry a government health warning. Its wording is misleading and it disguises a number of unstated assumptions both about the nature of the problem and about the nature of an effective response. Indeed, the question as stated invites a quite inappropriate sort of reply of the form 'Treatment A is best', with the further implication that all drug treatment

131

services should therefore offer this form of treatment. This is both unrealistic and undesirable. The issue becomes instantly more complex when the discussion is widened to include not merely the opiates but the whole range of other drugs that are abused.

For all types of drug problem requiring treatment, the intervention offered should be tailored to the needs of the particular individual. This apparently simple and uncontentious statement turns out to have complex and far-reaching implications if it is seriously applied in clinical practice. It is essential, for instance, that a thorough assessment should identify, *for each individual*, the nature of the problem and appropriate and achievable goals for treatment. In addition, the treatment process should identify as early as possible those particular factors that are likely to assist or hamper the achievement of the treatment goal(s).

Examples of types of treatment goal might include the following:

(1) Reduction of psychological, social or other problems not directly related to the drug problem.
(2) Reduction of psychological, social or other problems related to the drug problem.
(3) Reduction of harmful or hazardous behaviour associated with the use of drugs.
(4) Attainment of controlled, non-dependent or non-problem drug use.
(5) Attainment of abstinence from problem drug.
(6) Attainment of abstinence from all drugs.

These six examples are not, of course, mutually exclusive. It is possible, for example, to set as treatment goals the attainment of abstinence *and* the improvement of psychological functioning in areas unrelated to drug taking. It is, however, useful to distinguish between those treatments that are aimed *directly* at the drug problem and those that have an *indirect* or hypothetical relationship to the target problem.

One example of the indirect approach which has played a dominant role in influencing psychiatric thinking about drug dependence is related to the personality disorder model. In essence, this sees drug abusers and particularly addicts as having deep-rooted personality problems which lead to difficulties in many areas of their life (the abuse of drugs or alcohol being but one example). The treatment approach, which by implication is a long-term affair, is aimed at correcting the underlying personality defects so that after treatment the patient will no longer need to revert to drug taking. Addictive behaviour is therefore regarded as symptomatic of a more important problem (Kohut, 1977). The similarities between this formulation and that which relates symptoms and disease in physical medicine are considerable and may account for much of its persistence among medically trained clinicians.

It is only comparatively recently that the use of direct treatment approaches for the addictive disorders has become established and, therefore, made any substantial impact upon clinical practice. Direct treatment methods focus upon the specific behaviour and circumstances of the drug problem, and attempt to modify them as problems in their own right. This approach owes a good deal to other trends in clinical psychology. The description of assessment procedures for a behaviour modification programme offered by Kanfer and Phillips (1970) provides good general guidance for a direct treatment approach. The model of assessment does not attempt to describe the total personality but instead narrows its focus to those factors particularly relevant for treatment. Information is needed about the target behaviours, the reinforcement parameters maintaining them, opportunities in the patient's environment for maintaining other more desirable responses, and the patient's ability to observe and reinforce himself or herself. It is characteristic of such approaches that their data are often direct samples of behaviour in specific situations and not indirect and generalised signs of personality predispositions.

In the treatment of drug problems, it has unfortunately often been the case that the decisions about which treatment to offer have depended as much upon the orientation of the therapist as upon the difficulties of the patient. Therapists looking for intrapsychic difficulties have identified and treated such problems, while therapists concerned with behavioural functioning have tended to locate and treat problems at a more behavioural level. Not the least of the advantages of the assessment procedures used in the direct treatment approach (as advocated, for instance, by Kanfer and Phillips, 1970) is that they yield information which has clear, direct and specific relevance to the target problem. In contrast, dispositional diagnosis seldom gives any guidance about the type of treatment which is appropriate to modify the addictive behaviour. As a result the personality disorder model often leads to a non-specific treatment approach in which a vast range of unrelated procedures are lumped together in the vague hope that such an 'eclectic' or 'multimodal' package will be more likely to hit the target than any more specific procedure. However, the shotgun is not always a superior weapon to the rifle, and despite the popularity of such 'broad spectrum' approaches they have clear disadvantages.

There is evidence that the more techniques and procedures we apply in any treatment case, the more difficult it is for the patient to maintain compliance with the requirements of the programme (Hall, 1980). This is especially true where 'broad spectrum' shotgun packages are applied indiscriminately to a heterogeneous population such as drug addicts or alcoholics, and may be further aggravated by the failure of patient and therapist to agree upon what are the goals of treatment. The goals of treatment should be made fully explicit and should be mutually acceptable to both the patient and the therapist wherever possible. Failure to achieve this understanding can lead to considerable difficulties at later stages of treatment.

A further difficulty for many treatment packages is that many of the components tend to be aimed at initial behaviour change and not at the maintenance of any such change (Marlatt, 1982). One consequence of this is that there is often an imbalance in these programmes, with insufficient attention being paid to the maintenance of change.

The attempt to modify psychological or other problems that are assumed to be related to the drug problem may be seen as an end in itself. However, it is important to be clear about the goal at which such interventions are aimed. In some cases such attempts may be more profitably regarded as a means towards achieving a goal rather than as a goal in themselves. Some treatment interventions aimed at abstinence flounder as a result of seeking to improve social skills, or reduce anxiety, or obtain better housing accommodation, on the assumption that this will necessarily lead to an improvement in drug-taking behaviour.

Motivational interviewing and motivational milieu therapy

The term 'motivation' has a long and often dishonourable association with treatments for the addictions. In their discussion of some of the more outstanding misconceptions surrounding addiction, Einstein and Garitano (1972) point to the circularity in the way that this term has been so often misused.

> The general approach is that if the drug abuser patient gets better—translated that means he gives up his drugs of choice—he was a good and motivated patient and was able to profit from our professional expertise and skill. We cured him. If the patient continues his drug use, this is manifest evidence that he was not motivated, and a poor treatment risk who could not profit from our skill.

This circularity has been consistently misleading and unhelpful and has been a major factor in leading to a dissatisfaction with the concept of motivation. It is because of this sort of problem that it has been suggested that the concept of motivation is useless and should be discarded. However, it is not necessary completely to reject the term. It has been shown that when motivation is operationally defined (for example, in terms of the strength of the addict's desire for in-patient treatment), this is one of the principal determinants of how long addicts subsequently remain in an in-patient treatment programme (Gossop, 1978). The concept can therefore be rescued from circularity and it can be shown to relate to treatment response. However, it remains an inherently problematic concept, especially when used without clear definition. It is simplistic to regard motivation as unchanging or as an entirely 'internal' factor. However, the extent to which it changes in response to external social and environmental factors requires further investigation.

More recently, the term has re-emerged in relation to a form of treatment known as 'motivational interviewing'. Miller's original account of motivational interviewing describes its application with problem drinkers (Miller, 1983). Here, motivation is conceptualised as an interpersonal process, and the behaviour of the therapist is seen as having considerable influence on the subsequent attributions and behaviour of the client. Miller puts forward alternative views for mechanisms such as denial which he does not regard simply as inherent in the alcoholic but as a product of the way in which the counsellor has chosen to interact with the problem drinker. The aim of therapy is to increase levels of cognitive dissonance until a critical mass of motivation is achieved, at which point the client is willing to consider change alternatives. Miller uses the model of process of change (Prochaska and DiClemente, 1983, 1986) in his discussion and explanation of his model to project movement from precontemplation and contemplation to determination and action. In the six-step sequence for implementing motivational interviewing, Miller emphasises how important it is that the therapist initially adopts an almost exclusively empathic stance using the techniques operationalised by Carl Rogers. However, this process is soon modified to be subtly selective in its reflection so as to reinforce statements of concern and elicit self-motivational statements. The client then constructs his or her own inventory of problems related to drinking to express their concern and identify possible changes which they might consider. The role of the therapist is to encourage the active involvement of the client in the identification of the problem and in the cost–benefit analysis of the various available options, as described by Janis and Mann (1977). The approach is intended to enhance the importance of personal responsibility and the internal attribution of choice and control, and the therapist must help the client to avoid treatment 'short circuits' from low self-esteem, low self-efficacy and denial and the dangers of the 'alcoholic' label and of binary thinking (i.e. alcoholic vs not alcoholic).

One of the interesting features of Miller's model is the way in which Rogerian reflective listening is used selectively. The therapist must be aware that he is not just being reflective but is subtly steering the client towards change. One of the main purposes behind the Rogerian stance is the active involvement of the client. The therapeutic style is not truly reflective, as the client's comments are fed back in a modified form and are selected so as to increase dissonance. This selection must be a clandestine operation and the therapist should include doubts expressed by the client so as to preserve the credibility of the procedure. The patient's own terminology should be used as far as possible. As Miller says, 'the counsellor should not put words in the client's mouth, because this will be easily detected as a ploy'. There is a real concern that not only would this particular treatment contact be fruitless, but there may be a boomerang effect in which the individual realises he is being coerced and is then more likely to follow an exactly opposite course of action. The internal attribution of this moulded feedback generates dissonance which must then be directed in an appropriate direction. The therapist should not discuss treatment options or alternatives until this critical mass of motivation is reached; and even then the alternative intervention options should include the possibility of 'no special intervention' — self-directed change strategies as well as traditional treatment options should also be offered. The therapist assists the client in identification of appropriate goals and in the implementation of strategies to achieve these changes.

More recently, van Bilsen and his colleagues have used a similar approach with heroin addicts (van Bilsen and van Emst, 1986; van Bilsen, 1987, 1988). Van Bilsen and his colleagues describe their motivational milieu therapy (MMT) as a humanistic approach which should not be looked upon as a convincing process (i.e. convincing the client to do something about their drug use) but should be seen as the supervision of a process of decision making in which the client makes the decisions. They describe an approach very similar to that of Miller and summarise this as comprising three phases: the eliciting phase during which a non-judgemental style is adopted so as to obtain information on the attitudes and behavioural patterns of the subject; the information phase during which there is feedback from the therapist; and the negotiation phase during which therapist and client discuss the possible changes which the client may wish to implement. However, van Bilsen's description of the work of MMT seems closer to more traditional work in which the therapist assists the patient in decision making, and lacks Miller's intriguing inclusion of deliberate manipulation of the patient's own language during the feedback by the therapist so as to generate dissonance. Van Bilsen's approach may be regarded as more honest, but the price for this honesty may be a more dilute treatment in which all responsibility is placed with the client. The therapist may feel more comfortable with such an approach, but it may be that Miller's more Machiavellian approach will be more likely to bring about change despite its requirement for the therapist to be more actively involved in the identification and planning of the behaviour change.

Compulsion as a central feature of dependence

Compulsion may be regarded as a central and necessary feature of drug dependence (Gossop, 1989). It was included in the definition of drug dependence from the World Health Organization (1969):

> a state, psychic and sometimes also physical, resulting from the interaction between a living organism and a drug, characterised by behavioural and other responses that always includes a compulsion to take the drug on a continuous or periodic basis in order to experience its psychic effects, and sometimes to avoid the discomfort of abstinence.

As Russell points out in his discussion paper 'What is dependence?' (Russell, 1976), the notion of dependence is associated with negative affect experienced in the absence of the drug or other object; and the degree of dependence can be equated with the amount of this negative affect. A preoccupation with frequency, duration or amount of use should be avoided as it is the difficulty in refraining from use which should be considered as a central element of dependence. In discussing the concepts of covert dependence and of the similarities and dissimilarities with compulsive states, Russell points out that dependence will only be recognised when there is an attempt to resist or do without the drug or substance. As with compulsions, the crucial feature is the strength of the underlying urge.

More recently, Rankin (1986) has discussed the contribution of dependence and compulsion to our understanding of models of change, and has drawn attention to the central role played by drug- or alcohol-related cues. For example, Rankin and his colleagues found that an individual's degree of dependence was associated with the frequency and intensity with which cues triggered drinking behaviour (Rankin *et al.*, 1982). There has also been a lively debate about the value of the concept of craving in this context. Kozlowski and Wilkinson (1987) argued that 'craving' has been conceptualised in many different ways, each with different implications for research or for treatment. They suggested that the mismatch between the current technical uses of the term and its use in ordinary language is problematic in many cases and misleading in others. In particular, they suggested that it is unacceptable to explain the use of drink or drugs, relapse or 'loss of control' by invoking craving as a causative factor. This paper stimulated debate which highlighted the weaknesses surrounding the use of the term and clarified some of the issues. Marlatt, for example, drew attention to the value of seeing craving as 'a subjective state that is mediated by the incentive properties of positive outcome expectancies', and distinguished between cravings and urges: 'it is possible to conceptualise *craving* as a motivational state (often in response to external CS cues, and to define an *urge* as the behavioural intention' (Marlatt, 1987).

Cue exposure

An important development in the treatment of phobic and obsessive–compulsive behaviour has involved the use of treatments which have been variously referred to as flooding, exposure, participant modelling and response prevention. Such forms of treatment rely upon the idea that a strong urge to carry out a compulsion will go away if the urge is resisted. When applied to alcoholism, a programme may be designed in which the therapist first identifies those events that act as signals or cues for drinking (such cues may be internal feelings such as anxiety or depression, or external events such as particular bars or pubs): the alcoholic is then systematically exposed to these cues and is assisted to avoid drinking in response to them (Hodgson, 1982). It is further assumed that conditioning processes play an important role in the establishment of cues.

Examination of the role of classical conditioning in the experience of drug effects and subsequent dependence has produced apparently conflicting findings. On the one hand, conditioned euphoria may occur in the presence of drug-related cues (O'Brien *et al.*, 1974). However, there is also convincing evidence that the abstinence syndrome can be conditioned as a response to specific environmental stimuli in both animals and man (Wikler *et al.*, 1953; Wikler, 1965). Subsequent study has demonstrated the role of both unconditioned and conditioned drug effects as reinforcers (Stewart *et al.*, 1984). Equally, it has been found that both conditioned agonist effects and conditioned withdrawal are extinguished following repeated exposure of the conditioned stimulus in the absence of the original (unconditioned) stimulus (Siegel, 1983).

As outlined above, in the clinical setting, the patient is exposed to cues which would usually have triggered an episode of drinking or drug taking. During this exposure session, the patient may be supervised, may be in a protected environment in which there is no access to drink or drugs or may (in the case of alcohol) have previously taken an aversive drug such as disulfiram. The aim is to break down the stimulus–response relationship that has developed to alcohol itself and to various conditioned stimuli, by exposing the patient to the stimuli in sessions when these are not associated with the response of drinking. This approach may be used to achieve abstinence, but it has also been used as part of programmes aimed at controlled drinking (Heather and Robertson, 1986). O'Brien and his colleagues (1974) have used this same theoretical approach with opiate addicts, exposing them to drug-related cues such as needles and syringes and the drugs themselves. As yet it remains unclear to what extent this form of treatment will prove to be a valuable and practical clinical approach in the treatment of the addictive behaviours. Preliminary observations in opiate addicts have found that extinction of conditioned responses occurs following repeated exposure (Childress *et al.*, 1986).

Marlatt refers to several techniques that have relevance to the application of cue exposure as a treatment. He recommends that clients or groups of clients should be accompanied to actual high-risk situations for a 'dry run' practice session. Among various benefits he suggests that this might offer an opportunity for cue exposure during which previously learnt urges are allowed to extinguish in the presence of the original stimulus (Marlatt, 1985). He also deals with different strategies which the patient might employ during such a session so as to cope with the high-risk situation, and suggests that the patient might benefit from developing a sense of detachment by externalising the urge so as to moderate its influence. Marlatt also teaches his clients other tricks of the trade including 'urge-surfing' during which the client learns to go with the feelings of craving in the knowledge that there is bound to be a subsequent down-slope of the curve; and the 'Samurai' approach during which the client is taught to see the urge as an approaching enemy whose force can be countered by being forewarned. However, it is possible that these techniques may achieve their effect by increasing the coping skills and self-efficacy of the client, and that they may not be true examples of cue exposure in that so much attention is paid to cognitive modification of the stimulus–response relationship.

Intermediate goals

An urgent reappraisal of treatment approaches with injecting drug addicts is currently under way following the recent recognition of the particular risk of HIV infection among injecting drug users. During the 1970s there was a general trend for most treatment services in the UK to move towards an increasingly abstinence-oriented treatment system. However, as part of the need to respond to the threat of HIV infection, there has been a move back towards a recognition of the merits of helping drug users move away from injecting to non-injectable forms of drug use (e.g. oral only or smoking). Proponents of this view have strongly argued that drug treatment services should acknowledge the particular benefit of certain key changes—in particular the benefit that may be accrued from such blunting of the needle habit.

The recent report on AIDS and drug misuse (Advisory Council on the Misuse of Drugs, 1988) emphasises the importance of working with drug users towards achievable intermediate goals which may form the focus of work in the short term even though this may be in the context of a longer term work towards eventual abstinence. Attention would be focused on the safe passage through the immediate part of the journey so as to avoid a deterioration in the morale of client or therapist who finds the prospects of the total journey too daunting. Thus, client and therapist would work through a hierarchy of goals (sequentially and/or simultaneously) acknowledging the incomplete nature of each intermediate goal but recognising that each constitutes one further step forward in effecting the sought-after behaviour change (Strang, 1988, 1989). Treatment might thus be seen as working through a cascade of processes of change rather than simply one single cycle through the process.

Stallard *et al.* (1987) described the introduction of a relapse prevention programme for opiate addicts in Dundee. In this work they recommend consideration of a hierarchy of levels of outcome which assist in consideration of benefit: abstinence, using but not injecting, using but injecting with sterile equipment, using but not sharing equipment, and using and still sharing. Data are not yet available on the extent to which these goals might be realistically achievable for a broad group of drug users; nor is there guidance on the selection of appropriate goals within the hierarchy apart from the pragmatic approach described in the recent report on AIDS and drug misuse (Advisory Council on the Misuse of Drugs, 1988) in which identification of the next intermediate goal is simply dictated by consideration of the present nature of drug-taking behaviour.

The way in which a problem is perceived may influence the response to the problem. In his exploration of the move from contemplation to determination, Appel (1986) stresses the importance of breaking down the eventual goal into simpler component parts. Appel draws on work from attribution theory and problem solving, and suggests that there is value in constructing a 'goal tree' with simpler objectives at the lower levels and the final goal at the top. Subsequently, the therapist will need to assist the client in identifying actions that are needed to reach these goals, and as a result a 'decision tree' comprising these actions would be constructed.

One intermediate goal, and an intermediate stage of those treatments which are aimed at abstinence, involves withdrawal from drugs or 'detoxification'. The importance of this stage has often been overestimated, and there have been inappropriate expectations that detoxification alone could be expected to produce long-term abstinence. The research evidence, however, clearly shows that detoxification alone is not effective in this respect (Lipton and Maranda, 1983). None the less, this should not lead to an underestimation of the importance of the withdrawal phase of treatment. It is a necessary if not a sufficient condition for long-term abstinence. Nor should it be seen as merely a 'physical' process. The manner in which an addict responds to drug withdrawal is powerfully influenced by psychological factors. Anxiety-related factors, for example, appear to increase the severity of the withdrawal response, and to be a more powerful influence upon withdrawal symptoms than the dose of heroin upon which the addict was dependent prior to detoxification (Phillips *et al.*, 1986). One of the implications of this is that psychological procedures which reduce fears and anxieties about withdrawal could be expected to reduce withdrawal symptomatology. This was confirmed by Green and Gossop (1988) who found that providing addicts with accurate but reassuring information about withdrawal altered the nature of the withdrawal response. An informed group of addicts experienced lower peak withdrawal scores, and showed lower levels of residual withdrawal symptoms after the end of a methadone reduction schedule than a non-informed group of heroin addicts. In addition, the informed group was more likely to complete the detoxification programme. Psychological interventions can play a valuable role even during such an apparently 'medical' or 'physical' phase of treatment as detoxification.

Relapse and survival

It is surprising how little attention has been paid in the past to the study of relapse itself and the development of treatments which might prevent relapse or might moderate the damaging effect of such lapses. The idea of relapse as a problem in the addictions may be traced back to the nineteenth century when it was introduced as part of a growing redefinition of addictive behaviour as a treatable illness, with the notions of treatment and relapse being closely linked (Berridge, 1989). More recent work has been at some pains to disentangle these issues and to point out how the factors that are associated with the initial development of a drink or drug problem may be independent of factors that are associated with changing the behaviour (Marlatt and Gordon, 1985). It is important to distinguish both between the study of the relapse process and the clinical interventions that are intended to modify it, and also between relapse merely as an indicator of treatment outcome and relapse as a process in its own right (Gossop, 1989). Another useful distinction that has emerged from the empirical study of relapse is that between relapse and lapse. This conceptual separation helps to focus attention upon the various sorts of association that may exist between the two; a lapse may be seen as part of a transitional process which may or may not lead back to addictive use.

In recent years, one of the major contributions to the development of a specific relapse-prevention treatment package has been that of Marlatt, who has suggested that relapse prevention be seen as a self-management programme designed to enhance the maintenance stage of the habit-change process (Marlatt, 1985). The goal of relapse prevention is to teach individuals who are trying to change their drug-taking behaviour how to anticipate and cope with the pressures and problems that may lead towards a relapse, and relapse prevention is presented as a cognitive–behavioural treatment approach based upon the principles of social learning theory. The two most central factors of this approach are the notions of high-risk situations and the coping strategies available to the individual. In a series of studies of alcoholics, Litman and her colleagues put forward a model of survival which depended on the interaction between (a) situations perceived to be dangerous for the individual in that they may precipitate relapse; (b) the coping strategies available within the individual's repertoire to deal with these situations; (c) the perceived effectiveness of these coping behaviours; and (d) the individual's self-perception and self-esteem and the degree of learned helplessness with which they view their situation (summarised in Litman, 1986). They developed questionnaires to obtain information from clients on their responses, attitudes and strategies in their attempts to avoid relapse. These were the Relapse Precipants Inventory (RPI), Coping Behaviours Inventory (CBI), Effectiveness of Coping Behaviours Inventory (ECBI), and Dependence Inventory (Litman *et al.*, 1979, 1983a, 1984).

Several interesting features emerged from an analysis of data from these questionnaires. Contrary to expectations, avoidance was perceived by clients to be an effective coping behaviour for both social anxiety and lessened cognitive vigilance (Litman *et al.*, 1977). Relapsers were compared with survivors. Individuals with a multiplicity of coping styles were more likely to survive, and the factor for cognitive control on the ECBI was the strongest discriminator between relapsers and survivors. High scores on the RPI were associated with an increased likelihood of relapse, as were high scores on the factor for unpleasant affect on the RPI. From this work, Litman proposed her 'conceptual framework for alcoholism survival' (Litman, 1980), which looked at the stages of survival rather than viewing it as an all-or-nothing phenomenon. In the early stages of survival, avoidance and positive thinking are both viewed as effective coping behaviours; although at later stages in survival there will be greater use of positive thinking alone. Litman argues that this work provides further support for individually tailored treatment programmes which are designed according to the resources and vulnerabilities of each individual rather than their broad diagnostic category (Litman, 1986).

Relapse in former heroin addicts has recently been studied by Gossop and his colleagues. A group of 80 opiate addicts who had recently completed in-patient detoxification were followed up during the six-month period immediately after discharge. It was found that a disturbingly high proportion of subjects used opiates again soon after leaving treatment. Eighty-one per cent used opiates at least once during the six-month period, and in most cases the lapse occurred very soon after discharge; 11 used within the first 24 hours, and a total of 32 subjects (42%) had lapsed within one week. The authors concluded that the period immediately after leaving treatment should be considered a critical period during which the treatment group is at extremely high risk (Gossop *et al.*, 1989). However, the results of this study were more promising when looked at from a longer term perspective, since many of the subjects were able to avoid a full relapse to addictive use of opiates. At six months 45% of the sample were abstinent from all opiates (as confirmed by urine screening) and living in the community. Of the 11 categories of relapse precipitants included in the study, the three factors that were found to be most often associated with the initial lapse were negative mood states, cognitive factors, and external situations (Bradley *et al.*, 1989). Almost two-thirds of those who lapsed indicated that cognitive factors, usually some explicit decision or plan to return to opiate use, were implicated in their initial lapse. More than half indicated that some negative mood state (sadness, boredom, tension or anxiety) preceded their lapse. These associated factors occasionally occurred as single relapse precipitants, but more often they occurred as either clusters (several simultaneous relapse factors) or as sequences (one or more factors leading on to others).

Preventing relapse

Over the last couple of decades, the emphasis in treatment programmes has shifted, and greater attention is now being paid to ways of preventing relapse. The explanatory hypotheses for these treatment approaches are very varied. In their review of relapse prevention approaches in the alcohol field, Donovan and Chaney (1985) list models ranging from the neurological to the behavioural. As they point out, the popularity of models changes over time and reflects the dominant mode of thought at a given time in history.

An elaborate model has been developed by Marlatt and his colleagues for understanding and preventing relapse (Marlatt and George, 1984). Attention is turned away from an alleged preoccupation with detoxification to a consideration of after-care. There has been a mistaken emphasis on the problem of cessation of drug use, when what is required is more emphasis on the difficulties encountered in maintenance of the change once cessation has occurred. A central concept is that of the *high-risk situation* in which the individual has an increased likelihood of reverting to former drug-taking behaviour. In a study of 311 patients addicted to a variety of drugs, Marlatt found that high-risk situations could be grouped into negative emotional states (accounting for 35% of relapses), interpersonal conflict (16% of relapses) or indirect or direct social pressure (20% of relapses) (Marlatt and George, 1984). Craving and urges might be triggered by environmental and internal cues, and an important first task for the client is to develop a keen sense of awareness of the way in which these internal and external triggers may contribute towards the development of a high-risk situation. Clients are encouraged to keep regular diaries detailing use of drugs and the extent to which they have encountered possible precipitants of relapse and a summary of their response. The therapist may assist in conducting a behavioural analysis of these situations and teaches the client how to conduct such a behavioural analysis themselves. Structured problem-solving techniques are employed alongside rehearsal/role play. The client is warned of the dangers of the way in which covert planning may lead to relapse, and of apparently irrelevant decisions (AIDs) which may 'by chance' lead the client to happen to find himself outside his old drug dealer's house. The client must learn to spot early warning signals for these potential relapse situations.

On occasions when the client begins craving, he must allow the feeling to wash over and beyond him adopting a technique which Marlatt poetically refers to as 'urge-surfing'. On occasions when there is resolution breakdown and drugs are taken, then the client must reassume control, realising that drug use or abstinence is not an on/off behaviour, and thus avoid an undampened oscillation of perceived control which Marlatt terms the abstinence violation effect.

Thus specific intervention strategies should be considered which would include possible muting of the conditioned stimulus–conditioned response relationship, correcting of some identified physical or psychological handicap, or a relapse rehearsal so as to develop alternative coping strategies; and these should be supplemented by global self-control strategies such as the learning of new 'positive addictions' and consideration of strategies for stimulus control and stimulus avoidance.

Annis has presented a relapse-prevention model based on social learning approaches and in particular, self-efficacy theory. The self-efficacy model predicts that a successful treatment exerts its influence by enhancing the client's own efficacy expectations (defined as a judgement that one has the ability to execute a certain behaviour pattern (Annis, 1986)). Efficacy expectations will influence initiation, generalisation and maintenance of coping behaviours. The strength of the efficacy expectations will determine how long the coping behaviours will be maintained under stress. Thus the disease model and a reliance on absolute abstinence are regarded as counterproductive in so far as they minimise the client's own self-efficacy expectations. In addition, an outcome expectation based on a 'one drink–one drunk' philosophy is likely to become self-fulfilling so that the event of lapse becomes more catastrophic. Annis recommends systematic teaching of self-regulatory and social skills so that the recovering alcoholic is better equipped to cope with 'slips'. Self-efficacy theory predicts that treatment is effective only in so far as it increases the client's own expectations of what they can themselves achieve and maintain. Emphasis is placed on the importance of enhancing the coping abilities of recovering alcoholics with sporadic drinking episodes which occur after periods of abstinence. Annis uses her own questionnaires for eliciting information from alcoholics (e.g. the Situational Confidence Questionnaire and Inventory of Drinking Situations), following which performance tasks can be ranked according to the particular patient's ratings of self-efficacy. Treatment is seen as comprising two phases: phase 1, concerned with initiating changes in drinking behaviour, and phase 2 which deals with consolidation of this progress associated with mastery experiences. Annis (1986) predicted that the extent of progress during phase 2 will be influenced by four factors:

(a) a perceived high-risk situation;
(b) achievement of success through only moderate effort;
(c) primarily internal attribution of success; and
(d) the success being part of a more general improvement.

Conclusion

As the precise nature of new treatments becomes clearer, so the skills required from staff may be expected to become clearer, and so the deficiencies of the pre-existing service and skill mix become clearer. As new treatments and the active components of previous treatments are identified, it is necessary for the staff/skills mix of treatment services to be adjusted accordingly, and this will also expose a need for retraining of existing and new staff who will require training and supervision in the application of these new techniques.

Treatment programmes in the past have been notoriously badly defined, and there has been an unhelpful tendency to camouflage the treatment programmes in such a way that the boundaries of separate components seem to merge imperceptibly from one to the other. Thus enquiry has all too often been directed at global questions such as whether a particular treatment programme does or does not work. Greater attention needs to be paid to the study of the treatment process as well as to the more traditional type of outcome studies. Various psychological treatment approaches are currently being developed whose description and study constitute a significant challenge for the next few years. In comparison with physical and drug treatments, psychological treatments have not been given adequate attention—possibly because of the dominant medical influence and hospital base of many treatment services. The development of these new psychological treatments opens up exciting new areas which may contain novel strategies for intervening with the drug taker; and the greatest challenge of all may be the challenge to existing drug services that they should modify the service provided and the skill mix of their staff so as to change with the changing characteristics of drug takers themselves.

References

AIDS and Drug Misuse: Part I. Department of Health and Social Security (1988) Report of the Advisory Council on the Misuse of Drugs (London: HMSO).

Annis H.M. (1986) A relapse prevention model for treatment of alcoholics. In *Treating Addictive Behaviours: Processes of Change*, eds Miller W.E. and Heather N. (New York: Plenum Press), pp. 407–434.

Appel C.-P. (1986) From contemplation to determination: contributions from cognitive psychology. In *Treating Addictive Behaviours; Processes of Change*, eds Miller W.E. and Heather N. (New York: Plenum Press), pp. 59–89.

Berridge V. (1989) The end of optimism: the pre-history of relapse. In *Relapse and Addictive Behaviour*, ed Gossop M. (London: Routledge), 231–248.

Bradley B., Phillips G., Green L. and Gossop M. (1989) Circumstances surrounding the initial lapse to opiate use following detoxification. *Br. J. Psychiat.*, **154**, 348–353.

Childress A.R., McLellan A.T. and O'Brien C.P. (1986) Abstinent opiate abusers exhibit conditioned craving, conditioned withdrawal and reductions in both through extinction. *Br. J. Addiction*, **81**, 655–660.

Donovan D.M. and Chaney E.F. (1985) Alcoholic relapse prevention and intervention: models and methods. In *Relapse Prevention: Maintenance Strategies in the Treatment of Addictive Behaviours*, eds Marlatt A.G. and Gordon J.R. (New York: Guilford Press), pp. 351–416.

Einstein S. and Garitano W. (1972) Treating the drug abuser, problems, factors and alterations. *Int. J. Addictions*, **7**, 321–331.

Gossop M. (1978) Drug dependence: a study of the relationship between motivational, cognitive, social and historical factors, and treatment variables. *J. Nerv. Ment. Dis.*, **166**, 44–50.

Gossop M. (1987) What is the most effective way to treat opiate addiction? *Br. J. Hosp. Med.*, **38**, 161.

Gossop M. (1989) Introduction to *Relapse and Addictive Behaviour* (London: Routledge).

Gossop M., Green L., Phillips G. and Bradley B. (1989) Lapse, relapse and survival among opiate addicts after treatment: a prospective follow-up study. *Br. J. Psychiat.*, **154**, 348–353.

Green L. and Gossop M. (1988) The effects of information on the opiate withdrawal syndrome. *Br. J. Addiction*, **83**, 305–309.

Hall S. (1980) Self-management and therapeutic maintenance: therapy and research. In *Improving the Long-term Effects of Psychotherapy*, eds Karoly P. and Steffen J. (New York: Gardner).

Heather N. and Robertson I. (1986) *Problem Drinking* (Harmondsworth: Penguin).

Hodgson R. (1982) Behavioural psychotherapy for compulsions and addictions. In *Social Psychology and Behavioural Medicine*, ed. Eiser J.R. (Chichester: Wiley), 375–391.

Janis, I. and Mann L. (1977) *Decision Making A Psychological Analysis of Conflict, Choice and Commitment* (London: Collier Macmillan).

Kanfer F. and Phillips J. (1970) *Learning Foundations of Behaviour Therapy* (Chichester: Wiley).

Kohut H. (1977) Preface to *The Psychodynamics of Drug Dependence* (Washington, DC: US Government Printing Office).

Kozlowski L. and Wilkinson A. (1987) Use and misuse of the concept of craving by alcohol, tobacco and drug researchers. *Br. J. Addiction*, **82**, 31–36.

Lipton D. and Maranda M. (1983) Detoxification from heroin dependency. In *Evaluation of Drug Treatment Programmes*, ed. Stimmel B. (New York: Hawarth), 31–55.

Litman G. (1980) Relapse in alcoholism. In *Alcoholism Treatment in Transition*, eds Edwards G. and Grant M. (London: Croom Helm).

Litman G. (1986) Alcoholism survival: the prevention of relapse. In *Treating Addictive Behaviours*, eds Miller W. and Heather N. (New York: Plenum), 391–405.

Litman G.K., Eiser J.R., Rawson N.S.B. and Oppenheim A.N. (1977) Towards a typology of relapse: a preliminary report. *Drug and Alcohol Depend.*, **2**, 157–162.

Litman G., Eiser J., Rawson N. and Oppenheim A.N. (1979) Towards a typology of relapse: differences in relapse and coping behaviours between alcoholic relapsers and survivors. *Behav. Res. Ther.*, **17**, 89–94.

Litman G.K., Stapleton J., Oppenheim A.N. and Peleg, M. (1983a) An instrument for measuring coping behaviours in hospitalised alcoholics: implications for relapse prevention and treatment. *Br. J. Addiction*, **78**, 269–276.

Litman G.K., Stapleton J., Oppenheim A.N., Peleg M. and Jackson P. (1983b) Situations related to alcoholism relapse. *Br. J. Addiction*, **78**, 381–389.

Litman G.K., Stapleton J., Oppenheim A.N., Peleg M. and Jackson P. (1984) The relationship between coping behaviours, their effectiveness and alcoholism relapse and survival. *Br. J. Addiction*, **79**, 283–291.

Marlatt G.A. (1982) Relapse prevention: a self-control programme for the treatment of addictive behaviour. In *Adherence, Compliance and Generalisation in Behavioural Medicine*, ed. Stuart R.B. (New York: Brunner/Mazel).

Marlatt G.A. and Gordon J. (eds) (1985) In *Relapse Prevention*, (New York: Guilford), 329–378).

Marlatt G.A. (1987) Comment on Kozlowski and Wilkinson's use and misuse of the concept of craving by alcohol, tobacco and drug researchers. *Br. J. Addiction*, **82**, 42–43.

Marlatt G.A. and George W. (1984) Relapse prevention: introduction and overview of the model. *Br. J. Addiction*, **79**, 261–273.

Miller W. (1983) Motivational interviewing with problem drinkers. *Behav. Psychother.*, **11**, 147–172.

O'Brien C.P., Chaddock B., Woodey G. and Greenstein R. (1974) Systematic extinction of addiction associated rituals using narcotic antagonists. *Psychosomatic Med.*, **36**, 458.

Phillips G., Gossop M. and Bradley B. (1986) The influence of psychological factors on the opiate withdrawal syndrome. *Br. J. Psychiat.*, **149**, 235–238.

Prochaska J. and DiClemente C. (1983) Stages and processes of self-change of smoking: toward a more integrative model of change. *J. Consult. Clin. Psychol.*, **51**, 390–395.

Prochaska J. and DiClemente C. (1986) Toward a comprehensive model of change. In *Treating Addictive Behaviours*, eds Miller W. and Heather N. (New York: Plenum Press), 3–27.

Rankin H. (1986) Dependence and compulsion: experimental models of change. In *Treating Addictive Behaviours*, eds Miller W. and Heather N. (New York: Plenum Press), 361–374.

Rankin H., Stockwell T. and Hodgson R. (1982) Cues for drinking and degrees of alcohol dependence. *Br. J. Addiction*, **77**, 287–296.

Russell M.A.H. (1976) What is dependence? In *Drugs and Drug Dependence*, eds Edwards G., Russell M.A.H., Hawks D. and MacCafferty M. (Farnborough: Saxon House/Lexington Books), pp. 182–187.

Siegel S. (1983) Classical conditioning, drug tolerance and drug dependence. In *Research Advances in Alcohol and Drug Problems*, eds Smart, Glaser, Israel, Kalant, Popham and Schmidt (New York: Plenum Press), pp. 207–246).

Stallard A., Heather N. and Johnson B. (1987) AIDS and intravenous drug use: what clinical psychology can offer. *Bull. Br. Psychol. Soc.*, **40**, 365–368.

Stewart J., De Wit H. and Eikelboom R. (1984) Role of unconditioned and conditioned drug effects in the self-administration of opiate and stimulants. *Psychol. Rev.*, **91**, 251–268.

Strang J. (1988) Changing injecting behaviour: blunting the needle habit. *Br. J. Addiction*, **83**, 237–239.

Strang J. (1989) Intermediate goals and the process of change. In *AIDS and Drug Misuse: Understanding and Responding to the Drug Taker in the Wake of HIV*, eds Strang J. and Stimson G. (London: Routledge).

van Bilsen H.P. (1987) Heroin addiction and motivational milieu therapy: first results. Paper presented at the Summer Conference of the British Association of Behavioural Psychotherapy, UK.

van Bilsen H.P. (1988) Motivating drug users to change. In *New Directions in the Treatment of Drug Abuse*, ed. Bennett G.A. (London: Routledge).

van Bilsen H.P. and van Emst A.J. (1986) Heroin addiction and motivational milieu therapy. *Int. J. Addictions*, 21, 707–713.

WHO (1969) Expert Committee on Drug Dependence: 16th Report. *Tech. Rep. Ser.* No. 407 (Geneva: World Health Organization).

Wikler A. (1965) Conditioning factors in opiate addiction and relapse. In *Narcotics*, eds Wilner D.M. and Kassenbaum G.G. (New York: McGraw-Hill).

Wikler A., Fraser H.F. and Isbell H. (1953) N-Allylnormorphine: effects of single doses and precipitation of acute abstinence syndromes during addiction to morphine, methadone or heroin in man [post-addicts]. *J. Pharmacol. Exp. Ther.*, 109, 8–20.

7

Psychosocial Interventions

Brian Wells

Synopsis

This chapter on interventions deals first with the principles of treatment. An attempt is made to aid understanding of some of the mechanisms involved in the process of change. Secondly we address the issues of treatment priorities and goal setting. This is timely as the occurrence of HIV infection has prompted a radical review of drug addiction treatment on an international scale. For many, the treatment 'goalposts' have shifted and we are now in the centre of a debate in which a number of old chestnuts have reappeared, especially those issues that surround prescribing. Modes of intervention, non-professional and professional, that exist on both sides of the Atlantic are then addressed, and finally some brief comments concerning the training of staff and maintenance of staff well-being are offered.

Principles of intervention and treatment

It is worth noting that many problem drug takers, including some with severe dependence, never come anywhere near professional services. Recent research (Stimson *et al.*, 1988) indicates that many drug takers, with intravenous habits for up to ten years, have never had dealings with the law or professional workers. A surprising number are completely unaware of the existence of even well known 'street agencies'. The natural history of drug dependence is dealt with elsewhere (chapter 4), but it is now clear that the majority of drug takers are quite capable of detoxifying themselves, and often do so many times. Current estimates imply that only around 10% of drug users are involved with 'helping agencies', and it is therefore likely that many will alter their lifestyles and behaviour for reasons unrelated to professional intervention and treatment.

The process of change

In general, problem drug takers need to make changes. It is sometimes useful to think of them as people on a personal journey, making calls at various ports of life experience, some of which may include treatment interventions of various types, others being less well intentioned but equally important (visits to court, child-care conferences, etc.), and all of which together can assist in the bringing about of personal change that will hopefully lead to improved health and well-being.

Prochaska and DiClemente (1983) have described a process of change that may be facilitated in part by treatment, and this is represented in figure 7.1.

Figure 7.1   The process of change (from Prochaska and DiClemente, 1983).

Using this model, a client may be persuaded by family and friends to seek help, become increasingly aware of the chaos of his or her circumstances (contemplation) and agree to a programme of prescribed drugs (action) that removes the need for illegal activity such as prostitution and theft. This prescription may be maintained for a period of time to allow the client an opportunity to resolve difficulties.

An alternative example may be the assistance of withdrawal, using a tapering dose of medication that brings the client to a drug-free state. This form of action may then lead to 'maintenance' of the improved state via a period of specialist treatment and/or perhaps engagement in a self-help group such as Narcotics Anonymous (NA). Often, a combination of approaches using different goals over periods of time may be required in order to bring about fundamental change.

An important concept is that of the critical perceptual shift (figure 7.2) described by Litman. This provides a psychological framework for the phenomenon noted by a number of observers, namely the need for some form of 'rock bottom' or defenceless state to be reached before change is likely to occur (Litman, 1982).

Although Litman's work was conducted with clients suffering from alcohol dependence, there are many who feel that such a perceptual shift or form of cognitive restructuring is necessary before major change, such as

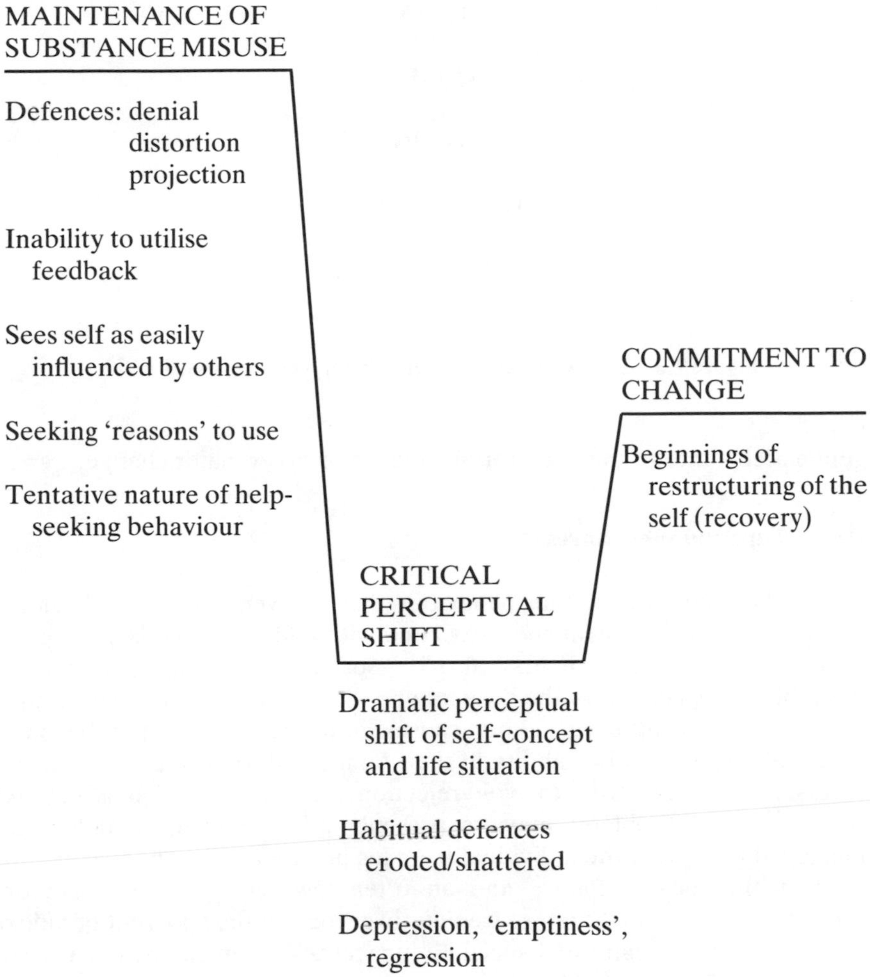

MAINTENANCE OF
SUBSTANCE MISUSE

Defences: denial
       distortion
       projection

Inability to utilise
  feedback

Sees self as easily
  influenced by others

Seeking 'reasons' to use

Tentative nature of help-
  seeking behaviour

COMMITMENT TO
CHANGE

Beginnings of
restructuring of the
self (recovery)

CRITICAL
PERCEPTUAL
SHIFT

Dramatic perceptual
  shift of self-concept
  and life situation

Habitual defences
  eroded/shattered

Depression, 'emptiness',
  regression

Figure 7.2   Critical perceptual shift (adapted from Litman, 1982).

a move towards abstinence, can be realised in someone with a moderate or severe history of drug dependence. A number of models attempt to explain the process of this cognitive/perceptual shift. Some workers describe a 'grief reaction' similar to that required during bereavement (figure 7.3).

Principles of treatment therefore include attempts that help the client move from denial to acceptance of his or her problems (precontemplation to contemplation, leading to action) via the necessary stages of the grief process, treating anger as a normal or healthy phenomenon, bargaining ('I'll just smoke dope at weekends', 'If I don't inject then I'm not really taking drugs') as an understandable resistance to change, and depressed mood as a normal reaction to loss (of the drugs), which can lead to an often

Figure 7.3   Stages of bereavement (from Kubler-Ross, 1969).

gentle acceptance of the need for abstinence or other major change.

Peer groups and subcultures

Drug taking involves human behaviour that is diverse and complicated. Although it may be illegal and associated with a lifestyle that is extremely harmful in some cases, it may also be 'socially acceptable' and indeed desirable in the context of the drug taker's life, subculture and peer group. However, problem drug taking causes difficulties as people become unreliable, unwell and a liability to their family and friends. Problem drug takers, therefore, in order to avoid rejection, may behave as if all is well. A deep denial of problems may be present and a number of 'defences' employed to prevent the individual from losing face and having to come to terms with repeated failure and an often low sense of self-worth or self-esteem. Workers therefore frequently encounter the apparent paradox of a client whose health and social circumstances are in chaos, but whose attitude may be seen as difficult, arrogant and manipulative.

Principles of treatment include the use of 'peer-group pressure'. Just as many drug takers start to experiment with chemicals in a context of peer-group or subcultural acceptability, so one of the most powerful ways of facilitating positive change seems to be via the persuasive forces that are invoked by a group of people moving in a particular direction. Such examples are seen in the worlds of fashion and pop music. Similarly, a number of treatment modalities (therapeutic communities, self-help groups, etc.) find the 'power of the group' to be a vital part of the treatment process.

Dignity and caring

A low sense of self-worth is common to many suffering from drug- and alcohol-related problems, and awareness of this has led to a recent move away from the more confrontational approaches to treatment. Many workers and agencies are finding that respect for the dignity of the client and developing a caring, empathic relationship provide results far more beneficial than did some of the previously used styles.

The priorities

The priorities of drug-addiction intervention vary according to the perspective from which they are viewed. Most workers agree that, if an individual is experiencing problems as a result of drug taking, the most logical and sensible way forward is to reach a point where the drugs can be removed from the person's life. This allows difficulties to be addressed without the added complications that result from a drug-taking lifestyle. Some contend that if individuals choose to continue taking drugs, they should be provided with adequate drugs for a period as long as necessary (maintenance), in order to remove those factors associated with the lifestyle (illegal activity, financial problems, etc.) that contribute to the overall difficulties.

There are many issues surrounding this long-term debate. In England the Drug Dependence Units (DDUs) were set up in the late 1960s largely to facilitate this latter viewpoint, following the recommendations of the Brain Committee. As time progressed and the number of opiate-dependent clients increased, clinicians became disillusioned with the notion of maintenance prescribing so that, by the early 1980s, most clinics in southern England were 'abstinence oriented' and would only take on new clients for purposes of detoxification. There were many (mostly using drug addicts) who objected to this policy and claimed that maintenance prescribing was working very well, allowing them to pursue a normal life that happened to include the daily ingestion of opioid drugs. A number of clinicians were also impressed by this view so that in the early 1980s there was a tendency for clinicians to belong to one or other of the abstinence/maintenance camps, although many continued to operate in a grey area, basing their clinical decisions on the assessment and apparent needs of individuals (*Druglink*, 1987). Similarly in the USA (where the prescribing of heroin or other injectable drugs to addicts is not permitted), services tended to develop along the lines of either abstinence-oriented treatment or methadone maintenance. In the USA a large number of well-staffed highly structured methadone maintenance programmes were developed, some of which were stricter than others in terms of their rules and selection criteria. In the UK, a smaller number received maintenance prescriptions in a less formal setting, mostly collecting their drugs from a local pharmacy on either a daily or more extended basis.

The situation as (very roughly) outlined above was severely jolted by the onset of HIV infection. By 1986 it had become clear that drug taking was to be a major vector for the spread of HIV. Workers grappled with the numerous issues around the management of this epidemic (modes of transmission, testing, the need for counselling, confidentiality, etc.). In particular the Advisory Council on the Misuse of Drugs held urgent meetings, and in 1988 produced a report sensibly pointing out that the prevention of the spread of HIV infection must now constitute the number one priority when considering the management of problem drug taking (DHSS, 1988).

The emergence of HIV infection has reopened the prescribing debate. There has been much comment on issues such as the legalistion of drugs (as opposed to the current state of prohibition). Some are calling for an almost generalised availability of drugs including injectable heroin, cocaine, amphetamines and other 'drugs of choice' that people may require. The basis for this controversial viewpoint is that drug takers will continue to take their drugs of choice in whatever way they please, irrespective of any attempts at treatment or intervention, until they reach a point when they 'mature out' of their drug-taking behaviour. Workers should therefore provide the opportunity for drug taking to continue in as healthy a manner as possible, until the person decides to make different choices. There are others who believe that drug takers are quite capable of altering their behaviour and that interventions and other life experience can assist in the facilitation of a cognitive/perceptual shift leading towards an altered (more healthy) lifestyle, if not complete abstinence from drug taking. The general availability of drugs on demand is viewed as likely to hinder this process of change, and so the debate continues.

A major problem in the prescribing debate involves the differing perspectives from which suggestions and claims are made. Whilst, on the one hand, it may seem entirely reasonable from an epidemiological viewpoint to provide maintenance drugs to a population of drug takers (e.g. the Hispanic drug-taking community on the Lower East Side of New York where HIV is rife), on the other, is this necessarily the wisest option to recommend to an individual who presents asking for help? The prescribing debate is conducted from the viewpoints of epidemiology, politics, clinical practice and anecdote. Often the perspectives become blurred and the issues therefore confused. Very little sound research data are available to support or refute claims that are made, and emotions that surround the subjects of HIV infection and individual 'freedom of choice' frequently obstruct clarity of thought.

Most workers agree that minimisation of the spread of HIV is a priority; that there requires to be greater availability of prescribed drugs and that the former 'high thresholds' of the DDUs (numerous attendances for urinalysis, demonstration of 'motivation', etc.) should be lowered. There is a need for greater flexibility of prescribing by doctors including general practitioners and other 'non-specialists' who should have access to specialist teams for advice and referral of cases that are problematic.

Much is said about the need for harm minimisation, for needle and syringe exchange schemes and for the provision of outreach workers to maximise contact with drug takers, attracting them into 'user friendly' services that can provide education and necessary health care. Given the shift in priorities, many such suggestions seem eminently sensible. Early research indicates, however, that workers may still be removed from the realities of the drug-taking world. Increased contact may be possible, but we remain unclear as to precisely how we may assist in the bringing about of real and consistent behavioural change.

Goal setting

Assessment

Drug taking constitutes a complex variety of behaviours and substances involving a range of individuals who come from all walks of life. A prerequisite of intervention and treatment is the engagement of a client into a trusting relationship with a worker or treatment agency for purposes of thorough assessment. This should involve a two-way exchange of information that allows mutual understanding of the relationship that the client has developed with substances, in the context of his or her life. Where possible, a family member or significant other person should participate in this process so that the priorities of an individual case can be clarified. Hopefully this will be followed, as described, by assistance in the process of change. Change that is real and of lasting benefit can only come about as a result of work done or steps taken by the client. The most practical way forward therefore is via the setting of realistic goals by mutual agreement. It is helpful to view goal setting from the perspectives of the immediate, short, intermediate and long term.

Case histories

Case 1

Roberto was a 24-year-old Italian living in a squat in central London with, at times, up to 30 other drug takers, mostly from Italy and Scotland. He had been injecting heroin for six years and was supporting his habit by shoplifting, having taken a variety of drugs since the age of 16. He had been hospitalised twice with hepatitis, and 18 months previously, whilst in jail in Italy, was told that he 'had the AIDS virus', following a compulsory blood test. He came to London to avoid further trouble with the police in Italy where he was wanted for several drug-related offences. He had a 19-year-old English girlfriend who did not inject drugs (but smoked cannabis occasionally), and who had been found to be 16 weeks' pregnant. She had not had a test for HIV antibody.

Case 2

Sharon was a 17-year-old who lived with her mother on an estate in south London and had left school two years previously with no qualifications. She had never worked. Since the age of 13 she had become drunk on most weekends, going to parties and pubs with friends who had given her strong lager. She said this had not caused her any problems and 'everyone else did it'. One year previously she had met Mick, aged 22, who introduced her to cannabis which they smoked together on a regular basis with no apparent ill effects. Nine months later Mick's dealer had no cannabis available so instead sold them Pakistani heroin which he said was 'more or less the same thing'.

Sharon found that heroin made her feel wonderful. Within a few weeks she had begun to experience 'flu-like symptoms which were relieved by smoking more. Over a period of some six weeks she had developed a habit of about a quarter gram of heroin per day.

She presented to the local Drug Unit, sullen, belligerent and in obvious opiate withdrawal, accompanied by an angry mother who had found blackened tin foil in her bedroom. Mother had been curious as to why Sharon had been borrowing so much money from her and other family members over previous weeks.

Case 3

James was a 34-year-old businessman who worked in the City, had been married for eight years and lived with his wife and three young children in their own house in a fashionable area of London. James first experimented with cannabis whilst at boarding school aged 17. He smoked cannabis on a regular basis at university, took LSD on two occasions and magic mushrooms on another. All of these experiences had been interesting but 'harmless experimentation'. He moved to London and began working in the City where he was rapidly promoted through his company so that by the time he married he was earning a good salary and making several business trips abroad each year. He and his wife enjoyed an active social life, and alcohol had been an unremarkable feature both at work and at home. Cannabis was consumed at odd times in a 'recreational manner'.

Two years previously a friend had introduced James to cocaine. He found that the odd 'line' taken intranasally made him feel good and seemed to help with increasing pressures at work. Within a year James was using cocaine on a daily basis and found that his alcohol intake had increased considerably. This use escalated so that by the time he presented for help he was 'freebasing' up to 3 g of cocaine per day, had taken Ecstasy (methylenedioxymethamphetamine) on several occasions and was drinking in excess of a bottle of spirits nightly in order to sleep. He had spent several hundred thousand pounds of his own capital and had been claiming exorbitant expenses at work. His employers were concerned and puzzled at his deteriorating performance over preceding months. Admission to a private clinic was precipitated by a convulsion that James had at work following a spell of several days in which he had seemed excitable and not his usual self having claimed openly that various colleagues were conspiring against him. His wife had been consulting a solicitor about possible divorce proceedings. Friends and family had been worried for some months about James's weight loss and increasing eccentricity.

The above three case 'vignettes' demonstrate clearly that, although all three individuals were in some form of personal crisis, each case has different priorities.

Roberto demonstrated a need for urgent improvement in his life circumstances in order to make an assessment of the relationship with his girlfriend, her likely HIV status and the wisdom of continuing her pregnancy in the light of any test results and counselling. Immediate and short-term goals included stabilising him on a mutually agreed dose of prescribed drugs (oral methadone), as continuing to inject is not advisable in someone who is seropositive to HIV. The couple were found alternative accommodation (the pressures or remaining in a drug-taking environment often interfere with health and decision-making ability) and an urgent appraisal of the pregnancy was made.

An intermediate goal, of Roberto's keeping regular contact with services able to provide him with a prescription, seemed sensible. In the circumstances it was not felt necessary that long-term goals should be agreed upon, although they were certainly borne in mind considering his HIV status.

Sharon clearly had some points to consider regarding her relationship with Mick, with her mother and with drug taking. An attempted short-term goal was the provision of a tapering dose of methadone to assist her withdrawal from heroin. This strategy allowed some counselling to take place and an intermediate goal included the notion that Sharon should attempt to get a job whilst continuing to attend on a regular basis. Again, long-term decision-making was felt not to be appropriate although it would become relevant should the situation continue to deteriorate.

James was clearly unwell and in danger of losing his family and career. Immediate management included assessment of the severity of his alcohol dependence and a thorough physical examination, with special investigations including urinalysis to identify any coincidental drug taking (e.g. high doses of benzodiazepines). James was advised to remain in residential treatment for a period of time allowing him to become completely abstinent from all drugs (including alcohol) and to receive counselling for his craving for cocaine. An intermediate goal included recommendations that he should remain abstinent from mind-altering substances for a substantial period of time, and receive introductions to specific therapies and self-help groups. Long-term goals included plans that involved abstinence from all drugs with any return to drinking being attempted cautiously, following 'educated' choices, in the full knowledge of his family and friends.

These cases only begin to touch on the enormous complexity of drug-taking behaviour and underline the need for detailed individual assessment. They also demonstrate that a wide range of services is required for the diversity of people and problems encountered in the field of substance misuse. (See Postcript, page 173.)

Modes of intervention

The community

The community provides a variety of interventions. Family, friends, employers, police, pharmacists, clergymen, ambulance drivers and members of the public all have a part to play in the life experience of a problem drug taker. Many 'interventions' are unplanned, and drug takers will sometimes change their behaviour as a result of an upset family, a wife threatening to leave and words of kindly advice (or otherwise) from the police.

The community includes organisations such as the Samaritans, Citizens' Advice Bureaux, self-help groups such as Narcotics Anonymous (NA), Alcoholics Anonymous (AA) and Families Anonymous (FA) and, in some areas, groups for using addicts (e.g. the Addicts Union), some specialising in those who are HIV positive.

The law

Many drug takers break the law in a number of ways and may present to treatment agencies via the police, the courts, probation services or as an alternative to prison, resultant upon law-breaking behaviour. In the USA it is estimated that 80% of all prisoners have committed some drug-related offence. The figures are less alarming in the UK, but there remains a need for considerable improvement in the training of those involved in the legal and penal systems. There is increasing evidence that drug takers may usefully be directed towards treatment by workers in the legal system. Members of the probation service have begun to take an interest in such treatment and in some areas have opened clinics and drop-in opportunities within probation offices. Initial results suggest that such work can be effective and of great benefit to what is sometimes an extremely disadvantaged client group.

There is also evidence that clients who are 'coerced' into treatment by the legal system are likely to do better than one may intuitively expect (from a client apparently lacking in self-motivation). Many drug takers leave prison and immediately return to drug use but a number who enter treatment (such as a therapeutic community), either directly from, or as an alternative to, prison, go on to do extremely well (Leukefeld and Tims, 1988). The legal system provides many valuable opportunities for interventions into problem drug taking; research and increased expertise in this area are required.

Whilst the issues that surround drug taking and crime are complicated and whilst there are many active 'criminals' who become drug users, there is little doubt that a large number of drug takers are treated inappropriately within the legal system.

The organisation of services

Services for substance misusers in the United Kingdom vary enormously in experience, expertise, derivation and source of funding. They may be from within statutory bodies such as the National Health Service, Social Services, the Probation Service, etc.; from 'non-statutory' or voluntary sector organisations such as Turning Point, Accept, Phoenix House, Broadway Lodge and numerous other charitable trusts; or they may be derived from the private sector as are various clinics, private doctors and counselling agencies.

Although political boundaries continue to exist, there is a tendency these days for greater co-operation to take place between the various bodies and agencies involved. Most workers agree on the need for a wide range of services. Increased communication and co-operation are leading to an improved network of services that are developing a healthy respect for each other. As statutory services recognise their own limitations and the expertise of other organisations, so funding is being organised with greater flexibility, all sectors becoming aware of the vital need for sound evaluative research.

In an attempt to simplify boundaries and recognise expertise, this chapter will refer to *general* and *specialist* services that may operate on a residential (in-patient), day-care, out-patient or community-oriented basis.

General services

Advice, assessment, counselling, referral and basic treatment may be obtained from a variety of sources. Some agencies offer telephone advice, occasionally on a 24-hour basis, and a number of services offer assessment to problem drug takers on either a walk-in or an appointment basis. The voluntary sector 'street agencies' (e.g. The Hungerford, Community Drug Project (CDP), etc.) still provide general services for drug takers, and some have become increasingly sophisticated and are able to offer specialist treatments in addition.

Community Drug Teams (CDTs)

Many parts of the country have little access to specialist services and those that exist are sometimes considered by drug users to be authoritarian and unapproachable. Recent years have seen the development of a number of models of 'community-oriented work'. It is hoped that much of the previously mentioned outreach and improved client contact will be achieved by CDTs working in urban areas.

The components and operation of CDTs will vary according to their location and circumstances. General principles include the use of a true multidisciplinary group of workers, operating from either a central base or a series of satellite centres, making use of hospital-based specialist teams for back-up and referral. In a rural area, therefore, a district CDT may consist of a trained community psychiatric nurse and social worker, coming to a particular area for sessions in a health centre with prescriptions being provided by a GP. This will constitute a satellite clinic with the regional team acting as a central base in the relevant urban area.

An urban Community Drug Team will ideally consist of a variety of generic workers with experience in the drug field. Such workers could be derived from the fields of nursing, medicine, psychology, social work, occupational therapy, youth work and 'non-statutory' drug agencies. Some teams are employing ex- (or even current) drug users and other 'streetwise' workers such as former prostitutes and ex-offenders who are considered likely to perform outreach in a real sense.

Community Teams need to provide a system of networking for all professionals that come into contact with drug takers. A needle/syringe exchange scheme in a drop-in centre or GP practice may provide a focus for activity. Some workers may offer specialist services, such as regular sessions in 'relapse prevention', while others may have particular interests such as women (pregnant or otherwise), gay men, ethnic minority groups and young people. A Community Drug Team can provide both general and specialist services, establishing links with other workers who can receive a major training input from members of the team. Community workers are also needed to facilitate important research in the field of behavioural change and HIV minimisation.

Withdrawal and detoxification services
In general, too much emphasis is placed on the need for medically supervised withdrawal from drugs and alcohol. Many medical and nursing students qualify believing that addiction treatment consists of detoxification and little else. Although its importance should not be minimised, it should be placed in perspective. With the exception of high-dose alcohol and sedative (benzodiazepines, barbiturates, etc.) dependence, withdrawal from drugs and alcohol rarely constitutes a medical emergency. Most problem drug takers are able to withdraw themselves on a 'DIY' basis, and much assistance and valuable information (such as the Blenheim Project booklet) may be forthcoming from workers operating in a general sense. Expertise in 'non-medical' approaches to withdrawal (keeping busy, groups, massage, exercise, etc.) needs to be developed. Use can be made of standardised withdrawal regimes when the comfort of the individual is the primary consideration, and there is no doubt that there will remain a need for admission to units of various types in order to remove clients from drug-taking environments and to provide expert support with the often difficult if not life-threatening complications of withdrawal.

Special services
Prescribing
There is sometimes a reticence or fearfulness around issues of prescribing displayed by the medical profession. This is usually based upon ignorance, lack of experience and mythology not dissimilar to that which exists within drug-using circles (the horrors of cold turkey, etc.). There is little doubt that, in order for drug takers to receive an adequate service, prescribing needs to take place on a number of levels, as follows.

(a) *Crisis intervention.* As mentioned, withdrawal from drugs is only life threatening when it occurs in the course of high-dosage sedative dependence. Practitioners in a primary care setting (GPs, casualty officers) require training, reassurance and the secure knowledge of access to specialist services (medical beds, Community Drug Team, psychiatrist with expertise in substance misuse, etc.) for clients who present in urgent need of a medically supervised withdrawal. City Roads, a well known London-based residential service, was originally set up to assist chaotic users likely to be taking barbiturates. They provide an expert 10-day withdrawal from drugs, making use of a standardised tapering dosage of medication and other symptom-alleviating techniques (massage, etc.), in the context of a three-week admission during which time a thorough assessment is made. This is often followed by referral onwards to relevant treatment. Although there are now fewer crises involving barbiturates, problems with alcohol and benzodiazepines present frequently enough.

Crisis intervention extends to other conditions where prescribing may be necessary, or a useful therapeutic move to engage clients in services likely to promote improved health. All fully registered practitioners should be aware of their ability to prescribe methadone and other symptom-alleviating drugs (clonidine, promazine, etc.).

(b) *Stabilisation and alleviation of symptoms; setting and attainment of goals.* No great expertise is required in prescribing a straightforward dose of drugs for stabilisation of a client prior to the setting of straightforward goals, such as referral to a specialist service or the provision of a tapering dose of cross-tolerant medication over an agreed period of time. Such prescribing can take place in a number of settings including general practice, casualty departments, emergency psychiatric services, hospital wards of any speciality and even in the workplace when necessary. What is required is the understanding that 'substance misuse' must be in the remit of all medical practitioners. It must also be possible for them to turn to specialist workers for advice, training and appropriate referral.

(c) *Specialist prescribing.* The prescribing of diamorphine, cocaine and dipipanone to drug-dependent individuals can only be undertaken by licensed doctors operating from designated premises, e.g. DDUs. Whilst opinion as to what constitutes 'specialist prescribing' varies, the following is suggested as sensible practice.

(i)   cases needing the prescription of drugs that require a special licence (as insisted upon by law);
(ii) cases where a mutually agreeable starting/stabilising dose cannot be found;
(iii) cases in which agreed goals cannot be met in reality (e.g. the client is unable to refrain from using 'street drugs' on top of a prescribed dose of, say, methadone);
(iv) possibly cases that require prescribing for a period longer than three to six months;
(v)   cases that require the prescription of antagonist drugs such as naltrexone (only a limited licence is available at present in the UK).

All such cases should probably be referred to a specialist service.

Relapse prevention (RP)
Currently something of a 'buzz' expression, the relapse prevention movement has emerged from workers (mainly psychologists such as Marlatt) who view addiction as a relapsing condition over which the client can

develop control when equipped with adequate strategies that assist in preventing a return to drug taking.

Essentially, an in-depth analysis of likely relapse factors (using cues, danger areas) is made by the worker and client, who then together move on to devise relevant coping strategies. Such strategies may include avoidance (say, of particular people, the area where the dealer lives, etc.), graded exposure to using cues and 'dangerous situations', sometimes via the use of imagery, photographs and videos, as well as real-life exposure. Some workers favour the use of rapid exposure (flooding), with or without the use of drugs that remove symptoms of anxiety (e.g. beta-blockers) thus providing the client with greater confidence.

Most drug workers are able to practise 'relapse prevention' techniques, often in conjuction with other forms of treatment and support such as attendance at self-help groups. Training and supervision in such behavioural/cognitive techniques is desirable and these are probably best provided by a clinical psychologist.

Increasingly, RP techniques are being used in conjuction with pharmaco-therapeutic agents such as disulfiram (Antabuse) when dealing with alcohol, and naltrexone when the drugs in question are opioids. The use of naltrexone in the UK is relatively recent and is still regarded by some as experimental. It has been in the US armamentarium for drug workers for the last ten years, more recently in combination with clonidine as an agent to facilitate rapid opiate withdrawal. In spite of the higher dose of opiate drugs taken in the UK, there are good indicators that naltrexone will prove to be useful, particularly when used in conjuction with cognitive–behavioural techniques as described.

Therapeutic communities (TCs)
The original therapeutic community was the Belmont (Henderson) Hospital as founded by Maxwell Jones. Subsequently Rapoport described four features of life in the therapeutic community that he felt were of importance in the facilitation of change (Rapoport, 1960, and see figure 7.4.)

PERMISSIVENESS
(permission to behave as if social constraints are not present)
↓
COMMUNALITY
(sharing of responsibility)
↓
DEMOCRACY
(sharing of decision-making process)
↓
REALITY CONFRONTATION

Figure 7.4 Life in the therapeutic community (from Rapoport, 1960).

Following similar principles, a number of therapeutic communities that provide specialist residential care for drug takers have evolved from a variety of philosophical origins.

The Concept Houses. The first such centre in the UK was Phoenix House. Taking its name from Phoenix House in New York, the original programme was modelled upon that of Synanon (a community whose origins began in the abstinence-based philosophy of Alcoholics Anonymous). Phoenix House provides a long-term programme ranging from 9 to 18 months, in which drug-free residents enter via a period of induction to work in the house. The work of the house is carried out via a number of departments (the kitchen department, garden department, maintenance department, etc.), with residents starting at the bottom of a crew and working their way up through a hierarchy to the eventual position of head of department. The working day is highly structured and involves performing tasks as directed by the department head, without any complaint or argument until the opportunity is presented in one of the regular 'encounter' groups that take place. Emphasis is placed on getting in touch with feelings that may not have been experienced for many years as a result of drug taking.

In the community there is a strong sense of belonging and being part of a 'family'. Once trust is established, the resident is encouraged to make use of the 'power of the group' in order to gain insight, become more aware of others and learn how to live in an environment where an ethos of supportive self-help and taking responsibility for each other predominates.

Living in such an environment intensifies normal experience so that seemingly trivial actions (e.g. leaving cigarette ash on the floor), can lead to a community response that will encourage the individual concerned to take more responsibility for him- or herself and the community. Emphasis is placed on the need for personal growth and on learning how to deal with difficulties in an adult manner without recourse to drug taking. What can seem to a visitor to be an environment that is abrasive and confrontative is in fact a 'safe society' based upon mutual caring and love.

The staff include a number of workers who are ex-residents, having themselves been former drug users. Role modelling and a number of psychological techniques (Gestalt, psychodrama, co-counselling, etc.) are used, and importance is attached to education, development of life skills and re-establishment of social and economic networks.

Eventually the resident will reach the 're-entry' phase of the programme in which he or she will reside in a nearby house, start work—often as a volunteer, or perhaps attend a college of further education. The community continues to provide group work and support for the senior resident who will sometimes help to supervise more junior members in the evenings and at weekends.

Drinking privileges are usually allowed during the re-entry phase, although some communities maintain a cautious attitude towards alcohol having experienced difficulties with residents developing alcohol problems, often within a short period of being granted their drinking privileges. Alcohol is the subject of education, counselling and watchfulness, some communities having now become alcohol free. An introduction to Narcotics Anonymous (NA) is a feature of several re-entry and after-care programmes. After-care has now become an important feature and can include rehousing and resettlement as well as regular attendance at supportive meetings.

The original American Concept House model has left several misconceptions that still remain among some professionals and drug users. In the late 1960s it was not uncommon for residents to have their heads shaved and to be placed on extremely strict 'work contracts', which, although not intended as punitive, certainly allowed the residents to get in touch with difficult feelings and frequently precipitated their departure.

Over recent years the Concept Houses have become far less confrontative and tough in their activities. These days there is emphasis on residents respecting one another and paying attention to features such as dignity, gentleness and mutual caring. These latter features have become emphasised with the advent of HIV infection.

There are now a number of Phoenix House communities in various parts of the UK. Other notable Concept Houses include Alpha House, Suffolk House, the Ley Community, Inward House and the Coolmine Community in Dublin.

Christian-based communities. These houses also operate on therapeutic principles but differ from the Concept Houses. The strict discipline, hierarchical structure and intensive group sessions are far less apparent. In general the Christian communities provide a more relaxed structure with greater emphasis on one-to-one counselling. Interpersonal difficulties are explored with the team leader. Improvement of self-esteem following a hard day's work, in the context of a (usually optional) Christian-based belief system, is encouraged throughout the programme, with bible readings, religious discussion and house meetings being part of the usual day. An introduction to churches of various denominations close to the resident's home takes place prior to discharge.

All of these communities are based upon abstinence. Most operate a single-sex policy and tend to provide relatively long-term programmes. The most well known include Yeldall Manor, Meta House (for women), Chatterton Hay and the Life for the World Trust. The Cokehole Trust is a house with Christian staff that provides a long-term programme without particular emphasis upon Christian principles.

General houses. A number of projects exist that vary in their approach but in general provide drug-free programmes for periods in excess of six months, with group and individual support being provided by the staff and community. Residents are usually encouraged to explore non-drug-taking lifestyles, and the community of residents is often included in the selection-for-entry process. Some examples include Elizabeth House, Cranstoun House, Oak Lodge, Face to Face and the Chester Substance Misuse Project.

Details of all the therapeutic communities in the UK may be obtained from SCODA, the Standing Conference On Drug Abuse, which acts as an umbrella organisation for non-statutory services. SCODA provides an excellent directory with detailed descriptions of individual houses, prog-rammes, selection criteria, etc. (SCODA, 1988). In recent years a number of therapeutic communities have been able to include the admission of couples and (in the cases of Phoenix House, London, and Phoenix, Sheffield) the accommodation of children.

Narcotics Anonymous (NA)
NA started in 1953 when a group of heroin addicts, following disagree-ments with the regular members, left their meeting of Alcoholics Anony-mous (AA) in Sun Valley, California, moved to a new location and applied the AA principles, steps and traditions to the illness of 'addiction' (as opposed to alcoholism). NA remained largely confined to California throughout the 1950s and 1960s. With the altered socio-cultural acceptance of drug taking that began in the late 1960s, pockets of 'recovery' started to appear in major cities across the USA. By 1980 there were an estimated 20 000 addicts recovering in NA, which had spread to other countries including Australia and Great Britain. Growth has remained consistent so that the most recent guesstimate from the World Service Office (December 1988) puts the worldwide membership at roughly 450 000 to 500 000 members (from 250 000 in 1986), attending around 14 000 groups in 43 different countries including Japan, India and El Salvador.

NA provides regular meetings in the community and institutions (clinics, prisons, etc.), where members who have experienced drug-related problems provide mutual support in a non-judgemental manner based upon the sharing of 'experience, strength and hope'.

A number of formats exist but a typical meeting will be either 'closed', for addicts only, or 'open', allowing the attendance of interested family, friends and professionals. It will last for 90 minutes, the first 40 or which are likely to include a member sharing his or her life story with the group (what it was like, what happened and what it's like now), or possibly sharing experience of a particular topic such as one of the 12 steps. The chairperson will then open the meeting and members will share from the floor in a manner that involves identification with the main speaker and very often a 'here and now' description of present-day events, difficulties, gratitude and matters relating to the process of recovery. Meetings are often lively with much hugging and displays of open friendship. Many members will move on to coffee shops and restaurants for a meeting with their 'sponsor' (usually someone of the same sex with whom particular issues can be shared), or simply for fellowship.

NA subscribes to the view that addiction is an illness for which there is no cure. Recovery can and will take place, however, by arresting the illness (becoming completely abstinent from all drugs including alcohol) and by active application of the individual to the suggested programme of recovery. This includes frequent attendance at meetings in early days, getting involved, learning how to use meetings and share openly in order to experience less isolation, greater confidence and a gradual enhancement of self-esteem.

Eventually it becomes important for the recovering person to develop a relationship with the NA 12 steps. These include an understanding of the need for complete abstinence, the notion of a 'power greater than oneself' (God as you understand him), often helped initially by making use of the power of the group; gaining deeper insight into one's circumstances and continued need for abstinence, making restitution to others for damage previously done and carrying the message of recovery to still suffering addicts (Step 12, 'We keep what we have by giving it away').

NA will accept people of either sex and of any age, race, colour, religion and sexual orientation. 'Very simply an addict is a man or woman whose life is controlled by drugs.' 'The only requirement for membership is a desire to stop using.'

NA-related treatment. Twelve-step-based treatment is available at a number of centres in the UK. It is sometimes referred to as the Minnesota Model, and most such centres operate a residential programme that includes a medically supervised detoxification followed by a 4- to 6-week programme of groups (based upon reality therapy), one-to-one counselling, writing a life story, individual assignments (work on anger, assertion, sexual issues, etc.), lectures, videos and audio tapes. Usually the resident completes the programme by moving through and working on the first five of the AA/NA twelve steps, being allowed to move from one to the other when the relevant counsellor and peer group of residents agree that he or she has a thorough grasp of a particular step and is ready to move on (peer evaluation).

Many clients move from primary treatment to a period in a drug- and alcohol-free halfway-house, where some form of employment is obtained and rigorous attendance at NA (and AA where appropriate) is initiated. An abstinence-based recovery in the 12-step fellowships is a vital part of the after-care provided by these treatment centres. Increasingly there is involvement of family members who are sometimes encouraged to enter into residential treatment themselves and then address their own recovery, via attendance at the family self-help groups Families Anonymous (FA) and Al-Anon. Most 12-step-based treatment centres in the UK are either charitable trusts which operate on a fee-paying basis with a certain number of beds available as 'assisted places', or remain in the private sector.

Services for families and 'family interventions'

Family members often provide a vital opportunity for intervention. Their involvement is frequently neglected by drug workers, mainly due to unwillingness on the part of the client, but when possible input from families should always be obtained during an assessment. Where the family can be engaged in ongoing treatment there is a greater likelihood that the client will be supported towards a more sensible way of life.

In the USA some treatment facilities, in particular those specialising in adolescents, insist on family involvement, sometimes on a residential basis, throughout treatment. Many centres practise a form of 'family intervention' in which family members gather together with the therapist and client, in order to present the facts to the using addict with a view to impressing upon him or her the need to engage in treatment. Sometimes referred to as 'tough love', such interventions can include an element of coercion that in effect gives the addict an offer that is difficult to refuse. Similarly, employers and colleagues from work may also be present to substantiate facts and offer additional motivation, usually by ensuring that employment will still be available provided that the principles of treatment are adhered to. There is increasing evidence that such methods of 'coercion' are likely to produce results comparable to those obtained when clients enter treatment of their own volition, although such measures remain controversial.

In the UK there is increasing awareness of the importance of family involvement. Some agencies operate a clinic for family members and a number of organisations now exist specifically for families of drug takers.

Child, adolescent and family therapy

Many children are affected by living with drug-taking parents, and many families are disrupted by an adolescent with drug-related problems. Formal (system-based) family therapy is an approach favoured by some. Although more widely available in the USA, centres of expertise also exist in the UK.

Plans exist for a central London unit which will provide care for pregnant drug takers from the antenatal period, through to confinement and subsequent after-care of mother and child. A likely combination of workers will include an obstetrician, paediatrician, drug workers, family therapists and a psychiatrist. Closer links are required between drug workers and departments of child and family psychiatry, many of which are dealing with problems relating to substance misuse (sometimes unknowingly). Many such departments have expertise in family therapy and are able to provide a valuable service to drug takers.

Co-dependence
Much interest is being generated by the concept of co-dependence. The term refers to various forms of 'dysfunction' that arise as a result of being in close contact with actively using addicts and/or alcoholics. Typically this may occur consequent upon having been raised in a household where one or other parent has been actively using for a number of years. The theory is that being in a 'dysfunctional' environment over a period of time gives rise to a number of traits that are likely to cause difficulties at some later stage. For example, some children with alcoholic parents will go on to marry people with alcohol-related problems or become alcoholics themselves. A number of 'signs and symptoms' have been described including a need to control; living life as a 'victim'; an inflexibility, said to derive from having allowed others to rule; and major problems with interpersonal relationships resulting from 'shame' and low self-esteem.

The same traits have been described in those adults closely involved with active addiction over periods of time, including the spouses of addicts/alcoholics and also professionals who have worked in the field for many years.

A number of self-help groups exist to cater for such 'dysfunctional' family members, Al-Anon, Families Anonymous (FA) and Adult Children of Alcoholics (ACOA) being examples. Many workers in the field are now encouraged to attend these groups and to address issues of co-dependence for their own well-being and for the development of professional 'detachment', thereby helping themselves to continue working with an often difficult, emotionally demanding client group without suffering from the insidious effects of overinvolvement.

The psychotherapies
Psychotherapy exists in a number of forms and on various levels. Drug workers require some knowledge of the range of therapies available, given the differing client groups of individuals, all of whom have their own personal requirements. It is unlikely that many active drug users will make good use of intensive psychodynamic therapy until they have been abstinent for some time and have undergone personal growth, attaining sufficient ego strength to enable the necessary psychodynamic work to take place. Drug takers at differing points in their drug careers, however, may well benefit from various forms of psychotherapy, be it supportive one-to-one counselling, attendance at an abstinence-oriented group or perhaps sessions with emphasis upon problem solving, social skills and assertiveness training. Many former drug users become fascinated by the process of growth and seek involvement in a range of psychotherapies (dynamic, transactional analysis, psycho-synthesis, etc.) in attempts to enhance their insight and well-being.

Spirituality

A number of drug takers move away from drug use and become involved in the development of some form of spiritual life. This may be an understanding of a 'power greater than oneself' as suggested by NA, it can be a form of organised religion perhaps rediscovered from childhood, or a type of yoga/meditation that may or may not incorporate a particular belief system. Many former users come to the understanding that they have been 'seeking' for most of their lives and have therefore embarked on a variety of mind-altering experiences, including those associated with drug taking.

A number of other 'substitution' activities are found in former addicts. These may involve vigorous exercise, exhilarating hobbies (parachute jumping, mountain climbing, etc.), and other interests that may be gratifying but that can lead to new problems (gambling, sexual promiscuity, over-eating, etc.).

Services for women and mothers

Women, in particular those who are pregnant, sometimes have special needs from workers in the sphere of substance misuse. At present specialist services for women remain scant and poorly organised, those with expertise being called upon usually at times of crisis. Such services require organisation. Well conducted research into issues around pregnancy and substance misuse (including subsequent infant care) is badly needed.

Services for ethnic groups

Substance misuse varies enormously throughout the world, many practices being based upon what is acceptable locally or within a particular culture. For example in Pakistan it is not uncommon for addicts to smoke in excess of 4 g of heroin per day. In Scotland and the North of England, drug-taking practices differ from those found in London and the South. Until recently there was an apparently small number of the Afro-Caribbean community using heroin (although many were dealing it). This has now changed and members of this community have recently been presenting to drug agencies with serious problems resulting also from the use of cocaine.

Experience in the USA demonstrates the usefulness of workers and organisations that specialise in ethnic minority groups. There are some who claim that the most successful way of facilitating behavioural change is to alter the beliefs and values of a culture (or subculture). In the UK, services for ethnic groups are scant but improving as awareness of the needs of minority groups increases.

Hospital-based rehabilitation

The days of the long-term (up to a year or more) hospital-based admission seem to be coming to an end, although such provision, whilst expensive, is still appropriate for a number of problem drug takers. Such units were set up in the late 1960s to deal with the client group of that time. The face of drug taking has changed dramatically since then and it is probable that the majority of today's drug users will benefit more from a community-oriented range of services than from a long admission to a medical institution (where traditional occupational therapy and nursing care predominate). The latter type of service is probably still of benefit to the more damaged and chaotic drug taker who requires a safe place to be, with supervised input until such time as he or she is ready to move on to more community-based facilities.

Dual diagnosis
The problem of psychiatric diagnosis in addition to substance misuse is one that is not dealt with satisfactorily in the UK. Whereas in the USA there are specialist units operating on a national basis to cater for such difficult clients, in the UK the problem is very much left to general psychiatrists, pain clinics, substance misuse teams and whomsoever can be involved.

There is a real need for such specialist services operating probably on a regional basis.

HIV infection service
Whilst HIV infection is a subject that should be familiar to all drug workers, there is a need for a specialist service able to deal with testing for HIV in a manner that preserves confidentiality. Little is known of any special needs that may be required by seropositive drug users developing HIV-related symptoms and illness. A number of specialist facilities are planned, including a terminal care unit that will be managed by ROMA (Rehabilitation of Metropolitan Addicts) in central London.

Rehabilitation of Metropolitan Addicts (ROMA). ROMA deserves mention as a unique service operating in central London. It provides accommodation and care for notified drug addicts most of whom are receiving prescriptions, on either a maintenance or reducing basis. ROMA constitutes a national resource, and in the current climate is a focus of much national and international interest.

Methadone maintenance programmes (MMP)
The UK does not have formal, highly supervised methadone maintenance programmes such as those existing in various US cities. Many clients are maintained on methadone from a number of centres but no formal programmes have yet appeared in the UK.

Discussions are taking place between interested parties on a national basis as to the usefulness of introducing a methadone programme in London, initially as an experiment. This could serve to answer a number of important questions, and whilst expensive is regarded by some as the way most likely to capture and retain particular groups of drug takers.

Conclusions

Professional training

Substance misuse is likely to be encountered by all professionals working in health care. It should be borne in mind that the use of chemicals may be a feature in any client/patient presenting with physical, psychological and/or social problems, either as a primary diagnosis or as a secondary contributing factor. An increased awareness concerning the use of chemicals and the necessary range of services is badly needed. Some training curricula barely touch upon the subject, and all too often the emphasis follows a particular (perhaps biological) perspective. Substance misuse is an enormous area and training may usefully be provided with input from a number of the social sciences. At postgraduate level it must include the recognition of expertise from all sectors, statutory, non-statutory and private where possible with real contact via visits, exchange schemes and placement experience. For example, there is no better way for a professional to understand the workings and usefulness of a therapeutic community than to spend a few weeks as a resident, working, living and experiencing the programme. An extraordinary number of senior psychiatrists, psychologists and social workers have never visited an open AA/NA meeting or drop-in street agency, although most make assumptions (often wrongly) concerning what takes place and how useful they may or may not be. Experiential involvement in substance-misuse treatments is now mandatory in many US medical training schemes, and this is to be applauded. It is to be hoped that British medical schools will respond to the importance of training in substance misuse and the addictions, particularly in the light of the HIV epidemic.

Staff well-being

Staff who work with substance misusers require training, supervision and personal support. These areas may be developed in a number of ways and will vary according to location and circumstances. Many teams now close down their service for a half a day a week in order to allow training, visiting, support groups and recreation to take place. Some organisations allow the regular scrutiny of an external consultant, and encouraging reports on the 'health' of these agencies are beginning to appear. Research and useful recommendations now surround the subjects of 'staff burn-out' and co-dependence, issues of particular importance to workers in the field of substance misuse. There is a need for flexibility and sensitivity towards fellow workers their values and well-being. Working in substance misuse can be tremendously rewarding. This is more likely in an atmosphere of professional respect, good humour and mutual caring.

Postscript

Case 1

Roberto was successfully stabilised on 60 mg of methadone daily and he and his girlfriend were found temporary accommodation in a different part of London. Following counselling and a negative HIV antibody test, the girlfriend announced that she had decided to have the pregnancy terminated (which she did in a private clinic) and was leaving to take up a place at college in Leeds.

An upset Roberto continued to attend the clinic for counselling and his prescription, and two months later he spontaneously decided to undergo withdrawal and to enter a Concept House. He successfully completed a three-week methadone reduction and entered a therapeutic community in London where he stayed for five weeks, seeming to engage in spite of language difficulties. He left somewhat impulsively for no reason that the staff could ascertain. Six months later his whereabouts were unknown.

Case 2

Despite pressure from her mother and encouragement from the DDU, Sharon was unable to make use of her tapering methadone regimen. Moving out of mother's flat to stay with Mick, she continued smoking heroin on a regular basis and was not seen for some four months, but kept sporadic telephone contact with her mother, who became actively involved in a local family support organisation.

Suddenly she reappeared at the DDU in a tearful and frightened state. Mick had been found dead in a public lavatory the previous night, presumably following an overdose of heroin that he had injected. He and Sharon had begun injecting the preceding month as it was cheaper than smoking heroin. She was also wanted for questioning by the police about circumstances surrounding Mick's death.

She was found a bed in a London crisis centre where she withdrew from heroin, underwent counselling and a (negative) test for HIV, made a statement to the police and was discharged after three weeks to attend an agency for support. One year later she remained free from heroin whilst living with her mother, and working as a trainee chef for a catering company. She attended a group at the agency on a monthly basis and was beginning to enjoy a social life with new friends whilst maintaining a healthy respect for alcohol, which in general she preferred to avoid.

Case 3

James spent four weeks in the clinic and then returned home to a suspicious wife who resented his working hard and then spending time in the evenings at NA meetings. James found NA difficult. It seemed like a clique with religious overtones, and although it was clearly of use to some people, after a month he decided it was not for him. Three weeks later he began to drink moderate amounts, after work with friends and in restaurants. His resolve not to use cocaine served him well for a further six weeks until his birthday, when he succumbed to 'just one line' as he was confident that it would not lead to difficulties. Within three months he had lost his job, and there was a court order preventing him from entering the family home after an incident in which he punched his wife (when she told him that divorce proceedings were going ahead). The weekend before he re-entered treatment he had freebased some 8 g of cocaine.

In addition to recommending abstinence and reattendance at self-help groups, the centre also made a thorough analysis of relapse factors and James left after three weeks, armed with a new belief system and a series of coping strategies. After six months of freelance work his old company re-employed him and he moved to the Los Angeles office where two years later he was well, attending NA and CA (Cocaine Anonymous) on a twice-weekly basis, had developed an interest in English vintage cars (the importation of which had become a lucrative hobby) and was contemplating marriage to his American girlfriend of nine months' standing.

References

DHSS (1988) *AIDS and Drug Misuse Part 1*. Report by the Advisory Council on the Misuse of Drugs (London: HMSO).

Druglink (1987) Vol. 2, Issues 4, 5, and 6 (London: ISDD Publications).

Kubler-Ross E. (1969) *On Death and Dying* (New York: Macmillan).

Leukefeld C.G. and Tims, F.M. (eds) (1988) *Compulsory Treatment of Drug Abuse: Research and Clinical Practice*. NIDA Research Monograph 86 (Washington, DC: US Department of Health and Human Services).

Litman G. (1982) Personal meanings and alcoholism survival: translating subjective experience into empirical data. In *Personal Meanings. The First Guy's Hospital Symposium of the Individual Frame of References*, eds Shepherd E. and Watson J.P. (Chichester: Wiley).

Prochaska J. and DiClemente C. (1983) Stages and processes of self change of smoking, and Towards a more integrative model of change. *J. Consult. Clin. Psychol.*, **51**, 390–395.

Rapoport R.N. (1960) *Community as Doctor* (London: Tavistock).
SCODA (1988) *Residential Rehabilitation Guide for Drug Dependents* (London: SCODA).
Stimson G.V., Alldritt L., Dolan K., Donoghoe M.C. and Lart R. (1988) Injecting equipment exchange schemes: a final report. Goldsmiths College, University of London.

Bibliography

Dixon A. (1987) *Dealing with Drugs* (London: BBC Books).
Druglink (Journal) (London: ISDD Publications).
Gossop M. (1982) *Living with Drugs* (London: Temple Smith).
Marlatt A. and Gordon J. (1985) *Relapse Prevention* (New York: Guilford Press).
Plant M. (1987) *Drugs in Perspective* (London: Hodder and Stoughton).

8

Medical Complications of Substance Abuse

Douglas Maxwell

Synopsis

Despite the efforts of regulatory agencies, the number of individuals abusing drugs, and the costs to society, continue to rise. In addition to the social and psychiatric complications which have been described in other sections of this book, substance abuse carries the risk of a number of potentially life-threatening medical hazards.

This chapter outlines the various ways drug abusers may present in a medical setting, and describes some of the health problems seen in such individuals, with particular attention to serious infections. Although medical complications are related more often to the style of abuse than to specific properties of the actual substance abused, the clinical features of three distinct categories of drugs of abuse—opiates, cocaine and volatile substances—are also discussed.

Recognition of drug abuse

In view of this growing problem it is important that general practitioners and staff working in hospitals be alert to the possibility of drug abuse, and aware of the varied medical problems drug abusers may experience (Louria *et al.*, 1967; Ghodse *et al.*, 1981; Horn *et al.*, 1987).

Staff should be particularly alert for the possibility of drug abuse in young individuals. Consider whether the problem might be due to drug intoxication, withdrawal, or one of the complications of drug abuse. Check for the presence of injection sites. If in doubt a urine sample can be screened for drugs.

The recognition and assessment of drug abusers are dealt with in chapter 5, but the following list, while not exhaustive, illustrates the range of acute medical problems likely to be encountered by those engaging in a drug-abusing lifestyle, presenting to various hospital departments.

Casualty department/emergency room

Overdose with intoxication or coma
Respiratory failure (common after opiate overdose)
Trauma (may follow drug intoxication or result from drug-seeking behaviour)
Bizarre behaviour (might suggest drug psychosis or withdrawal)
Atypical or unusual pain in patients requesting analgesics (might also suggest withdrawal)

The monitoring of drug-related problems by hospital emergency departments is a good method for detecting changes in prevalence of drug misuse, as well as changes in patterns of substances abused (Ghodse *et al.*, 1981).

Medical wards

Unexplained fever
Any acute or chronic infection (especially skin, joints)
Unexplained cardiac murmurs and endocarditis
Venous or arterial thrombosis
Jaundice, or abnormal liver function
Lymphadenopathy or other features of immunosuppression
Munchausen syndrome

Surgical wards

Abscess
Acute abdomen
Intestinal obstruction ('body packers')
Vascular problems
Trauma (such as road traffic accidents or burns)
Rhinitis or rhinorrhoea

Genito-urinary clinic

Venereal disease

Obstetric unit

The baby born to an addict mother faces an uncertain future and it is vital to recognise the problem early. In addition to disorders of fetal growth and development, and risk of transmitted infection from the mother, withdrawal effects should be anticipated in the newborn infant. The prognosis for very low birth weight infants born to addicted mothers is gloomy, with significantly increased infant mortality and handicap rates. Indeed it has been suggested that very preterm or low birth weight infants of addicted mothers should be placed in the care of social services and discharged not to the parents but to a foster home. This important topic is discussed more fully in chapter 10.

If the circumstances raise the possibility of a drug-related health problem, the clinician should:

(1) Take a detailed drug history.
(2) Check with Home Office whether the patient is on the Drug Register.
(3) Treat the immediate medical problem rationally, but do not prescribe heroin or other opiates unless there is objective evidence of the opiate abstinence syndrome, when oral methadone may be given.
(4) Get expert advice from the nearest Drug Dependency Unit. Engage the patient in treatment of the drug problem, involving the local DDU and medical social workers.

Multiple health problems associated with drug abuse

The many medical problems seen in drug abusers may be conveniently considered under the headings of lifestyle disorders; overdoses; effects of withdrawal; complications of the mode of drug administration; and infections.

Lifestyle

Many addicts lead a chaotic and unsettled life. Self-neglect (and sharing crowded, unsatisfactory accommodation) may contribute to the higher prevalence of tuberculosis in this group. Severe malnutrition is uncommon, but may occur in those who neglect themselves and their diets in pursuit of drugs. Dental decay is also frequently present. Prostitution may be resorted to by female addicts to sustain their drug habit, and this brings with it the risk of venereal disease as well as assault. Violent injury is a hazard faced by those who engage in illegal activity and who associate with the criminal fraternity in order to procure or sell drugs. Drug abusers are also at greater risk of accidental injury (such as burns, head injury or road traffic accidents) when intoxicated or withdrawing from drugs.

Overdose

This is the most common cause of death in drug abusers (Louria *et al.*, 1967). Accidental overdose may be due to loss of tolerance to the drug (for example after returning to a previously tolerated dose following a period of abstinence), to impaired judgement, or as a result of unrecognised alteration in the purity of the administered drug. Accidental overdose may also occur after packages of illicit drugs have been swallowed or concealed in the vagina or rectum by international couriers to avoid detection—the 'body packer syndrome' (Lancashire *et al.*, 1988).

Overdose may also be intentional, due to coincidental depression or psychotic illness. The increased risk of suicide and deliberate self-poisoning in drug abusers is discussed in chapter 9.

Withdrawal

Complications of drug withdrawal are usually the result of withdrawal psychosis, although somatic manifestations of withdrawal are also well recognised. Drug withdrawal is discussed in chapter 5, and the psychiatric features are described in relation to specific drugs in chapter 9. Tables 8.1 to 8.3 list the typical symptoms and signs following abstinence in physically dependent opiate, benzodiazepine and barbiturate addicts.

Table 8.1 Withdrawal features in physically dependent opiate addicts

Grade of abstinence	Signs	Hours after last dose		
		Heroin	Morphine	Methadone
0	Craving for drugs, anxiety, drug-seeking behaviour	4	6	12
1	Yawning, perspiration, running nose, lachrymation	8	14	34–48
2	Increase in above plus mydriasis, pilo-erection, tremors and aches, anorexia, irritability, abdominal cramps	12	16	48–72
3	Increased BP and pulse, tachypnoea, insomnia, nausea, restlessness	18–24	24–36	
4	Increase in above plus febrile facies, vomiting and diarrhoea, weight loss	24–36	36–48	

Complications of mode of administration

(a) *Intra-arterial injection* can cause spasm or vascular trauma, and in

Table 8.2   Features of benzodiazepine abstinence/withdrawal

Short term*	Long term+	
	Psychological	*Somatic*
Anxiety	Apprehension	Paraesthesia
Tremor	Perceptual distortion	Pain
Insomnia	Hallucinations, delusions	Ataxia
Nausea	Paranoid thoughts	Visual disturbances
Vomiting	Unreality, depersonalisation	Gastrointestinal symptoms
	Agoraphobia	Influenza-like symptoms
	Depression	Metabolic and endocrine
	Craving	symptoms

* Short-term symptoms may occur 3 to 10 days following discontinuation of treatment with a long-acting benzodiazepine, and within 24 hours after abrupt withdrawal of a benzodiazepine with a short half-life.
+ Long-term features may appear in the first 3 to 10 days, and may last for months.

Table 8.3   Progressive signs of barbiturate–sedative intoxication and abstinence

Intoxication	Abstinence/withdrawal
1. Depression of superficial skin reflexes	1. Weakness
2. Fine lateral gaze nystagmus	2. Restless, tremulous, irritable
3. Coarse rapid nystagmus	3. Insomnia
4. Diminished deep tendon reflexes	4. Rising or elevated temperature
5. Minimal ataxia	5. Tachycardia (>100/min) and drop in BP with rise in pulse rate on standing
6. Slurred speech	6. Increased muscle tone, fasciculations, twitching
7. Pseudo-ptosis	7. Brisk reflexes, coarse tremor, ankle clonus
8. Positive Romberg's sign	8. Fibrillary twitchings of upper eyelids on loose closure
9. Thick speech	
10. Moderate ataxia	9. Distorted perception (e.g. walls appear curved)
11. Nystagmus on forward gaze	
12. Somnolence	10. Anorexia, nausea, vomiting, abdominal cramps
13. Severe ataxia with falls	
14. Confusion	11. Dilated pupils
15. Difficulty in arousing	12. Convulsions (occasionally status epilepticus)
16. Semi-comatose with small pupils	
17. Respiratory depression	13. Psychosis with visual (less frequently auditory) hallucinations, confusion, paranoid ideas, formication and delirium (especially at night)
18. Shock with dilated pupils	
19. Death	

some cases can result in gangrene necessitating amputation (Lancashire *et al.*, 1988).

(b) *Intravenous injection* may be followed by superficial thrombophlebitis or deep vein thrombosis and pulmonary embolism. Other postthrombotic complications include limb swelling and venous ulcers (Louria *et al.*, 1967; Yeager *et al.*, 1987; Lancashire *et al.*, 1988).

Inadvertent injection of drugs into nerves can cause paraesthesia or hyperaesthesia, and paralysis has occasionally been reported. Drugs may be mixed ('cut') with adulterants such as brick dust, talc or even strychnine which when injected may be responsible for complications such as granuloma formation in lungs (Glassroth *et al.*, 1986) or liver. Needle embolisation to the lung has also been reported.

(c) *Inhalation* of heroin may be responsible for precipitating asthma or acute bronchitis. Forced inhalation of drugs (such as cocaine) to enhance the effect has been associated with pulmonary complications such as pneumothorax (Cregler and Mark, 1986). Asphyxiation may result from the use of a plastic bag placed over the head to inhale volatile substances (Anderson *et al.*, 1986; Watson, 1986), or from vomiting and aspiration.

(d) *Intra-nasal administration* of cocaine (snorting) results in rhinitis and, if prolonged, nasal damage with perforation of the septum (Cregler and Mark, 1986).

Infection

Undoubtedly the most serious health risk faced by addicts, particularly those who inject their drugs, comes from infection. The increased risk of tuberculosis as a result of poor social conditions, malnutrition and self-neglect has already been mentioned. Prostitution and promiscuous behaviour contribute to an increased prevalence of venereal disease. In addition, as a result of sharing contaminated needles, or poor aseptic injection techniques, drug abusers are exposed to a variety of other bacterial, viral and occasionally fungal infections. Immunosuppression after HIV infection is another important risk factor to TB and opportunistic infections in those who inject.

Infection at the site of injection frequently causes cellulitis, and occasionally cutaneous abscess formation (Louria *et al.*, 1967). Chronic suppurative skin infections associated with the habit of 'skin popping' (repeated subcutaneous injection) may be complicated by amyloidosis which is emerging as a major cause of nephropathy in those who inject their drugs (Neugarten *et al.*, 1986). Septicaemia can result in lung, kidney and brain abscesses, and involve other organs including joints and bone (Chandrasekar and Narula, 1986), heart valves (Reisberg, 1979; Chambers *et al.*, 1983) and blood vessels (mycotic aneurysms). Drug abusers who inject are also at risk of transmission of hepatitis viruses from infected needles and syringes, which can result in acute and chronic liver disease (Kunches *et al.*, 1986; Novick *et al.*, 1986). Perhaps of greatest concern is the recognition that drug abusers are becoming a significant reservoir of HIV infection, and pose a major health risk to the community at large (Acheson, 1986; Adler, 1986; Brettle *et al.*, 1987).

Serious infections in drug abusers

While drug abusers are at increased risk of many infections, the following serious infections—endocarditis, hepatitis and HIV infection—merit special consideration.

Infective endocarditis

Infective endocarditis is a well recognised complication of the illicit use of intravenous drugs, with an incidence conservatively estimated at 1.5 to 2 cases per 1000 addicts at risk per year (Reisberg, 1979). The age and sex of drug addicts with infectious endocarditis reflect the prevalent use of heroin by young males. From a number of reports the average age of patients with narcotic-associated endocarditis was 29 years, whereas the average age of patients with endocarditis in the general population was found to be 50.

Valve involvement

Most non-addict patients with endocarditis have an underlying cardiac abnormality that predisposes them to infection. In contrast, addict patients with infective endocarditis usually present with acute endocarditis caused by organisms capable of attacking normal cardiac valves, and have a substantially lower incidence of underlying cardiac disease.

The majority of narcotic addicts with endocarditis will have their infection localised to the tricuspid valve. A much smaller number have concomitant involvement of the pulmonary, mitral and aortic valves. However, for the small proportion of addicts with underlying rheumatic valvulitis, infective endocarditis commonly affects valves on the left side of the heart, as is the case for non-addicts with infective endocarditis.

The preponderance of right-sided endocarditis is unique to infection associated with intravenous substance abuse. Almost invariably the tricuspid valve has been thought to be normal prior to infection, and *Staphylococcus aureus* is the micro-organism most often implicated (Reisberg, 1979; Chambers *et al.*, 1983). Other organisms occasionally responsible include various species of *Streptococcus*, and gram-negative bacilli especially *Pseudomonas aeruginosa*. Rarely *Candida* species may infect the tricuspid valve, but this and other organisms of low virulence may require prior valve damage before they can cause endocarditis. It has been suggested that intravenous drug abusers (IVDA) may damage their valves by bombardment of the endothelial surface with particulate material present in the injected material. This could lead to deposition of platelets and fibrin, and subsequently trapping of bacteria or fungi in the developing platelet–fibrin thrombus. In support of this hypothesis was the necropsy finding of talc granulations in the subendothelium of the tricuspid valve of an addict with infective endocarditis.

Source of infection

In some addicts with infective endocarditis the source of infection is not difficult to find, for example where cutaneous abscesses or septic thrombophlebitis are present. There is also evidence that addicts with *Staph. aureus* endocarditis frequently carry this organism in nose, throat or skin of ante-cubutal fossa (figure 8.1). Other studies indicate that individuals who repeatedly inject themselves have a higher rate of carriage of *Staph. aureus* than those who do not. Despite the unsterile practices involved in the preparation of illicit drugs for intravenous injection, cultures of narcotics, other powders for injection and injection paraphernalia rarely reveal pathogenic bacteria.

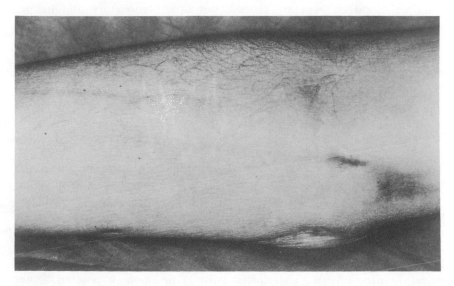

Figure 8.1 Cubital fossa of an intravenous drug abuser showing thrombophlebitis.

Clinical features

The majority of patients present with features of an acute infection, with duration of illness of under a week. Staphylococcal endocarditis in particular is distinguished from endocarditis due to other causes by its acute onset and fulminant course manifested by multiple septic and embolic complications. Patients infected with less virulent organisms may have symptoms for three weeks or more. The frequency of pulmonary symptoms depends on the presence or absence of right-sided endocarditis, and the pulmonary manifestations of tricuspid endocarditis—pleuritic chest pain, cough and dyspnoea—may dominate the clinical picture. On examination typical cutaneous manifestations of infective endocarditis such as petechiae, subungual splinter haemorrhages and Osler's nodes are present in up to 50% of the patients. Many patients are found to have a cardiac murmur, and almost all will eventually develop one some time during hospitalisation. Other physical findings are due to embolic or suppurative complications. Neurological signs are common, ranging from confusion to coma. Impaired renal function due to immune glomerulonephritis, and intra-abdominal emboli, are other well recognised complications.

Investigations

Multiple blood cultures are crucial, but other laboratory findings are non-specific. Most patients have a neutrophil leucocytosis, and microscopic haematuria is found in half. Echocardiography can be a very useful investigation in suspected infective endocarditis in IVDA (figure 8.2), by documenting the valve lesion, and can also occasionally demonstrate vegetations.

Treatment and prognosis

Treatment of infective endocarditis in intravenous drug abusers follows the same principles as for infective endocarditis in the general population. There is evidence that better results are obtained where cardiologists and physicians with an interest in infective diseases cooperate in joint management of the patient. Apart from prompt treatment with appropriate antimicrobial therapy, the two major determinants of outcome are the organism responsible for producing infective endocarditis, and the affected valve(s). Infections of the tricuspid valve with *Staph. aureus* and other gram-positive cocci have a favourable prognosis and can usually be treated successfully with antibiotics alone. However, staphylococcal infection of the aortic and mitral valve often leads to valvular incompetence and the development of cardiac failure.

Progressive heart failure is the most common identifiable cause of death in drug addicts with endocarditis, and in patients with progressive failure unresponsive to medical management cardiac surgery, with excision of the infected valve and replacement, is indicated. A second indication for valve replacement is inability to eradicate the infection with antimicrobial agents alone. This most commonly occurs with infection due to gram-negative

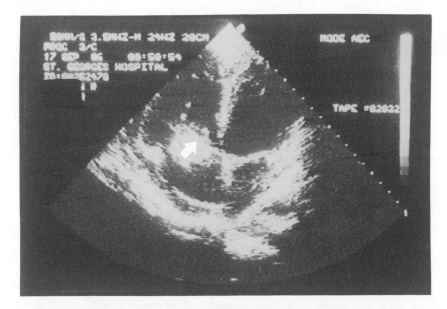

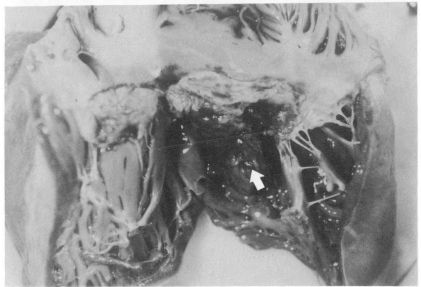

Figure 8.2 Echocardiograph and post-mortem heart of an intravenous drug abuser with tricuspid endocarditis. Arrows indicate vegetations on tricuspid valve. (Courtesy of Mr Graham Leech.)

bacilli (such as *Pseudomonas* or *Serratia*) and fungi (e.g. *Candida*). Cure of fungal endocarditis almost always requires surgical removal of the infected valvular tissue (as current antifungal agents are ineffective in penetrating fungal vegetations) together with prolonged antimicrobial therapy.

Substance Abuse and Dependence

Viral hepatitis

The viruses responsible for hepatitis A, B, D (delta infection) and non-A, non-B hepatitis can all be transmitted by contaminated blood. Study of IVDA has shown a greatly increased incidence of markers of past infection with hepatitis A and B, and of elevated liver enzymes, compared with non IV drug users (Kunches *et al.*, 1986; Novick *et al.*, 1986). Sera in dilutions of up to 10^{-7} can transmit hepatitis infection if introduced parenterally, while up to 1 ml of undiluted serum is required to transmit infection by the oral route. Thus it is not surprising that there is a high prevalence of acute and chronic liver disease as a result of parenterally acquired viral hepatitis in IVDA. The risk of developing cirrhosis is increased if alcohol is also abused.

Hepatitis B

Acute clinical hepatitis B is a notifiable disease in the UK, and in countries like the UK, where exposure is uncommon before adult life, good estimates of clinical incidence provide a better means of surveillance than prevalence studies in the population. The regular Public Health Laboratory Service (PHLS) Communicable Disease Reports provide a reliable estimate of trends in incidence for acute clinical hepatitis B.

Annual totals of reported cases to the PHLS remained similar at about 1000 from 1975 to 1980, of whom 18% were drug abusers. There was an

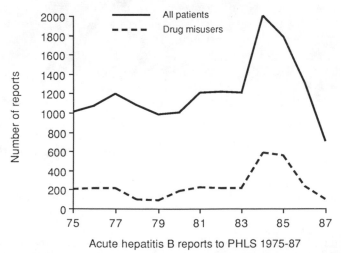

Acute hepatitis B reports to PHLS 1975-87

Figure 8.3 Acute hepatitis B reports to Public Health Laboratory Service 1975–1987 showing proportion of cases in drug misusers. (Courtesy of Dr Sheila Polakoff and the editor of *The Lancet*.)

increase to more than 1200 in each of the years 1981–1983, and in 1984 the total reached almost 2000 with a marked rise in the number of drug abuse associated cases (figure 8.3). However, a substantial fall occurred in 1986 in both the total numbers and the numbers of drug abuse associated cases. Various explanations were offered for this reversal in the trend, including the temporary exhaustion of susceptibles among drug abusers (if this is so, another increase can be expected later); possible reduction in IVDA, or that abusers are not sharing syringes to the same extent as formerly; or possibly that some drug abusers who are still susceptible to the infection have been vaccinated.

Delta virus

Delta antigen was initially detected as nuclear immunofluorescence in liver cells of patients with chronic hepatitis B. It is now known to be a unique but defective transmissible hepatitis virus with an RNA genome too small to allow complete independent replication. Multiplication of hepatitis B virus is required to permit delta replication and to provide the protein coat for the delta virus. It is distributed worldwide in association with hepatitis B carriers and cases of hepatitis B, many but not all of whom are drug abusers (Raimondo *et al.*, 1982).

There are two basic categories of delta infection. 'Co-infection' refers to simultaneous infection with hepatitis B and delta virus. Hepatitis B takes some time to begin its replication, and until it does delta virus cannot replicate. Most cases (95%) of co-infection run a benign course similar to that of ordinary hepatitis B. Progression to chronic hepatitis B + D occurs in under 2%. 'Superinfection' with delta occurs where a patient was infected with hepatitis B some months before acquiring delta virus, or is already a chronic hepatitis B carrier. Since the hepatitis B virus is already replicating, it can allow delta to replicate simultaneously. This commonly results in a very severe infection. Delta superinfection is associated with a significantly higher number of fulminant hepatitis cases, and is also associated with a very high rate of progression to chronic active hepatitis (70–90%).

The mode of transmission is similar to parenteral spread of hepatitis B. Sharing of syringes and needles is an important factor, and serological evidence of infection is found frequently in drug addicts. In the Dublin epidemic of hepatitis B among IVDA which started in 1980, over 40% had markers of delta infection. In Western Europe delta infection is largely confined to drug abusers and their close, usually sexual, contacts. In the USA markers of delta infection are also frequently present in individuals (e.g. haemophiliacs) who have had multiple transfusion of blood products from commercial donors. Extensive screening of blood donations for HBsAg should by now have considerably reduced the risk of delta infection in multiple transfused individuals, but IVDA continue to be an easy target. Because of the possibility that delta infection can suppress hepatitis B surface antigen, it is recommended that all drug abusers with jaundice, whether or not they are HBsAg positive, should be tested for delta antigen.

Non-A non-B hepatitis

This is a heterogeneous group defined on the basis of absence of specific hepatitis markers in patients with elevated transaminases unrelated to any known cause of liver injury. Both faecal/oral and parenteral transmission have been implicated, and non-A non-B infections have been reported to account for between 6 and 48% of acute hepatitis in hospitalised patients. Parenteral drug abuse is a recognised risk factor, and there is a high frequency of progression to chronic hepatitis and cirrhosis.

Screening

In the UK and other low-prevalence countries pre-screening before hepatitis B immunisation is not normally cost effective. However, subjects who belong to a group at high risk of hepatitis B, such as IVDA, should be screened, and if negative have a course of hepatitis B vaccine to prevent acute hepatitis B and progressive liver disease such as chronic hepatitis, cirrhosis and hepatocellular carcinoma. Antibody to hepatitis B core antigen (anti-HBc) is the optimal prevaccination test, as other markers are often absent.

Sexual contacts

Sexual contacts of IVDA with hepatitis B should be tested for HBsAg and anti-HBs. Anti-hepatitis B virus immunoglobulin (HBIG) is given immediately and 1 month later if the first exposure to the infected person was within 48 hours. If tests for both HBsAg and anti-HBs are negative, the patient should also be vaccinated. Simultaneous administration of HBIG and vaccine does not decrease the efficacy of the vaccine.

Immunisation

Outbreaks of fulminant hepatitis B (and delta infection) among IVDA emphasise the need for early immunisation in this group. The full course of hepatitis B vaccine requires an initial intramuscular injection, which is repeated one month and six months later. Seroconversion is satisfactory in susceptible IVDA, indicating that hepatitis B vaccine is immunogenic in this population (Kunches *et al.*, 1986). As yet there is no vaccine for delta infection, but in hepatitis B negative subjects infection by delta virus is also prevented by hepatitis B immunisation, as this virus replicates only in the presence of hepatitis B infection.

There is a high incidence of HBs antigenaemia in IVDA, which almost certainly reflects decreased immunocompetence. If these individuals are also unable to eliminate the delta agent, the stage will be set for perpetuation of delta agent infection and a rising incidence of chronic liver disease.

The incidence of acute hepatitis B in health-care workers is generally low, and the risk comes from blood contact rather than patient contact. However, staff who work in contact with drug abusers are regarded as being at higher risk, and should be offered immunisation.

Infants

Infants born to hepatitis B virus carrier mothers should be given both active and passive immunisation at birth. Infants of mothers who are HBV-DNA positive (indicating active viral replication) are most at risk of acquiring hepatitis B, and combined active and passive immunisation of such infants has been shown to have a success rate of over 80% in keeping infants HBsAg negative at one-year follow-up. Infants born to HBsAg-positive mothers who were HBV-DNA negative have a low risk of becoming HBsAg positive, and immunisation may not be necessary in such infants. The failures may represent *in utero* infections.

Chronic hepatitis

This is defined as liver inflammation (recognised by elevation of transaminases) persisting for more than six months, and can be characterised histologically into relatively benign (chronic persistent hepatitis—CPH), or progressive (chronic active hepatitis—CAH) forms on the basis of liver biopsy appearances.

The efficacy of anti-viral drugs (such as vidarabine and its analogues) and interferon is being evaluated in chronic hepatitis B and chronic non-A non-B hepatitis. The decision to treat patients with chronic hepatitis B is based on the presence or absence of HBV replication (assessed in serum by measuring HBV-DNA, HBV-DNA polymerase or HBe antigen, and in liver by immunohistological detection of HBc antigen) and liver cell inflammation (assessed by serum transaminases). Interferon given subcutaneously for a 16-week course may induce HBe seroconversion in about

20% of patients, and is currently the basis for further improvement by combination with other drugs.

In general, results depend on the duration of infection and the integrity of the patient's immune response. Patient compliance is also important with prolonged intramuscular therapy, and this is seldom optimal with IVDA.

HIV infection and AIDS

A new disease complex, subsequently defined and named the Acquired Immune Deficiency Syndrome (AIDS), was first recognised when cases of *Pneumocystis carinii* pneumonia and Kaposi's sarcoma were reported among homosexual men in the USA in 1981. The disease has become an important pandemic worldwide, and it is now realised that groups other than homosexual males, in particular IVDA, are at risk (Acheson, 1986; Brettle *et al.*, 1987).

The striking features of the original cases were the unusual and recurrent opportunistic infections and tumours associated with a character-istic cellular immune defect, recognised by a reduction in helper T cells (T4 cells). It is now known that AIDS is caused by a retrovirus, the Human Immunodeficiency Virus (HIV), formerly known as the Human T Lym-photrophic Virus Type III (HTLV III) or Lymphadenopathy Associated Virus (LAV).

Clinical features and diagnosis

The spectrum of HIV infection extends from the acute infectious illness, through asymptomatic infection to the persistent lymphadenopathy syn-drome (PGL). The most important factor for progression to AIDS is the length of infection. Data from cohort studies of HIV-infected individuals suggest that 50–75% may progress to symptomatic disease in 10 years.

The great majority of patients with AIDS present with an opportunistic infection (tumours are less common) which can be localised or widely disseminated involving any system in the body. Prominent constitutional symptoms include fever, weight loss and fatigue. These symptoms are often associated with specific findings in the lungs, gastrointestinal tract or central nervous system. Multiple opportunistic infections may be present, and are typical of the advanced phases of the disease. There is a tendency for infections to recur, and deep organ involvement with fungi, parasites and DNA viruses is unlikely to be eradicated.

Pneumocystis carinii pneumonia is the most commonly reported infec-tion and accounts for almost half of reported opportunistic disease. Kaposi's sarcoma (figure 8.4) is the second most common associated disease, but appears to be of declining importance. Other diseases indicative of defective underlying cellular immunity include *Candida* oesophagitis, disseminated cytomegalovirus (CMV), cryptococcal infection, chronic mucocutaneous herpes simplex, cryptosporidiosis, CNS toxoplasmosis and disseminated atypical mycobacterial infections (Young, 1987).

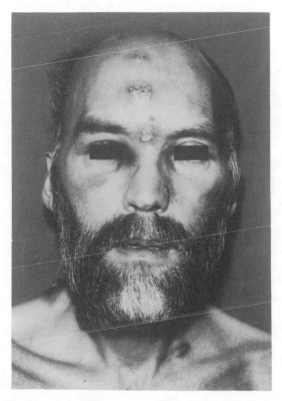

Figure 8.4   Multiple cutaneous lesions of Kaposi's sarcoma in a patient with AIDS. (Courtesy of Dr Mark Wansbrough-Jones.)

Classification and diagnosis of HIV infections

The US Centers for Disease Control (CDC) *clinical* classification identifies four mutually exclusive categories of HIV infection. Some established terms (such as AIDS) will probably remain in use. However, the new classification should allow better separation of subgroups for scientific study.

Group 1. Acute infection

Group 2. Asymptomatic infection
Group 3. Persistent generalised lymphadenopathy (PGL)
Group 4. Other disease
    A Constitutional disease
    B Neurological disease (e.g. dementia)
    C Secondary infectious disease
    C1—specified secondary infectious diseases specified in CDC surveillance definition of AIDS
    C2—other specified secondary infectious diseases
    D   Secondary cancers (including those in CDC AIDS definition)
    E   Other conditions

The CDC now emphasises the results of *laboratory* tests for HIV infection, and the revised definition of AIDS for surveillance purposes can be summarised as follows:

(1) *Without laboratory evidence of HIV infection.* Where test has not been done or result is inconclusive, any of 12 indicator diseases (e.g. *Pneumocystis carinii* pneumonia; extrapulmonary cryptococcosis; Kaposi's sarcoma in patient under 60) are, if diagnosed definitively, diagnostic of AIDS provided other causes of immunodeficiency have been excluded.

(2) *With laboratory evidence of HIV infection.* Regardless of the presence of other causes of immunodeficiency, any of the 12 indicator diseases, plus any of a further list of 12 additional indicator diseases (such as HIV encephalopathy and 'slim' disease) all may be defined as AIDS.

(3) *With laboratory evidence against HIV infection.* This excludes AIDS unless *all* other cases for immunodeficiency have been ruled out, and the patient has definitive *P. carinii* pneumonia or both one of the primary 12 diseases indicative of AIDS *and* a T helper/inducer cell count below 400/mm^3.

The five routes to a diagnosis of AIDS are summarised in figure 8.5.

Transmission of HIV infection

The virus is fragile and survives poorly outside the body. It is transmitted by three routes, requiring close contact.

Sexual contact
Both heterosexual and homosexual genital contact. This has important implications for the spouses and partners of IVDA. Since female drug abusers often turn to prostitution to support their lifestyles, this constitutes another important mode of spread of HIV to the heterosexual non-drug-

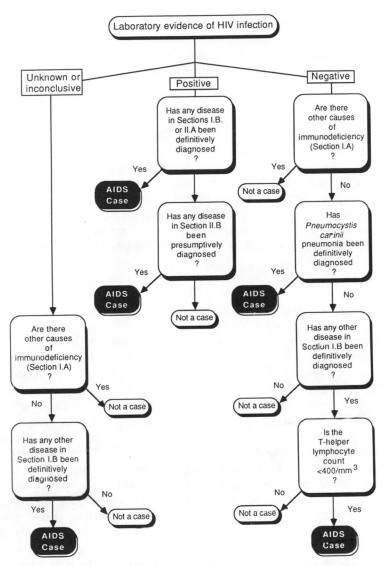

Figure 8.5 Flow diagram showing the revised CDC case definition for AIDS.

using population (Brettle *et al.*, 1987). Although HIV is not transmitted by casual contact, it has been identified in saliva, and there are anecdotal reports of transmission from kissing and bites.

Blood to blood spread

The risk is relatively small from blood and blood products, except for commercially produced factor VIII, and has been virtually eliminated in developed countries. Far more important is the sharing of blood-contaminated syringes and needles by IVDA. Widespread HIV infection among IVDA is largely due to more extensive blood contact from the habit of 'booting' and sharing 'works'. Smaller risks come from needle stick injury to health workers, and from transplantation of HIV infected organs.

Materno-fetal spread

The infant of an infected mother is at great risk of vertical transmission of infection via transplacental spread or at parturition. HIV seropositivity in newborn infants is not sufficient evidence for HIV infection, since maternal antibodies cross the placenta and may persist for up to 15 months. New, highly sensitive molecular biology techniques which allow detection of DNA sequences in infants of seropositive mothers suggest that the risk of transmission in pregnancy is 30–40% in infants of IVDA. Female HIV carriers should be persuaded to practice safe sex and to avoid pregnancy since this appears to accelerate the onset of illness/AIDS in asymptomatic carriers.

HIV infection and AIDS in drug abusers

Studies of IVDA have suggested that transmission of HIV may be facilitated by transfer of small amounts of blood during the widespread practice of sharing needles and syringes. Transfer may be facilitated by the habit of 'booting'—redrawing blood into the syringe and reinjecting it. Knowledge of the risks involved in this practice appears to have altered risk-taking behaviour in some addicts (Robertson *et al.*, 1988). Other studies indicate that sharing of syringes is associated with a feeling of community among some drug users, and not necessarily due to a shortage of injection equipment. These findings are obviously relevant to needle/syringe exchange schemes (Marks and Parry, 1987).

In the USA, after homosexual and bisexual men, IVDA are the group at greatest risk of AIDS and account for about 25% of all AIDS patients reported to the Communicable Diseases Center (CDC) (of whom about 8% were both IVDA and homosexual or bisexual men). In 1984 in the USA the incidence rates of AIDS in heterosexual IVDA was estimated at 168 cases per 100 000 drug users. Fifty-five per cent of children with AIDS were born to mothers who were drug users or whose spouses were IVDA. Prisoners (many of whom also abuse drugs) are also at high risk for HIV infection: the great majority of prisoners with AIDS or who were HIV positive gave a history of IV drug abuse.

In Europe the situation is at present rather different, with WHO reports indicating that only 8% of all AIDS patients are IV drug abusers. However, there are wide regional differences. In the UK IVDA accounted for only 3% of the cumulative total of AIDS patients reported to the DHSS in 1988 (well below numbers reported for homosexual/bisexual men or haemophiliacs) while in Spain and Italy the figure is well over 30%.

In Europe the prevalence of HIV antibody also varies widely among drug abusers, from 6% in England to 37% in Spain, 44% in West Germany and 76% in Italy. Within the UK there are also major differences. In Scotland 60% of IVDA are now HIV positive. HIV positivity in drug abusers has been correlated with a longer duration of drug abuse, a greater likelihood of sharing needles and syringes frequently, and an increased prevalence of serum markers of hepatitis B infection.

The outbreak among Edinburgh drug addicts (Brettle *et al.*, 1987) may explain the fact that 20% of people found to be HIV positive in the UK live in Scotland, which accounts for only 10% of the UK population. Since there is a substantial risk to their sexual contacts, this situation has serious implications for their partners and children.

Prevention of HIV infection in IVDA
Health education
Measures to prevent the transmission of HIV through transfusion of infected blood and blood products (through self-deferral of high-risk blood donors, HIV antibody testing, and heat treatment of plasma factors) have achieved prevention in two important areas, but the groups at risk constitute only a tiny minority of the epidemic.

There is no immediate prospect of a vaccine, and prevention of HIV infection for the vast majority at risk, including the growing numbers of IV drug abusers, will have to depend on effective and unambiguous health education. It is vital that drug abusers be educated in the methods of HIV transmission, and be persuaded to adapt their behaviour to avoid sharing needles and syringes, advised of the crucial need to practice methods of 'safer sex', and warned of the dangers of prostitution (Acheson, 1986).

The continuing decrease in hepatitis B incidence in UK drug abusers since the peak recorded in 1984 gives some hope that this lesson has been learned by drug misusers (Robertson *et al.*, 1988). HIV-infected women must also be advised against pregnancy, and consideration given to termination if HIV infection is found in the early antenatal period.

Provision of needles and syringes
The best solution is never to start IV drug use. For those to whom this counsel of perfection has come too late and are unable to stop the habit, it is vital that, if illicit drugs are used parenterally, the injection equipment is clean and will not act as a vector for HIV infection.

The provision of free needles and syringes on a replacement basis has been advocated by some authorities to reduce needle sharing among IVDAs, since this, rather than heterosexual intercourse, seems to be the more important route of transmission in drug abusers. Indeed the alarming increase in HIV infection in drug addicts in Edinburgh occurred after a period when the availability of drugs, needles and syringes was vigorously suppressed. Although there is some evidence to suggest that IVDA prefer to share syringes because this promotes a feeling of community, preliminary experience of a free syringe exchange programme for drug addicts in Liverpool has been encouraging (Marks and Parry, 1987), and similar programmes are being evaluated elsewhere.

Health workers and health educators must convince the authorities that measures to control the spread of HIV through drug abuse are even more pressing than drug abuse itself. This is an area of considerable controversy, but to ignore this (or any other aspect of HIV control) is to put at risk the whole community with a terrible escalation of the epidemic.

Treatment

There is no specific treatment, but zidovudine (formerly AZT), a reverse transcriptase inhibitor, has shown immunological, virological and clinical benefits in patients with fulminant HIV infections. These benefits are often at the expense of toxic effects—notably bone marrow suppression, and other dideoxynucleoside analogues are being evaluated. Opportunist infections should be recognised and treated promptly (Young, 1987). It is also important to recognise the need for psychosocial counselling for patients and their families, who have to come to terms with depression and death and the effects of HIV infection on relationships and sexuality (Miller, 1987).

Unlike other members of AIDS-risk groups, many drug abusers suffer severe social problems and do not have the support of self-help groups. Many lead unsettled, chaotic lives, default on out-patient appointments, and are not easy to cope with in hospital, where security and violence may be problems. Urgent planning is required to deal with the inevitable rise in numbers of these 'bed-blocking young' and the concomitant medical and social problems.

Medical complications related to the substance abused

While most medical problems associated with substance abuse can be explained by complications of the method of abuse, the specific characteristics of the drug abused are also relevant. Three major categories of drug will be briefly considered: opiates, cocaine and volatile substances.

Opiates

Opiates, particularly heroin, remain the most important drugs of abuse.

Over 90% of addicts hospitalised for medical complications of their habit have been taking heroin (often in combination with other drugs). Apart from overdose, most of the medical complications of opiate abuse are a consequence of infection and thrombophlebitis following injection (Louria *et al.*, 1967). They can be summarised as follows.

Overdose

The most dreaded complication of narcotic abuse is estimated to kill 1% of addicts annually. Most overdoses are inadvertent and result from a lack of awareness of the potency of the drug. Analyses of street 'heroin' have shown an enormous range of concentrations, from no trace (filler only) to over 70%. Other overdoses result from loss of tolerance, for example in the abstinent addict who returns to the habit, or the neophyte who imitates a drug-tolerant colleague and injects what is for him an inordinately large amount. Overdose causes stupor with irregular, slow, gasping respirations. Coma, pulmonary oedema and respiratory arrest may supervene. Treatment is with the opiate antagonist naloxone. It should be remembered that this drug is itself potentially dangerous if given to severely addicted individuals as it may precipitate sudden exaggerated withdrawal.

Infections

The most commonly seen infections are cellulitis, abscesses at the site of injection and bacteraemia. Hepatitis, one of the most frequent infectious complications requiring hospitalisation, and infective endocarditis, due to a wide variety of organisms, have been discussed in some detail in an earlier section of this chapter. Tetanus and malaria were formerly widely recognised complications of IVDA, but are no longer seen. In their place have come human immunodeficiency virus (HIV) infections which have established a reservoir among IVDA and now pose a threat to a wider community.

Pulmonary complications

These may take a number of forms. Pulmonary oedema is a poorly understood and often fatal complication of heroin overdose. Embolic pneumonia, with or without lung abscess, is easily explicable on the basis of bacteraemia or right-sided (tricuspid valve) infective endocarditis. Bacterial pneumonias are also common in IVDA. They may be the result of depression of the cough reflex by opiates, but cannot be correlated with debility or coma. Finally foreign body embolisation to the lungs (cotton fibres, talc and even broken segments of needles) is a well recognised finding in IVDA, and may result in granuloma formation, arteritis and ultimately pulmonary fibrosis.

Obstetric complications

There is higher fetal loss in pregnancy. In addition to disordered fetal growth and development, and transmission of serious infections from the mother, withdrawal effects should be anticipated in the newborn infant. The prognosis for very low birth weight infants born to addicted mothers is very gloomy, with significantly increased infant mortality and handicap rates. This subject is discussed in more detail in chapter 10.

Volatile substances

A wide range of volatile lipid-soluble substances, mostly halogenated or unsubstituted hydrocarbons, may when inhaled cause changes in mood or consciousness (central nervous system effects similar to those of acute alcohol intoxication), or in some cases hallucinations and visual disturbances. The abuse of these substances to get a 'high' is popularly but inaccurately known as 'glue sniffing' or 'solvent abuse' (Anderson *et al.*, 1986).

The major categories of volatile substances inhaled include gas fuels (mainly butane); solvents in glues (mainly toluene); other volatile agents (such as cleaning agents and correcting fluid thinners) and aerosol sprays.

Organ damage

In view of the cerebral effects of volatile substances, there has been concern that continued abuse might cause significant *brain* damage. However, reports are contradictory. Some anecdotal reports and uncontrolled studies of small groups of solvent abusers indicate that long-term abuse of toluene-containing substances may be associated with brain dysfunction, especially balance control and impairment of intellect and memory. Brain scans suggest that this may be accompanied by cerebral atrophy. There is no agreement on the mechanisms involved. Direct toxicity on the brain is not proven, and other factors such as hypersensitivity reactions, hypoxia following inhalation, or even nutritional deficiency may be implicated. A recent large carefully controlled study of abusers showed no evidence for neuropsychological impairment, but did not exclude the possibility of a harmful effect from chronic abuse.

Other medical complications include *bone marrow* suppression resulting from the effects of inhaling substances containing *n*-hexane, which was previously used in adhesives. This problem is unlikely to recur since *n*-hexane has now been banned. Apart from the brain, the other organs most likely to be affected by abuse of volatile substances are the *liver*, *kidneys* and *heart* (*Lancet*, 1988). Despite the large numbers of individuals involved in solvent abuse, there have been few reports of hepatotoxicity or renal dysfuntion. Interpretation of these reports is difficult as various factors may have been responsible, singly or in combination, including concomitant viral infection and alcohol abuse, as well as individual hypersensitivity. It seems that the great majority show no evidence of chronic physical disease as a result of abusing volatile substances (Watson, 1986).

Deaths

Whereas there is uncertainty about organ damage following solvent abuse, there is no doubt that deaths are associated with this practice (Anderson *et*

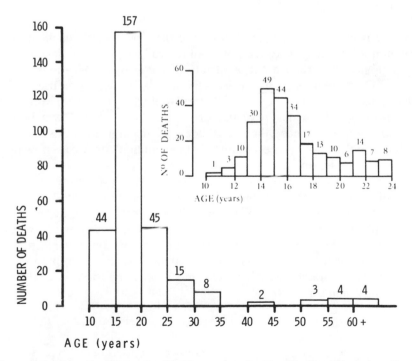

Figure 8.6 Age distribution in deaths associated with volatile solvent abuse in the United Kingdom, 1971–1983. (Courtesy of Professor H.R. Anderson and the editor of the *British Medical Journal*.)

al., 1986). Despite an increased awareness of the hazards of abusing volatile substances, and efforts to prevent abuse and reduce risks among abusers, there appears to have been an increase in the number of deaths from this form of substance abuse in the UK in recent years, with an annual death rate now exceeding 100. In 1983, 2% of all deaths of males between 10 and 19 years of age were attributed to solvent abuse (figure 8.6). Although this number is small in comparison with alcohol-related mortality, it is disturbing that the great majority of fatalities are in otherwise fit young males.

Although glues are most widely abused, misuse of other volatile products appears to be more hazardous. This may be because the techniques used are more dangerous, or the substances themselves are more toxic. Over half the deaths are attributed to the direct toxic effects of the substances. These are possibly due to cardiac arrhythmias, as there is evidence that volatile substances sensitise the heart to the effects of sympathetic stimulation. The remaining deaths are thought to have resulted from trauma as a result of intoxicated behaviour; the method of inhalation (plastic bag over the head); or inhalation of stomach contents.

Cocaine

Cocaine is becoming recognised as one of the most dangerous illicit drugs in common use today, with the potential to produce profound dependence, psychological disturbance and a variety of medical complications. In the past it was so expensive that price served as a barrier to its use, but as cocaine has become less expensive its availability has increased. Moreover, as a result of the widespread but erroneous belief that it is a benign, non-addicting substance, there has been an upsurge in its use in both Britain and the USA. It is estimated that five million Americans now use it regularly (Cregler and Mark, 1986).

Cocaine was first introduced as a locally acting anaesthetic, but its systemic effects on the nervous system are probably mediated by alterations in synaptic transmission. Cocaine blocks the presynaptic uptake of the neurotransmitters noradrenaline and dopamine, producing an excess of transmitter at the post-synaptic receptor sites. Activation of the sympathetic nervous system by this mechanism produces vasoconstriction, an acute rise in arterial pressure, tachycardia and a predisposition to ventricular arrhythmias and seizures.

Complications

These pharmacological actions provide a rational basis for the medical complications of cocaine abuse, which are as follows.

(a) *Cardiovascular complications*, including acute myocardial infarction, have been temporally associated with cocaine use. This drug represents a potential hazard to anyone with coronary heart disease because of increase in heart rate, systolic blood pressure and myocardial oxygen demand. The occurrence of acute myocardial infarction in a young patient who does not have the usual coronary risk factors should raise the possibility of coronary spasm related to cocaine use. In addition to life-threatening arrhythmias, rupture of the ascending aorta and cerebrovascular accidents have been reported. These effects are probably related to adrenergic stimulation and sudden rise in blood pressure.

(b) *Neurological complications*. Headaches are commonly noted after cocaine use, and are probably a result of drug-induced hypertension, as is stroke. Cocaine also lowers the seizure threshold, and convulsions were among the earliest known adverse effects.

(c) *Gastrointestinal complications*. Severe bowel ischaemia and gangrene have been described after oral use. This is again thought to be a direct pharmacological effect of the drug, stimulating α-adrenergic receptors in the gut, leading to vasoconstriction and reduced blood flow. Intestinal ischaemia should be considered whenever a cocaine user experiences severe abdominal pain.

(d) *Pregnancy complications*. Cocaine use during pregnancy carries significant risks. Its use is associated with lower gestational age at delivery, increase in preterm labour and delivery, lower birth weights and delivery of small for gestational age infants. There are reports of abruptio placentae (probably also due to transient drug-induced hypertension), and the spontaneous abortion rate is even higher than among women who use heroin in pregnancy. There is some evidence that infants are at higher risk of malformations, perinatal mortality and behavioural disturbances.

(e) *Route of administration*. Other acute and chronic complications of cocaine use depend on the route of administration, purity and sterility. Intra-nasal administration is most popular via sniffing ('snorting'), but it can also be smoked in the more volatile free alkaloid ('crack') form ('freebasing'). Less commonly it is taken orally, vaginally, sublingually or rectally, and can also be injected (Cregler and Mark, 1986).

Prolonged intra-nasal administration can lead to chronic inflammation with rhinitis, rhinorrhoea, ulceration and ultimately perforation of the nasal septum.

Granuloma formation and pulmonary oedema have been reported after smoking freebase, and deep, prolonged or forced inhalation has resulted in barotrauma (spontaneous pneumothorax, pneumomediastinum).

Studies of recreational drug users suggest that, for the great majority who take the drug infrequently, serious problems are rare. The most common unwanted effects are lassitude and irritability. However, cocaine is a dangerous drug with many similarities to amphetamine and other centrally acting stimulants such as phenmetrazine. Acute anxiety and psychosis (similar to but of shorter duration than amphetamine psychosis) have been recorded.

Death

Overdose of large quantities causes depression of medullary centres and death from respiratory and cardiac arrest. These risks depend not only on the dose but also on the purity which may vary from 25 to 90% when purchased on the street. Fatal overdose may also be with suicidal intent. Other cocaine fatalities have resulted from accidental overdose arising from attempts by drug couriers (known as 'body packers' in the US, and in the UK as either 'stuffers' or 'swallowers') to conceal packages of the drug within body cavities (Lancashire *et al.*, 1988).

Most deaths after cocaine use are attributed to generalised convulsions, respiratory failure or cardiac arrhythmias.

References

Acheson E.D. (1986) AIDS: A challenge for the public health. *Lancet*, **1**, 662–666.
Adler M.A. (1986) AIDS and intravenous drug abusers. *Br. J. Addiction*, **81**, 307–310.
Anderson H.R. *et al.* (1986) Recent trends in mortality associated with abuse of volatile substances in the UK. *Br. Med. J.*, **293**, 1472–1473.
Brettle R.P. *et al.* (1987) Human immunodeficiency virus and drug misuse: the Edinburgh experience. *Br. Med. J.*, **295**, 421–424.
Chambers H.F. *et al.* (1983) *Staphylococcus aureus* endocarditis: clinical manifestations in addicts and non-addicts. *Medicine (Baltimore)*, **62**, 170–177.
Chandrasekar P.H. and Narula A.P. (1986) Bone and joint infection in intravenous drug abusers. *Rev. Infect. Dis.*, **8**, 904–911.
Cregler L.L. and Mark H. (1986) Medical complications of cocaine abuse. *New Engl. J. Med.*, **315**, 1495–1500.
Ghodse A.H. *et al.* (1981) Drug-related problems in London accident and emergency departments. *Lancet*, **2**, 859–862.
Glassroth J. *et al.* (1986) The impact of substance abuse on the respiratory system. *Chest*, **91**, 596–602.
Horn E.H. *et al.* (1987) Admissions of drug addicts to a general hospital: a retrospective study in the northern district of Glasgow. *Scott. Med. J.*, **32**, 41–45.
Kunches, L.M. *et al.* (1986) Seroprevalence of hepatitis B virus and delta agent in parenteral drug abusers. Immunogenicity of hepatitis B vaccine. *Amer. J. Med.*, **81**, 591–595.

Lancashire M.J.R. *et al.* (1988) Surgical aspects of international drug smuggling. *Br. Med. J.*, **296**, 1035–1037.

Lancet (1988) Editorial. Complications of chronic volatile substance abuse. *Lancet*, **2**, 431–432.

Louria D.B. *et al.* (1967) The major medical complications of heroin addiction. *Ann. Int. Med.*, **67**, 1–22.

Marks J. and Parry A. (1987) Syringe exchange programme for drug addicts. *Lancet*, **1**, 691–692.

Miller D. (1987) *Living with AIDS and HIV* (London: Macmillan).

Neugarten J. *et al.* (1986) Amyloidosis in subcutaneous heroin abusers ('skin poppers' amyloidosis'). *Amer. J. Med.*, **81**, 635–640.

Novick D.M. *et al.* (1986) Chronic liver disease in abusers of alcohol and parenteral drugs: a report of 204 consecutive biopsy proven cases. *Alcoholism (NY)*, **10**, 500–505.

Raimondo G. *et al.* (1982) Multicentre study of prevalence of HBV-associated delta infection and liver disease in drug addicts. *Lancet*, **1**, 249–251.

Reisberg B.E (1979) Infective endocarditis in the narcotic addict. *Progr. Cardiovasc. Dis.*, **XXIII**, 193–204.

Robertson J.R. *et al.* (1988) HIV infection in intravenous drug abusers: a follow up study indicating changes in risk-taking behaviour. *Br. J. Addiction*, **83**, 387–391.

Watson J.M. (1986) *Solvent Abuse. The Adolescent Epidemic?* (London: Croom Helm).

Yeager R.A. *et al.* (1987) Vascular complications related to drug abuse. *J. Trauma*, **27**, 305–308.

Young L.S. (1987) Treatable aspects of infection due to human immunodeficiency virus. *Lancet*, **2**, 1503–1506.

9

Substance Abuse and Psychiatric Problems

James Edeh

Synopsis

Most people who self-medicate are polydrug abusers. It is therefore relevant to consider aspects of psychopathology complicating dependence on multiple drugs and then proceed to examine separately the psychiatric complications of each specific class of drugs and the social consequences.

The changing drug scene presents an intriguing picture. Bromide abuse and dependence on barbiturates and methaqualone appear to have faded into the past, but drugs previously unrecognised for their abuse-dependence potential, for example benzodiazepines, dihydrocodeine and buprenorphine, are now in fashion. The pattern of use, such as sharing of injecting equipment or the practice of cocaine freebasing, and the availability of designer drugs produced by sinister molecular modifications, add new dimensions to a catalogue of complications, a clear understanding of which is essential to clinical evaluation and treatment of patients. More recently, Ecstasy (MDMA, i.e. 3,4-methylenedioxymethamphetamine), a synthetic analogue of MDA (3,4-methylenedioxyamphetamine), has become a popular recreational drug, particularly among party goers, to induce euphoria or increase sociability.

Psychopathology complicating dependence on multiple drugs

Drug-induced and drug-withdrawal psychoses

The clinical presentation of drug-induced psychosis varies considerably depending on the substance used. Unlike most toxic states, the patient suffering from amphetamine psychosis is usually well orientated, retains intact memory function and appropriate level of consciousness and is not confused (Connell, 1966). Symptoms abate rapidly on cessation of drug use. Except for delusions there is usually no progressive deterioration of thought process. Stereotyped body movements are common. There may be haptic hallucinations or delusions of infestation by microorganisms, although these are more common in cocaine psychosis. With high doses of amphetamines or a mixture of amphetamines and other drugs, there may be a transient toxic psychosis superimposed on the amphetamine reaction so that delirium, confusion and disorientation become manifest.

In cannabis and LSD psychoses, perceptual changes, visual illusions, hallucinations and depersonalisation are more marked, and flashbacks may occur several months after drug ingestion.

A drug-withdrawal psychosis typically occurs with sedative–hypnotics, particularly barbiturates and alcohol. There is marked delirium, disorientation, insomnia, and visual and sometimes auditory hallucinations. Some patients withdrawing from benzodiazepines have described hallucinatory experiences.

Depression and anxiety

Dependence on drugs may coexist with affective symptoms which may become more pronounced during drug withdrawal or detoxification. Clinical experience with heroin addicts on methadone treatment gives the impression that many use drugs for the relief of anxiety and/or depression. These symptoms are at times manifest but may be masked. Reduction in methadone regimens often results in increased affective disturbance.

McLellan *et al.* (1979) reported increased depression scores in patients with sedative–hypnotic dependence compared with opiate or stimulant users. Female subjects and those with low socio-economic status predominated, so that acute life stress situations as well as drug effect may be contributory. Profound depression may follow withdrawal from stimulant drugs, such as amphetamines, and may be resistant to treatment with tricyclic antidepressants.

Personality characteristics and deterioration

Earlier work on the personality characteristics of drug addicts focused on their ego pathology and inability to deal with narcissistic crisis and aggression. 'Addictive' personalities (inebriates) were thought to lack impulse control and resort readily to drug-taking and abuse of other substances. Dependence on potent drugs is then followed by a gradual downward slide in psychosocial functioning, disturbance of interpersonal relationships, delinquency and criminality, with a possibility for 'maturing-out' of this process as age advances, in either the late thirties or early forties. Other views, supported by high P scores on the Eysenck Personality Inventory (EPI), associate assertiveness, aggression, hostility and coldness to human relationships with drug-taking. More recent work disproves the concept of the addictive personality. The finding (Steer and Schut, 1979) that only 23.3% of heroin addicts displayed extreme levels of hostility also brings into question the theory that hostility is a primary affect underlying addiction.

Other aspects of personality disturbance deserve mention; substance use and dependence in Munchausen syndrome or in eating disorders (anorexia nervosa and bulimia) pose intriguing questions. It has been suggested that a disorder of impulse control manifesting with compulsive gambling may occur intermittently and simultaneously with substance abuse and severe psychiatric disability. Pathological spending (Glatt and Cook, 1987) shares some similarities with pathological gambling as a form of psychological dependence incorporating the element of thrill or sensation seeking.

Deliberate self-poisoning and suicidal behaviour

Suicidal behaviour in association with drug dependence has been estimated at 5 to 17 times higher than expected in the general population (Murphy et al., 1983). There is a high correlation between the prescription of drugs and their selectivity for overdosage, which suggests that availability is a good predictor of which drug will be used for deliberate self-poisoning.

The pattern of drug overdose and mortality over the past three decades provides a fascinating narrative on the changing trend in drug-using behaviour. Bewley et al. (1968) reported only 69 known deaths of non-therapeutic heroin addicts up to the end of 1966; most deaths were attributed to overdose, suicide and septic complications. Methylamphetamine or cocaine mixture with heroin was incriminated as a factor in these deaths. Ghodse et al. (1978) reported 134 deaths from drug addiction investigated by coroners in Greater London (January 1970 to December 1974); over three-quarters were aged 30 years or under; 78% were male and barbiturate overdose accounted for over half of the deaths.

A striking reduction in the misuse of barbiturates, more related to reduced availability of prescriptions for hypnotic drugs over the past decade, is reflected in a decrease in the number of drug-dependent individuals presenting in the accident and emergency departments of London's hospitals with repeated overdoses (Ghodse et al., 1986). However, the reduction in the proportion of overdoses involving barbiturate hypnotics appears to have been achieved against the background of increased episodes of self-poisoning with minor tranquillisers, especially the benzodiazepines.

Sexual dysfunction

Although intravenous opiate addicts (those addicted to heroin, morphine, methadone, etc.) often equate their drug experience with sexual orgasm, diminished libido and impaired sexual performance are common sequelae of prolonged dependence. Male heroin addicts on methadone treatment generally report decreased interest in sex, impotence and delayed ejaculation; females complain of amenorrhoea. It has been suggested (*American Journal of Psychiatry*, 1980) that suppression of luteinising hormone (LH) release from the pituitary followed by a secondary drop in plasma testosterone levels is the basis of reduced sexual performance in the male patient. Cocaine is reputed to enhance sexual pleasure or induce hypersexuality but a decrease in sexual performance is associated with long-term use.

Gossop *et al.* (1974) compared sexual functioning in two groups of 54 patients with equal numbers of male and female users of narcotics ($N = 30$) and amphetamines ($N = 24$). Intravenous narcotic users showed a greater disturbance of sexual activity. Females as a group were more impaired; however, there was no difference in the incidence of sexual perversion between the groups on narcotics and amphetamines.

Cognitive impairment

The relationship between dependence on psychoactive drugs and cerebral deficits has been extensively investigated but the results are inconclusive. The suggestion that cannabis causes brain damage has little or no validity. Similarly neuropsychological investigations of LSD users have yielded contradictory findings. The most consistent data on cerebral dysfunction in the drug-using population have been more closely related to dependence on alcohol and sedative–hypnotics. Even in a population of polydrug abusers, few have shown cerebral deficits.

Opiates given in doses commonly used in clinical practice have no measurable EEG effects and do not impair cognitive functioning or performance of visual and motor-perceptual tasks (Hendler *et al.*, 1980). By contrast, dependence on sedative–hypnotics (barbiturates and benzodiazepines) in heroin addicts is more likely to produce cognitive impairment.

Acquired Immune Deficiency Syndrome (AIDS)

Intravenous drug use and the sharing of injecting equipment have been identified as important in the transmission of the human immunodeficiency virus (HIV). Features of HIV infection vary from the acute viral illness and antibody detection in some individuals to asymptomatic status in others, AIDS-related complex (ARC) or frank AIDS, as the end-stage, manifested commonly by opportunistic infections and tumours (e.g. *Pneumocystis carinii* pneumonia and Kaposi's sarcoma, respectively).

Depression, toxic confusional state and dementia described in the non-addict population have also been reported among intravenous drug abusers. In addition, patients with neurotic and paranoid premorbid personalities may present with AIDS phobia (AIDS panic or AIDS-induced psychogenic state). However, attitudes among drug addicts to the risk of AIDS appear polarised. Ghodse *et al.* (1987) observed that a hard core of drug abusers continues to share syringes despite the risk of AIDS. The authors studied two overlapping groups (Table 9.1): those who use syringes after someone else and those who allow others to use their syringes. The data suggest that sharing of syringes is associated with a feeling of community among drug users and not only with a shortage of injecting equipment, and is therefore unlikely to be influenced by needle/syringe exchange schemes. Prevention of HIV infection among intravenous drug abusers must emphasise, in addition to other measures, health education and AIDS-related behaviour change.

Table 9.1 Sharing of injection equipment by 212 drug abusers (Ghodse *et al.*, 1987)

	Number (%) using injection equipment after someone else	Number (%) allowing someone else to use injection equipment after themselves
Never	35 (16)	61 (29)
Previously but no longer	158 (75)	87 (41)
Yes but only with someone well known	11 (5)	40 (19)
Yes with anyone	8 (4)	24 (11)
Total	212 (100)	212 (100)

Psychiatric complications of specific drugs

Opiates

Dependence on opiates (heroin, morphine, methadone, etc.) as a medical and social problem is often recognised because of widespread infections which may complicate parenteral self-administration, and because of the financial difficulties, criminality, strained relationships and general social instability consequent on a drug-using lifestyle. The rapid development of tolerance and dependence results in withdrawal symptoms on abrupt cessation of drug use or relative abstinence. Heroin overdose may occur if a regular user stops for a time and then resumes drug use at a previous dose level.

The nature of psychopathology in opiate dependence is not clearly understood, but psychiatric assessment using standardised instruments points to significant depression, anxiety and antisocial tendencies, and may partly explain the concomitant abuse of other substances. Dependence on alcohol and sedative–hypnotics in heroin addicts on methadone treatment has a high incidence of medical complications and mortality and presents a serious therapeutic challenge. The prevalence of problematic alcohol use has been reported to range from 10% to over 50% depending on the characteristics of the treatment population (Roszell *et al.*, 1986).

Barbiturates

These drugs, generally classified as short-acting (heptabarbitone), medium-acting (amylobarbitone (Amytal) and pentobarbitone (Nembutal)) and long-acting (phenobarbitone) have a depressant effect on the central nervous system varying from mild sedation to profound sleep and unconsciousness. There is an upper limit to the dose of barbiturate to which tolerance develops so that intoxication is a common feature of dependence. A withdrawal syndrome develops usually 8–36 hours after the last dose, and in serious cases may lead to convulsion and drug-withdrawal psychosis marked by delirium, disorientation and visual hallucination.

Barbiturate overdosage, deliberate or accidental, reached alarming proportions in the 1960s and 1970s. A voluntary curb on prescribing in the mid-1970s, and the inclusion of barbiturates in 1985 within the controls of the Misuse of Drugs Act, have taken the steam out of concern over their use. However, barbiturates continue to appear in street heroin, and therefore the danger of a fatal overdose persists.

Non-barbiturate hypnotics

Before barbiturates were replaced by benzodiazepines, a number of non-barbiturate hypnotics (e.g. glutethimide, meprobamate, methaqualone) became available and were thought to be relatively safe, but proved to be equally dangerous. Methaqualone (Mandrax) became a common drug of abuse and dependence, and in some subjects produced psychotic behaviour.

Benzodiazepines

About one and a quarter million of the UK population take benzodiazepines (e.g. diazepam (Valium), chlordiazepoxide (Librium) and lorazepam (Ativan)) for more than a year (Lader and Higgitt, 1986). These drugs are primarily used for treatment of anxiety and insomnia, relief of muscle tension and as anticonvulsants.

Benzodiazepines have a place in the emergency treatment of stress reactions and disturbed behaviour, but measured against the benefits the risk of short-term prescribing may impair psychological functioning, including psychomotor performance, central processing ability and tasks involving vigilance. Anterograde amnesia may occur even on therapeutic doses and could promote mental mechanism of denial in situations of unresolved conflict, such as acceptance of loss and bereavement. Psychological dependence develops rapidly but physical dependence may be masked until an abstinence syndrome manifests when drug use is abruptly terminated, and this is more likely to occur with the short-acting benzodiazepines. Sixty per cent of patients who stop benzodiazepines after several months' treatment will have no withdrawal effects, 10% return to their pre-existing anxiety levels and 30% have a withdrawal syndrome (Tyrer, 1987).

Benzodiazepine withdrawal syndrome is clearly distinguishable from the re-emergence of pre-existing anxiety and characteristically comprises insomnia, headaches, sweating, difficulty in concentrating, tremors, muscle spasms, sensory disturbance and panic attacks. Rebound anxiety, rebound insomnia, increase in REM sleep and dysphoria almost invariably follow abrupt drug withdrawal. Epileptic seizures, hallucinatory experiences and confusional states may occur. Depression may either have been present and not diagnosed prior to prescribing or follow long-term use. Chronic benzodiazepine dependence may cause cognitive dysfunction, though neurophysiological tests and computerised tomography (CT scanning) have shown conflicting findings.

Cocaine

A single dose of cocaine produces a brief euphoric state followed by a depression and a strong desire to continue to use it. As with other psychoactive drugs, the direct physical and behavioural risks of cocaine are dependent on dose, route of administration and pattern of use. Cocaine chewing and sniffing or snorting have traditionally been the main routes of self-administration. More recently, intravenous injection, sometimes in combination with heroin (speedball), and inhalation (smoking) of pure cocaine 'freebase' or 'crack' as distinct from the salt/acid (cocaine hydrochloride) are becoming the preferred routes of administration, with potential for rapid overdose.

Feelings of hyperactivity and hypersexuality are often associated with cocaine. High doses may cause anxiety, irritability and sleep and appetite disturbance, and ultimately a drug-induced psychosis with paranoid and schizophrenia-like features. Psychic dependence commonly occurs, but evidence for a physical dependence is less convincing. Feelings of insects or bugs under the skin (Magnan's signs or cocaine bugs) are characteristic, particularly during chronic, heavy cocaine use. Drug withdrawal results in rapid improvement, although depression and apathy (the 'crash') may follow.

Amphetamines

The administration of low doses of amphetamines (Benzedrine, Dexedrine, Methedrine) has been reported to exacerbate psychotic symptoms in schizophrenic patients, as well as to cause a paranoid psychosis in otherwise healthy individuals. Connell (1966) described a paranoid psychosis in a setting of clear consciousness, and associated with stereotyped movements and haptic hallucinations, although very rarely a toxic confusional state may be seen. In a majority of cases, amphetamine taking may only manifest with acute anxiety states, restlessness, rapid or slurred speech, unusual cheerfulness or euphoria, teeth-grinding movements, insomnia, anorexia, weight loss, and ataxia. On cessation of drug taking a protracted depression may supervene; this is more likely to occur with methylphenidate (Ritalin), closely related to amphetamine, and a combination of amphetamines, e.g. Durophet.

Sympathomimetic drugs such as ephedrine and other amphetamine-related compounds exert similar effects. Fresh leaves of the khat shrub commonly chewed by ethnic minorities from East Africa and the Arab emirates contain cathinone, chemically related to amphetamine, and have stimulant properties. Abuse often leads to psychic dependence, elevation of mood, anorexia and insomnia, and in extreme cases a paranoid psychosis.

Lysergic acid diethylamide (LSD)

Bewley (1967) classified the adverse reactions to LSD into three groups:

(i)   acute panic reactions;
(ii) recurrence of symptoms while abstaining from the drug, more likely to occur after multiple ingestion;
(iii) prolonged psychosis.

LSD experience depends largely on the characteristics of the user, his or her expectations and the setting. Typically there are changes in perception, commonly visual, and these are often illusions though hallucinations may occur. The intensity and content of the experience may be rewarding or frightening (a 'bad trip'), and accidental death or suicide has been known to occur during acute panic reactions. Flashbacks or spontaneous re-occurrence of LSD-induced experience may follow drug use, several months after initial exposure. Similar effects have been reported with other hallucinogenic drugs such as mescalin and psilocybin.

Cannabis

The role of cannabis in the escalation of drug abuse and dependence has been a subject of speculation. The question of dose–effect relationship also remains unanswered, and whether cannabis causes a psychosis in an otherwise healthy subject or merely precipitates abnormal behaviour in a predisposed individual. Smoking of cannabis as a recreational activity has a high prevalence in the age group 15–34 years, and a large population use it regularly without adverse effect. It is argued that antisocial behaviour, abuse of alcohol and depression associated with chronic use of cannabis tend to precede rather than complicate psychic dependence. 'Reversed tolerance' to cannabis has been described, but its clinical significance is unclear in view of the persistence of cannabinoids in the body long after supervised abstinence. Adverse effects on memory and the possibility of brain damage have no firm support. The 'amotivational syndrome' characterised by a diminution in ambition, productivity and motivation has been described in chronic users.

There is an abundance of literature in support of the view that cannabis can give rise to acute short-lived psychosis, though a chronic psychosis persisting long after drug use has ceased is less convincing (Edwards, 1983; Ghodse, 1986). Cannabis psychosis typically presents with complex perceptual distortions, depersonalisation, derealisation, transcendental experience, affective disturbance, panic and a paranoid colouring. Flashbacks may occur spontaneously or may be precipitated by further cannabis use.

Phencyclidine hydrochloride

Phencyclidine (angel dust), commonly used in the USA, is associated with aggressive, impulsive, dangerous and violent behaviour, including murder and self-mutilation. It was originally found to produce a state of serenity in laboratory monkeys. Early research was directed at its use as a surgical anaesthetic for humans and then as a veterinary tranquilliser. Smoked in crystal form, with or without cannabis, it produces hyperactivity, euphoria, and hypomanic, delusional and hallucinatory states.

Volatile substances

Despite advances in laboratory detection of a variety of volatile hydrocarbons and their classification by chemical composition and pathology, studies of psychiatric complications have lagged behind those of central nervous system (CNS) and systemic toxicity. Toluene, the main ingredient of glues and other volatile compounds, has been frequently implicated. Ron (1986) provides an impressive review of relevant literature.

Acute psychological effects of volatile substance abuse (VSA) are similar to those observed in alcoholic intoxication, notably an initial excitatory effect on the CNS followed by a depressive phase, illusions, delirium, and perceptual and behavioural disturbances. Accidents and assaults may occur in a state of impaired judgement, ataxia and feelings of omnipotence. Chronic encephalopathy and cerebellar degeneration with cognitive impairments have been described. It is generally agreed that VSA is largely a group activity and is usually a transient phenomenon, most users being in the age group 10–19 years. Dependence is almost entirely psychological and only a minority progress to illicit drugs and alcohol. Affective symptoms are marked and those who show delinquent behaviour or psychiatric morbidity tend to be solitary users and come from disturbed family background.

Approved recreational drugs

A detailed discussion of the psychiatric complication of dependence on alcohol is beyond the scope of this present chapter and readers should refer to a standard text. Chlormethiazole, often prescribed to suppress the alcohol withdrawal syndrome, has abuse-dependence potential and should be prescribed with caution. Fatal poisoning in chronic problem drinkers on chlormethiazole maintenance treatment has been reported (Horder, 1978).

Cessation of cigarette smoking in most people results in anxiety, irritability, inability to concentrate, hunger and a craving for cigarettes. Helping people to stop smoking must first deal with an overwhelming anticipation of failure. In neurotic individuals, conflicts previously obscured or masked may re-emerge. Anxiety, restlessness and insomnia may also occur with heavy consumption of caffeine (caffeinism), and symptoms of caffeine withdrawal have been described. Excessive use of caffeine in chronic psychiatric patients may cause exacerbation of their symptoms.

Miscellaneous substances with abuse-dependence potential

Psychic dependence on anticholinergic drugs (benzhexol (Artane), benztropine (Cogentin), procyclidine (Kemadrin), etc.) may give rise to a toxic psychosis, particularly among thrill-seeking adolescents. Expectorants often used to suppress unproductive coughs may contain codeine, dextromethorpan (Terpin), pseudoephedrine or antihistamine, and in conditions of abuse and dependence may cause a toxic psychosis. Abuse of steroids in sports is a growing problem, and steroid psychosis should be considered in circumstances of bizarre behaviour. It is indeed impossible to give an exhaustive list of drugs with dependence potential; some currently unrecognised are added to the list from time to time.

Social impact of drug dependence

For the individual the stigma of being labelled an addict is as much a social hurdle as the difficulty in giving up the drug-using lifestyle itself. Fear of disclosure of the habit to family and friends often results in attempts at concealment; the individual is forced into the status of an unwilling liar. Disclosure either by chance or intention may lead to strained relationships and alienation. Finding money to maintain the drug habit often results in debts, criminal activities and prostitution. Many drug addicts live in squats and are unemployed; suicide and mortality are higher than expected for the general population. The medical and legal cost to society, the value of property lost through burglary and shoplifting, and social security payments add up to a colossal sum and a huge slice of the British economy. With the growing problem of HIV infection and AIDS, there is a need to re-think preventive strategies and to keep the measures adopted under constant review.

References

American Journal of Psychiatry (1980) Editorial. Sex and heroin. *Amer. J. Psychiat.*, **137**, 951–952.

Bewley T.H. (1967) Adverse reactions to illicit use of lysergide. *Br. Med. J.*, **iii**, 28–30.

Bewley T.H., Ben-Arie O. and James I.P. (1968) Morbidity and mortality from heroin dependence. I: Survey of heroin addicts known to Home Office. *Br. Med. J.*, **i**, 725–726.

Connell P.H. (1966) Clinical manifestations and treatment of amphetamine type of dependence. Symposium: Non-narcotic addiction. *J. Amer. Med. Assoc.*, **196**, 718–723.

Edwards G. (1983) Psychopathology of a drug experience. *Br. J. Psychiat.*, **143**, 509–512.

Ghodse, A.H. (1986) Cannabis psychosis. *Br. J. Addiction*, **81**, 473–478.

Ghodse, A.H., Sheehan M., Stevens B., Taylor C. and Edwards G. (1978) Mortality among drug addicts in Greater London. *Br. Med. J.*, **ii**, 1742–1744.

Ghodse H., Stapleton J., Edwards G., Bewley T. and Al-Samarrai M. (1986) A comparison of drug-related problems in London Accident and Emergency Departments, 1975–1982. *Br. J. Psychiat.*, **148**, 658–662.

Ghodse A.H., Tregenza G. and Li M. (1987) Effect of fear of AIDS on sharing injection equipment among drug abusers. *Br. Med. J.*, **ii**, 698–699.

Glatt M. and Cook C.C.H. (1987) Pathological spending as a form of psychological dependence. *Br. J. Addiction*, **82**, 1257–1258.

Gossop M.R., Stern R. and Connell P.H. (1974) Drug dependence and sexual dysfunction. A comparison of intravenous users of narcotics and oral users of amphetamines. *Br. J. Psychiat.*, **124**, 431–432.

Hendler N., Cimini C.T. and Long D. (1980) A comparison of cognitive impairment due to benzodiazepines and to narcotics. *Amer. J. Psychiat.*, **137**, 828–830.

Horder J.M. (1978) Fatal chlormethiazole poisoning in chronic alcoholics. *Br. Med. J.*, **i**, 693–694.

Lader M.H. and Higgitt A.C. (1986) Management of benzodiazepine dependence—update. *Br. J. Addiction*, **81**, 7–10.

McLellan A.T., Woody G.E. and O'Brien C.P. (1979) Development of psychiatric disorders in drug abusers. *New Engl. J. Med.*, **301**, 1310–1314.

Murphy S.L., Rounsaville B.J., Eyre S. and Kleber H.D. (1983) Suicide attempts in treated opiate addicts. *Comp. Psychiat.*, **24**, 79–89.

Ron M.A. (1986) Volatile substance abuse: a review of possible long-term neurological, intellectual and psychiatric sequelae. *Br. J. Psychiat.*, **148**, 235–246.

Roszell D.K., Calsyn D.A. and Chaney E.F. (1986) Alcohol use and psychopathology in opioid addicts on methadone maintenance. *Amer. J. Drug Alcohol Abuse*, **12**, 269–278.

Steer R.A. and Schut J. (1979) Types of psychopathology displayed by heroin addicts. *Amer. J. Psychiat.*, **136**, 1463–1465.

Tyrer P. (1987) Benefits and risk of benzodiazepines. In *The Benzodiazepines in Current Clinical Practice*, eds Freeman H. and Rue Y., International Congress and Symposium Series (London: Royal Society of Medicine Services).

Bibliography

Edeh J. (1989) Volatile substance abuse in relation to alcohol and illicit drugs. Psychological perspectives. *Human Toxicol.*, **8**, 313–317.

Ghodse H. (1989) *Drugs and Addictive Behaviour: A Guide to Treatment* (Oxford: Blackwells).

The Royal College of Psychiatrists (1987) *Drug Scenes. A Report of Drugs and Drug Dependence* (London: Gaskell).

10
Problems of Maternal Substance Abuse

Hamid Ghodse

Synopsis

Interest in the effect of maternal drug abuse on the child dates back nearly a century when maternal addiction to morphine was the main problem. Since then the problem has diversified because of the phenomenon of multiple drug use and the higher prevalence of psychotropic drug use by women. Now, it involves a wide variety of drugs with a consequent complexity of the associated problems for both mother and child.

Maternal drug abuse may affect the child at every stage of its development: the intra-uterine environment may not be optimal, the neonatal period may be complicated by a drug withdrawal syndrome, and, if drug abuse continues, the child's physical, emotional and behavioural development may be adversely affected by growing up in a drug-taking environment. All of these problems have been compounded within the last decade by the advent of AIDS.

This chapter explores all of these areas but recognises that because drug abuse is often associated with environmental stress and/or personality disorder (and may be merely symptomatic of them), any adverse effects that are observed may not be due specifically to drug abuse but to the whole combination of circumstances, and that it is rarely possible to draw firm conclusions about causality. It follows that treatment approaches, while including the management of the drug problem, must be broad-based and sensitive to the specific needs of the individual mother and her child.

Introduction

The abuse of drugs by women of child-bearing age is not a new or even a surprising phenomenon, but, with the possible exception of the abuse of prescribed psychotropic drugs and 'over-the-counter' analgesics, male drug abusers have always outnumbered female drug abusers. This remains the case today but the gap is closing, so that most epidemiological studies now show a steadily increasing proportion of young females abusing a wide

216

range of drugs. This situation has serious implications not only for the women, often no more than girls, who are engaging in this dangerous practice, but also of course for the children whom they are likely to conceive. Any drug abuse by a pregnant woman or by a mother is always a cause for serious concern. That she should engage in such self-damaging behaviour is worrying enough, but the risk of harm to a vulnerable fetus, neonate, infant or child immediately intensifies that concern considerably.

General effects

There is a widely held belief that drug abuse is associated with low fertility. There is no doubt that this is true as far as opiate abuse is concerned because opiates interfere with ovulation, resulting in abnormal menstrual cycles or even amenorrhoea (Gaulden *et al.*, 1964; Stoffer *et al.*, 1969). This effect is probably mediated by the effect of opiates on the hypothalamus, and in opiate addicts pregnancy is most likely to occur when the woman is 'drug-free'—for example after release from prison. There is very little evidence about the effect of other drugs on fertility, but for all drug abusers it is very difficult to disentangle the pharmacological effects of their drugs of abuse from the effects of their lifestyle. For example, they may be poorly nourished, suffer from frequent infections and, constantly preoccupied with the need to obtain drugs, have a highly stressful existence. All of these factors may contribute to low fertility.

The infectious complications of drug abuse are well known and do not require repetition. In the context of drug abuse by women, however, it is important to remember that it is not uncommon for them to obtain the money they need to finance their drug habit by prostitution. Thus they are at particular risk from sexually transmitted diseases. At present, attention is mostly focused on AIDS but 'older' diseases, such as syphilis and hepatitis, are still around and still pose a threat to both the drug abuser and her unborn child. It is not only severely dependent addicts with an expensive drug habit who are at risk in this way. The altered mental state consequent on the abuse of psychoactive drugs may facilitate casual sexual relationships so that young drug abusers, perhaps experimenting with the new 'acid-house' culture but not (yet) physically dependent on drugs, may also be infected.

Integral to the problems of maternal drug abuse, at every stage, is the immaturity of the mother. Often, she is genuinely youthful—perhaps no more than a teenager—but even when she is chronologically older, immaturity of personality is frequently noted. She may be socially isolated because of her drug use and have little opportunity for role modelling. Pregnancy, labour, delivery and motherhood, all of which can be daunting even for mature women with good networks of social support, may be quite overwhelming for a drug abuser. She will undoubtedly require special care and support throughout pregnancy and probably for a long time after the baby is born, to offset her physical and emotional disadvantages so that she has the best possible chance of delivering a healthy child and of being a good parent.

Pregnancy

One immediate problem is that the diagnosis of pregnancy and hence the initiation of antenatal care may be delayed. An opiate abuser for example may attribute her amenorrhoea to her drug use and not realise that she is pregnant until well into pregnancy when her increasing weight and enlarging abdomen become apparent. Some women are so scared of the consequences of discovery of their drug abuse that they just stay away from all health-care professionals. This late presentation may be particularly disadvantageous for those living in poor environmental conditions and with poor nutrition who really need the vitamin and mineral supplementation routinely provided during pregnancy. Others may attend antenatal clinics but are frightened to admit their dependence and conceal it from obstetricians and other caring agencies.

Congenital abnormalities

One cause of severe anxiety to the pregnant drug abuser is the fear that her baby will suffer congenital deformity because of her drug taking. In fact there is little hard evidence that any of the common drugs of abuse are teratogenic. The drug that received most attention on this score was LSD because it can produce chromosomal damage in human leucocytes in culture and because abortion and congenital malformation follow its injection into rats, mice and hamsters (*British Medical Journal*, 1968). The significance of these observations for humans is not clear, and there is no firm evidence that LSD is teratogenic in man (Malleson, 1971; Fernandez *et al.*, 1974). Cannabis too has been suspected of causing limb deformities in humans (Tylden, 1973), but this is a condition of high background incidence so that anecdotal accounts of its occurrence in the children of cannabis abusers do not constitute conclusive evidence on this point. Furthermore, in a study which confirmed maternal reports of drug consumption by urine testing, Zuckerman *et al.* (1989) found that a positive urine assay for cannabis was not significantly associated with minor or major congenital abnormalities. There was, however, a suggestion, although not a statistically significant association, that women with a positive assay for cocaine were more likely to have a child with either a constellation of minor congenital abnormalities or one major abnormality.

It should be pointed out, however, that the majority of drug abusers are poly-drug abusers and may not know or recollect which drugs they took during the critical period of teratogen sensitivity, early in pregnancy. Even if they do remember, illicit drugs are often impure and may be contaminated with unidentified adulterants that may themselves be teratogenic. It is therefore extremely difficult to make categorical statements about the risk of congenital deformity in babies born to drug abusers. Although none of the common illicit drugs of abuse has been implicated as a specific teratogen, abusing drugs during pregnancy is a violation of the general principle that no unnecessary drugs should be taken at this time.

Fetal Alcohol Syndrome (FAS)

There is, however, no doubt that alcohol is a teratogen, causing a characteristic syndrome in affected fetuses. The essential features of the fetal alcohol syndrome (FAS) are growth deficiency, facial dysmorphia and central nervous system deficiency. Sulaiman *et al*. (1988) found that alcohol consumption equivalent to more than 120 g absolute alcohol per week, was related to shorter gestational age, smaller head circumference and smaller weight babies than those born to non-drinking mothers. Thus affected babies are 'small for dates' at birth, often with the impairment of growth affecting girth more than length, so that the baby seems undersized and skinny. After birth there may be a failure to thrive, despite every effort to improve growth, perhaps because the baby's body has less fatty tissue than normal. The facial appearance is also abnormal with a short palpebral fissure and hypoplastic upper lip; there may also be a short, upturned nose and flattened profile and sometimes cleft palate and hare lip are present. Central nervous system deficiency is manifest by mental retardation, and microcephaly is often obvious. The combination of a small head with the characteristic facial anomalies make FAS children an identifiable group. A number of other congenital abnormalities may also occur, involving the heart, the eye, the kidney or the external genitalia; haemangiomas may be seen on the skin (Clarren and Smith, 1978).

The mechanism of FAS is not known. It has been suggested that alcohol may cause a reduction in blood levels of glucose or oxygen to which the developing brain is sensitive. Alternatively, FAS may be due to a breakdown product of alcohol rather than to alcohol itself (Sclare, 1980). It appears, however, that there is a spectrum of severity of the effects of alcohol on the child, according to the level of daily consumption—although it it not clear whether binge drinking or sustained drinking is more harmful. Nor is it clear whether the use of other drugs in association with alcohol potentiates the teratogenic effect. This may be an important factor for drug abusers, many of whom take alcohol in combination with a whole range of other psychoactive substances.

Low birth weight

In numerical terms, a far greater problem than teratogenicity appears to be
that of low birth weight, which has frequently been reported in babies born
to women dependent on opiates (Finnegan, 1975; Ghodse et al., 1977).
Olofsson et al. (1983) reported that among 89 infants born to opiate-
addicted women, 20% were preterm and 31% were light for gestational
age, and there are many studies with similar findings (Gregg et al., 1988).
The significance of low birth weight is its association with infant morbidity
and mortality, but once again it is difficult to be sure whether these adverse
effects should be attributed to opiates or to the often unsatisfactory
lifestyle of the mother. It has been suggested, for example, that periodic
episodes of opiate withdrawal during pregnancy might restrict fetal growth
by reducing placental blood flow. Repeated episodes of infection and
maternal undernutrition might also be significant. Almost certainly, all of
these factors are important. In their study of the effect of maternal
consumption of cannabis and cocaine on the newborn, Zuckerman et al.
(1989) reported that the infants of women with a positive assay for either
drug weighed less at birth and were shorter than the infants of non-users.
In addition, babies born to cocaine users had a significantly higher
incidence of premature delivery and had a smaller head circumference,
perhaps indicating a smaller brain. In their discussion of the possible
mechanisms by which these drugs affect fetal growth, they point out that
even a single dose of cannabis, because of its long half-life, may lead to
prolonged exposure of the fetus to the drug. In addition cannabis, like
cigarette-smoking, may impair fetal oxygenation by substantially increasing blood carboxyhaemoglobin levels. Both cannabis and cocaine increase
maternal heart rate and blood pressure, and cocaine causes uterine
vasoconstriction—another cause of fetal hypoxia. The ability of cocaine to
cause low birth weight is independent of the maternal undernutrition which
is often present; this is partly due to the appetite-suppressant effect of
cocaine and partly to the lifestyle of many cocaine users.

Little is known about the effects of other drugs of abuse on intra-
uterine development, but many, probably the majority, of those who abuse
illicit drugs also smoke and drink alcohol regularly too. Both of these drugs
are known to be associated with low birth weight so that identifying the
specific effects of additional drugs is difficult.

Physical dependence

Special problems arise when the mother is physically dependent on a
particular class of drugs such as opiates or sedative–hypnotics and takes
them regularly during her pregnancy. If the drugs cross the placenta, which
many of them do, the fetus is constantly exposed to them too and

effectively becomes dependent on them, suffering withdrawal if the mother is deprived of her drugs. This may precipitate fetal distress or death or induce premature labour. On the other hand, if the mother takes a drug overdose, this may also affect the fetus adversely. Maternal dependence on sedative–hypnotic drugs is particularly hazardous for the fetus because it is often associated with a chaotic lifestyle and alternating episodes of intoxication and withdrawal with rapidly fluctuating blood levels of the drug.

AIDS in pregnancy

Another difficult problem that has to be confronted at this very sensitive time is AIDS. All pregnant addicts should be encouraged to be tested for HIV antibodies, and if positive should receive advice and counselling so that they can make an informed decision about whether to continue with the pregnancy or whether to seek termination. There is a 25–40% risk of the virus being transmitted from mother to fetus, the risk being higher if the woman is experiencing symptoms and has a low T4 count. Contrary to early beliefs, pregnancy does not appear to precipitate the onset of the illness nor to worsen the mother's prognosis. Unfortunately, information about the baby's HIV status is not available instantly at birth and indeed it may be some time before an unequivocal statement can be made about whether or not the baby is infected. Thus the pregnant addict has to cope with a long period of anxiety and guilt and is likely to need considerable support. Those who decide on termination of pregnancy have to come to terms with the fact that, in our present state of knowledge, it is highly unlikely that they will ever be able to have a child—a sadness they share with women who have been diagnosed as HIV-positive before becoming pregnant and who have decided not to have children. In addition to good family planning advice, these women, most of whom are likely to be very young, need special help to cope with their inevitable pain and grief.

Management of Pregnancy

There is no doubt that the preferred management of a pregnant drug addict is to help her to come off drugs as comfortably and as early in pregnancy as possible. Ideally, this will be achieved by at least 2 months before the expected date of delivery to ensure a non-addicted infant, even if there is some uncertainty about dates.

Opiate-dependent patients should be stabilised on methadone which should then be withdrawn gradually to avoid precipitating fetal distress or premature labour. The withdrawal programme should be individually tailored according to the severity of dependence, stage of pregnancy and the patient's motivation. Some patients may not be able to cope with being drug-free and some may present too late in pregnancy for complete withdrawal to be feasible. In this situation, the patient should be maintained on the lowest possible dose of oral methadone. Pregnant barbiturate addicts must be weaned off their drugs and encouraged to adopt a more stable lifestyle.

Amidst all the natural concern for the welfare of the fetus, it is important to remember that the mother is also very vulnerable. Normal fears about the health of her baby are compounded by feelings of guilt about the effects of her drug use and, in addition, she may be suffering grave doubts about her adequacy as a mother. It is not surprising that severe anxiety is common and, at a time of considerable emotional stress, when she probably feels more in need of her drugs than ever before, she is having to cope with drug withdrawal or at any rate dose reduction. Nevertheless her motivation to come off drugs may be high at this time because she knows that there is a greater risk of her newborn child being taken from her at birth, or at least being placed on the 'At Risk' register if she is still taking drugs at the time of birth.

Because of difficulties such as those described here, it is very important that all encounters between pregnant addicts and health-care professionals should be handled with tact and sensitivity so that these very vulnerable individuals are attracted into and are retained in treatment and that nothing deters them from seeking further help.

Birth and the neonate

Neonatal abstinence syndrome

In addition to the problems posed by prematurity and low birth weight are those due to a neonatal abstinence syndrome. This is most commonly seen in babies born to mothers dependent on opiates but also occurs with other types of physical dependency. It arises because the blood-borne supply of drugs on which the baby has also become dependent during its intra-uterine life is abruptly cut off at birth. Gregg *et al.* (1988) reported that it occurred in one-third of babies born to mothers who had inhaled heroin during pregnancy. Babies born to mothers dependent on opiates are hyperactive, irritable and restless with tremors and sometimes convulsions. They may have gastrointestinal disturbance with vomiting, and sleep disturbances, which persist after other manifestations of the abstinence syndrome have subsided, have also been reported (Pinto *et al.*, 1988). The onset of the neonatal abstinence syndrome depends very much on the duration of action of the opiate on which the mother is dependent. In an infant born to a heroin-dependent mother, signs are usually apparent within 24 hours, but may be delayed to the second or third day. In infants born to methadone-dependent mothers, the withdrawal syndrome does not usually start until 48–72 hours after birth and may be delayed even later. It is important to realise that the neonatal abstinence syndrome does not always occur and that its development depends on the dose of opiate being taken by the mother, the duration of her dependence and, to a certain extent, the timing of the last dose in relation to the time of delivery. Adulterants in drugs obtained illicitly may also affect the manifestations of the abstinence syndrome.

Treatment should be initiated if withdrawal signs are observed which progressively become more numerous or more severe. Chlorpromazine is generally recommended as the drug of choice, and once symptoms are well controlled the dose should be reduced in a step-wise fashion every two or three days. If the mother continues to take opiates, breast-feeding has been advocated on the grounds that they are believed to be secreted into breast milk and can thus ameliorate the abstinence syndrome. Theoretically, however, the administration of opiates in any form to the infant after delivery is contraindicated, and there is always a risk that any metabolic changes induced by exposure to them *in utero* may be accentuated by their continued use. Prophylactic treatment, with chlorpromazine or any other drug, is not recommended because it is unjustifiable to expose those who are not going to manifest the withdrawal syndrome, or those who will do so only mildly, to yet more unnecessary drugs. Instead the baby should be observed carefully so that, if signs of withdrawal do occur, they are recognised and treated promptly. Problems may arise when the mother's drug use is not known or suspected, so that diagnosis of the baby's condition is delayed.

Maternal dependence on sedative–hypnotic drugs such as barbiturates and benzodiazepines is also associated with a neonatal abstinence syndrome. The signs in the newborn baby are similar to those of opiate withdrawal but their onset is often delayed, sometimes for up to 4–7 days after birth, because of the long duration of action of many of these drugs. This delay may be dangerous as mother and baby may be discharged from hospital before the withdrawal syndrome becomes apparent, especially if the mother's dependent state was not diagnosed. If treatment is necessary, phenobarbitone is a logical choice to minimise the risk of convulsions, with the dose being reduced very gradually once the baby's condition has stabilised.

Stimulant drugs such as amphetamine and cocaine can also cause a neonatal abstinence syndrome although some of the signs once attributed to maternal amphetamine abuse may have been due to concomitant abuse of opiates—illustrating the difficulties of identifying the specific effects of particular drugs when poly-drug abuse is common. Babies born to cocaine users appear apathetic and listless.

The child

Whether or not the neonate experiences withdrawal, many studies have identified abnormal behavioural patterns in children exposed to drugs *in utero*. Perhaps this is only to be expected if that most delicate organ, the brain, is exposed to potent psychoactive substances throughout the vulnerable period of its development. Most studies have been concerned with children born to opiate-dependent mothers, but it would not be surprising if exposure to other psychoactive drugs were also detrimental.

For example, Householder *et al.* (1982) described babies born passively addicted as more irritable, more restless, more hyperactive, and experiencing more sleep and feeding difficulties than their non-addicted counterparts, and similar behaviour patterns were reported by Strauss and Reynolds (1983). Reduced cuddliness at 24 hours and increased tremulousness at 48 hours have also been described. With older children, developmental delays have been observed, particularly in habituation to visual stimuli and in complex motor skills (Davidson and Short, 1982), and Wilson *et al.* (1979) reported that preschool and school-age children who had been exposed to heroin *in utero* showed deficits in perception, quantitative skills and memory while their parents described them as impulsive, difficult, aggressive and lacking in self-control. Olofsson *et al.* (1983) who followed up 72 of 89 children born to opiate-addicted women for one to ten years after birth, found only 25% to be physically, mentally and behaviourally normal while 56% were hyperactive and aggressive with lack of concentration and social inhibition.

The development of these behavioural difficulties has a varied course. Householder *et al.* (1982) reported no symptoms between the ages of 4 to 6 months whereas Hans and Manus (1982/3), who reported on a longitudinal assessment at 4 and 12 months, found attention deficits emerging at 12 months when problems in motor coordination, that had been apparent at 4 months, were disappearing. They suggested that the earlier motor symptoms may have resulted from delayed or prolonged withdrawal, while the later attentional problems indicated a new, more permanent, neurobehavioural syndrome.

Of course when maternal drug use persists after birth and the neonatal period, it may be very difficult to distinguish the behavioural and developmental patterns which might be attributed to intra-uterine exposure to opiates from those which might be attributed to the impact of the mother's drug use on the child's environment. This distinction, between the direct toxic effects of the substance misused and the secondary environmental–interactive effects, is central to any exploration of the effects of parental drug use on children (Hutchings, 1985). Such an exploration is currently of the greatest importance: drug use is now widespread and attracts public condemnation and, at the same time, the subject of inadequate parenting and child abuse is at the forefront of public concern. The ability of drug abusers to care for their children is being questioned— sometimes in the courts.

For example, in December 1986, a 15-year-old Berkshire girl was received into care after she revealed to her teacher during a school discussion on drug abuse that her mother took heroin. At the initial hearing of the case the girl was deemed to be in 'moral danger' whilst being cared for by her mother who was receiving injectable methadone from a private doctor. Another case involved an addicted baby born to an opiate-dependent mother. The House of Lords ruled that the effect of a mother's drug addiction on her unborn baby can be taken into account by magistrates considering the care of the child if, and only if, the mother's drug misuse continues after the birth. This decision suggests that activities prior to a child's birth should not be seen as evidence of unsuitable parenting although, once the child is born, parental drug misuse may be seen as affecting the child's health and proper development and may therefore be a consideration in the court's decision regarding the child's future.

What is significant about both of these cases is that the courts saw parental drug misuse as an important factor in their assessment and their consequent decision to make and uphold care orders on both a baby and a 15-year-old. One should note, in passing, that this is routine in some countries where every child of a drug-using parent is perceived to be at risk of abuse or neglect by reason of their parents' drug taking. The opposite point of view is that children of drug users are no more or no less at risk than children born to any other group of parents, but undoubtedly the reality lies somewhere between these two opinions—that some children are at risk and some are not. Preliminary research suggests that abuse is no more common by drug-using parents than by the rest of the population, but that there is an increased incidence of injury as a result of accident associated with drug use.

In fact, information about the effect of parental drug abuse on children is hard to come by. While it is indisputable that being conceived, carried by and born to a woman who uses heroin or methadone may have serious physical consequences, and may place an infant temporarily at a disadvantage, far less is known about the consequences of opiate use by the mothers of children past the infant stage. Even less is known about the effects of other forms of drug abuse, and virtually nothing about the consequences of paternal drug abuse.

While studies have tended to focus on the negative, short-term effects of addiction during pregnancy, there have been few longitudinal investigations of the more long-term consequences. Of the studies carried out, a number lack adequate controls and often the parents', usually the mother's, drug use is the only variable considered. The Berkshire magistrates who deemed a 15-year-old to be in moral danger by virtue of her mother's methadone use would have been able to find scant evidence to support or refute their decision.

There are of course many studies apparently demonstrating that addicts make poor parents. For example Densen-Gerber and Rohrs (1973) state that addiction must be designated as a *prima facie* criterion of unfitness as a parent, but offer little evidence in support of their assertion. The report of a study carried out in the late 1960s by the Child Welfare Research Programme at Columbia University (Fanshel, 1975) levels some sweeping accusations at heroin-addicted parents describing them as unpredictable, unreliable, promiscuous and uncooperative. The study involved some 95 children with one or both parents addicted, who were placed in the care of the Jewish Child Care Association, New York. The findings are significant, but apply only to a specific group whose circumstances necessitated the children's removal from home. Hejanic *et al.* (1979) found that children raised in a home where the father is an opiate addict function cognitively less well, with teenagers showing earlier and stronger antisocial trends than their peers. They also noted a 'surprising' absence of 'other psychopathology' among the children of addicted parents.

However, the limitation of much of the work on parental drug use and its impact on children is its failure to acknowledge that drug use is often closely associated with other psychological and social problems. Thus, as well as substance-use disorders, the 18 methadone-maintained women described by Manus *et al.* (1984) were more likely to show evidence of other psychological dysfunctioning or personality disorders. Similarly, when Bauman and Dougherty (1983) compared 15 mothers on methadone maintenance and their 15 preschool children with 15 non-addicted mothers and their children, they found that the methadone-maintained women demonstrated personality characteristics such as impulsivity, irresponsibility, immaturity and self-centredness. Observations of their behaviour indicated that they exhibited a more threatening, disciplinarian attitude towards their children and that their children seemed to be more disruptive and hyperactive. In contrast, Colten (1982) found that addicted mothers seldom used physical punishment, and other studies have commented that addicted women fail to communicate adequately with their children, with some mothers actively avoiding communication (Wellish and Steinberg, 1980; Bernstein *et al.*, 1984).

These deficits in parenting, if and/or when they occur, should be seen in the psychosocial context in which they arise. A number of studies have drawn attention to the childhood experience of the addicted parent, frequently identifying significant disturbances. For example, maternal overprotection was reported by both opiate addicts and alcoholics (Bernardi *et al.*, 1989) although, according to these authors, the opiate addicts they studied experienced parenting which was more disturbed than that of the alcoholics and was more likely to include paternal overprotection. Lief

(1985) found that in most cases the addicted parent had as a child experienced impatient, harsh and ineffective discipline, and, having internalised this parental model, it was extremely difficult for them to adopt a different approach with their own child. Another observation was that drug addicts' mothers had severe difficulty in allowing the individuation of their child with whom they became overinvolved. Colten found that this failure to differentiate was perpetuated when the child grew up and became a parent so that they tended to rely on their own mother's support and assistance more heavily than their non-addicted counterparts. Similar childhood experiences were reported by another group of opiate addicts (Schweitzer and Lawton, 1989) who perceived their early parenting as 'high protection and low care' and judged their parents as cold, indifferent, controlling and insensitive.

Perhaps as a result, lack of confidence was commonly identified among addicted mothers. Rosenbaum (1979), for example, described pregnant addicts as beginning their careers as mothers with extreme guilt and a sense of failure. Colten commented that although these mothers did not differ in their feelings towards, and perceptions of, their children, nor in most of the activities they engaged in with them, they did differ in their perceptions of their own capabilities, demonstrating a high level of concern about the adequacy of the care they were offering. These doubts tend to be reinforced by the pervading public view of addicted mothers so that a sense of failure and low self-esteem, often deriving from the home experience, is reinforced by society at large (Escamilla-Mondanaro, 1977; Jeffries, 1983).

In situations such as these, it is frequently impossible to establish which is the cause and which is the effect in the relationship between poverty, deprivation, a disturbed family background, depression and the misuse of drugs. What is clear is that all are factors that are likely to affect parents' ability to care for their child.

Implications for treatment

Mothers who use drugs may have received poor parenting themselves, they may be living in poor environmental circumstances and they may be experiencing difficulties in their adult relationships. As a result of these background factors the addicted mother is likely to have a diminished opinion of herself as a parent. This, combined with a prevailing sense of guilt, is reinforced by society's indignation at the idea of an addicted mother.

It is likely that these feelings of inadequacy and fears for their children's future are central to the addicted mother both when she is pregnant and when the child is born. As a result of fear some women will avoid or delay seeking treatment of their addiction. They may fear that their feelings of inadequacy will be confirmed and that they will face condemnation and criticism and, at worst, that they will be seen as an unfit parent and the child(ren) taken away from them. There may also be other practical deterrents such as inadequate facilities for children attending treatment agencies with their parents, a lack of domiciliary services for parents tied to the home by young children, poor public transport and low income.

While the first responsibility of any agency involved with addicted or drug-abusing parents is to protect the well-being of the child, this may often be most effectively exercised in co-operation with the parent(s). Therefore, in order to protect the children, it is vitally important to encourage the parents to seek help. Services need to create an atmosphere of acceptance, and facilities must be provided that overcome some of the practical problems parents might encounter when seeking treatment. In the early stages of treatment it is sometimes useful to establish that the health-care professionals and parents have a shared objective: ensuring the health and happiness of the child(ren). Such a shared objective can help to create a working alliance and may facilitate the processes of assessment and the development of an appropriate treatment plan.

Because drug misuse occurs in families where other environmental, psychological and emotional problems also exist, a co-ordinated response involving various agencies is usually appropriate. The first stage is to make a thorough assessment of the family's problems, and from the start several disciplines need to be involved. In the case of a pregnant addict, the team would include antenatal and obstetric workers in addition to health-care professionals from the psychiatric, medical and child-care disciplines. An assessment should involve both community-based professionals—health visitor, general practitioner, community psychiatric nurse, social worker—and specialists from the local drug treatment agency—psychiatric nurse, psychiatrist, psychologist and social worker. There may also be other significant people who should be involved—the probation and education services or the police, for example. However, the benefits of casting the net wide and involving as many parties as possible must be weighed against the addicts' right to a confidential service. Where child abuse or neglect has been identified, the parent(s) have automatically waived their right to confidentiality. In cases where neglect or abuse is not apparent, decisions have to be made in accordance with what seems to be in the child's best interests. It is important that responsibility for co-ordinating an assessment be clearly established. Where abuse or neglect has occurred, this responsibility will lie with the local authority, but in other cases it may be necessary to appoint an individual to take on the responsibility.

As with any child-care assessment, attention should be paid to both the physical and emotional care offered by the addicted parent(s). In addition to the aspects of care usually addressed, the impact of the parents' drug misuse on the functional and emotional life of the family needs to be explored in detail. Once a picture of the family's pattern of life has been established, intervention may be planned which protects the child(ren) from risk and builds on the strengths within the family and its network.

It is important, for example, to establish who is the prime carer, whether he or she is involved in drug misuse and what drugs are being used and how. If the drugs are of reliable quality and are being used in a 'stable' way, the impact on the care of the child(ren) may be less than an unstable and erratic pattern of use involving alternating periods of intoxication and withdrawal.

When parents recognise and acknowledge the potential impact their drug misuse might have on their capacity to provide adequate care for their child(ren), it is more likely that a working alliance may be established between the family and the social/medical agencies. However, when parents deny the potential effects and risks, the task of ensuring the child's safety and well-being is made more difficult.

Generally it is not appropriate for parents to involve their children in the practices and rituals surrounding their drug misuse. A worker making an assessment may need to explore in some detail how, for example, the drugs are procured: whether the parents take the child(ren) with them when they go to buy drugs or whether they leave them alone in unsafe circumstances. It is also important to establish whether the parents become intoxicated in the presence of their child(ren) and, if they do, if the children are then at risk within the home. The children may, for example, be at risk of infection or accident as a result of needles and drugs being left about the home.

The worker may also wish to explore the types of interaction that occur within the family. Does the parental drug misuse affect the degree and quality of the interactions between parent and child? Are the children expected to assume duties and responsibilities above and beyond those that are appropriate for their age? Are the parents able to place the needs of their children above their own desire to use drugs?

The aspects of family life mentioned here are not intended to represent a complete list of the ways in which a child might be affected by growing up in a drug-taking environment, but they serve as an indication of how a child may be put at risk. This risk is obviously greater if it is the main care-provider (or the only care-provider in a single parent family), usually the mother, who is dependent on drugs, although many of the risk factors are independent of which parent is involved. The age of the child concerned is also relevant. Younger children are at greater physical risk of neglect and of accidental injury, and there may be clear evidence of failure to thrive. Older children, although better able to fend for themselves physically, are more likely to recognise drug-taking and to understand its significance, and so may be more emotionally vulnerable.

In summary, therefore, while parental drug misuse does not necessarily result in child abuse or neglect, it indicates that the family is in need of special attention and that it may require particular support. The challenge facing agencies and individuals working with families where drug misuse occurs is to protect the children whilst avoiding reinforcing feelings of alienation and inadequacy in the parents.

References

Bauman P. and Dougherty F. (1983) Drug-addicted mothers' parenting and their children's development. *Int. J. Addictions*, **18**, 291–302.

Bernardi E. *et al.* (1989) Quality of parenting in alcohol and narcotic addicts. *Br. J. Psychiat.*, **154**, 677–682.

Bernstein V. *et al.* (1984) A longitudinal study of offspring born to methadone-maintained women. Dyadic interaction and infant behaviour at 4 months. *Amer. J. Drug and Alcohol Abuse*, **10**, 161–193.

British Medical Journal (1968) Editorial. LSD and chromosomes. *Br. Med. J.*, **2**, 778–779.

Clarren S.K. and Smith D.W. (1978) The fetal alcohol syndrome. *New Engl. Med. J.*, **298**, 1063–1067.

Colten M.E. (1982) Attitudes, experiences and self perceptions of heroin addicted mothers. *J. Social Issues*, **38**, 77–92.

Davidson D.A. and Short M.A. (1982) Developmental effects of perinatal heroin and methadone addiction. *Phys. Occup. Ther. Paediat.*, **2**, 1–10.

Densen-Gerber J. and Rohrs C. (1973) Drug addicted parents and child abuse. *Contemp. Drug Probl.*, **2**, 683–695.

Escamilla-Mondanaro J. (1977) Women: pregnancy, children and addiction. *J. Psychedelic Drugs*, **9**, No. 1.

Fanshel D. (1975) Parental failure and consequences for children. The drug-abusing mother whose children are in foster care. *Amer. J. Public Health*, **65**, 604–612.

Fernandez J. *et al.* (1974) Cytogenetic studies in the offspring of LSD users. *Br. J. Psychiat.*, **124**, 296–298.

Finnegan L.P. (1975) Narcotics dependence in pregnancy. *J. Psychedelic Drugs*, **7**, 299–311.

Gaulden E.C. *et al.* (1964) Menstrual abnormalities associated with heroin addiction. *Amer. J. Obstet. Gynecol.*, **90**, 155–160.

Ghodse A.H. *et al.* (1977) The effect of maternal narcotic addiction on the newborn infant. *Psychol. Med.* **7**, 667–675.

Gregg J.E.M. *et al.* (1988) Inhaling heroin during pregnancy: effect on the baby. *Br. Med. J.*, **i**, 754.

Hans S.L. and Manus J. (1982/3) Motoric and attentional behaviour in infants of methadone maintained women. *Probl. Drug Dependence*, 287–293.

Hejanic B.M. *et al.* (1979) Children of heroin addicts. *Int. J. Addictions*, **14**, 919–931.

Householder J. *et al.* (1982) Infants born to narcotic-addicted mothers. *Psychol. Bull.*, **92**, 453–468.

Hutchings D.E. (1985) Prenatal opioid exposure and the problems of causal inference. In *Current Research on the Consequences of Maternal Drug Abuse* (NIDA Research Monograph No. 59), ed. Pinkert T.M. (Rockville, MD: NIDA), pp. 6–19.

Jeffries S. (1983) Heroin addiction. Beyond the stereotype. *Spare Rib*, **132**, 6–8.

Lief N. (1985) The drug user as a parent. *Int. J. Addictions*, **20**, 63–97.

Malleson N. (1971) Acute adverse reactions to LSD in clinical and experimental use in the United Kingdom. *Br. J. Psychiat.*, **118**, 229–230.

Manus, J. *et al.* (1984) A longitudinal study of offspring born to methadone maintained women. Design, methodology and description of women's resources for functioning. *Amer. J. Drug Alcohol Abuse*, **10**, 135–160.

Olofsson M. *et al.* (1983) Investigation of 89 children borne by drug-dependent women. *Acta Paediat. Scand.*, **72**, 403–410.

Pinto F. *et al.* (1988) Sleep in babies born to chronically heroin addicted mothers. A follow up study. *Drug Alcohol Depend.*, **21**, 43–47.

Rosenbaum M. (1979) Difficulties in taking care of business: women addicts as mothers. *Amer. J. Drug Alcohol Abuse*, **6**, 431–446.

Schweitzer R.D. and Lawton P.A. (1989) Drug abusers' perception of their parents. *Br. J. Addiction*, **84**, 309–314.

Sclare A.B. (1980) The foetal alcohol syndrome. In *Women and Alcohol*, eds Camberwell Council on Alcoholism (London: Tavistock Publications), pp. 53–66.

Stoffer S.S. *et al.* (1969) After cessation of narcotic addiction. *Obstet. Gynaecol.*, **33**, 558–559.

Strauss M.E. and Reynolds K.S. (1983) Psychological characteristics and development of narcotic-addicted infants. *Drug Alcohol Depend.*, **12**, 381–393.

Sulaiman N.D. *et al.* (1988) Alcohol consumption in Dundee primigravidas and its effect on the outcome of pregnancy. *Br. Med. J.*, **i**, 1500–1503.

Tylden E. (1973) The effects of maternal drug abuse on the fetus and infant. *Adverse Drug Reaction Bull.*, **38**, 120–123.

Wellish D. and Steinberg M. (1980) Parenting attitudes of addict mothers. *Int. J. Addictions*, **15**, 809–819.

Wilson G.S. *et al.* (1979) The development of preschool children of heroin addicted mothers: a controlled study. *Pediatrics*, **63**, 135–141.

Zuckerman B. *et al.* (1989) Effects of maternal marijuana and cocaine use on fetal growth. *New Engl. J. Med.*, **320**, 762–768.

Bibliography

Chiang C.N. and Lee C.C. (eds) (1985) In *Prenatal Drug Exposure: Kinetics and Dynamics*, NIDA Research Monograph No. 60 (Rockville, MD: NIDA).

Ghodse A.H. *et al.* (1977) The effect of maternal narcotic addiction on the new born infant. *Psych. Med.*, **7**, 667–675.

Riley D. (1987) The management of the pregnant drug addict. *Bull. Roy. Col. Psychs.*, **11**, 362–365.

11

Substance Abuse and Prevention Strategies

Nicholas Dorn

Synopsis

The role of health and welfare practitioners in substance abuse prevention is discussed in relation to three areas: their involvement in multi-agency co-ordination; a concept of prevention which takes in health, social, legal and financial considerations at levels of the individual, family and community, and wider society; and their facilitation of educational efforts. As far as working with others at local level is concerned, there are as yet unsolved problems around the question of central government's policy of localisation of responsibility for prevention strategy and for its funding. Positively, there are prospects for a broadening of the concept of minimising drug-related harm, from health considerations (in which containment of HIV looms large), to wider questions of how to reduce social distress (e.g. of family members) and how to reduce legal harm and other forms of drug-related problems (e.g. by diversion of drug users out of the criminal justice system). Educational interventions in the mass media (including local radio), schools and youth clubs are described as powerless to reduce drug use directly but as potentially useful in reducing drug-related harm and as facilitating other goals, such as enhancing public understanding and involving young people in lively and intellectually rigorous investigation of a multifaceted social problem. The contribution of health and welfare professionals to 'solving' drug problems is described in terms of damage limitation in the shorter term, with the possibility of an enhancement of their role as active citizens in the longer term. Modesty and openness to a variety of voices may be the better parts of valour.

Introduction

What is the role of health and welfare practitioners in relation to substance abuse prevention? This chapter is introduced by a brief but broad sweep through recent trends in British prevention policy, noting the increasing weight given to law enforcement in the late 1980s. It then looks at the context in which health and welfare professionals work together and with others at local level, and finally considers prevention in educational systems such as schools.

During the 1960s the British drug problem was primarily an urban phenomenon, restricted to a few cities and coastal places. Indeed it was to be found mainly in central London. During the 1970s the problem spread from city centres to broader areas of cities and suburbs, partly as a result of displacement as a consequence of law-enforcement attention being paid to city-centre dealing sites. It also began to increase across Britain, including more small towns. By the mid 1980s drug problems were recognised as having taken hold across the country, with special concentrations in some cities—London, Liverpool, Edinburgh and Bristol, for example. Not only had the total volume of imports of drugs increased since the 1970s, but also an extensive distribution system (or a variety of distribution systems alongside each other) had sprung up.

The elevation of 'drugs' to the level of a nationwide problem in the UK led to developments at the level of national policy co-ordination and local action. At national level, the Home Office was for the first time nominated as the lead Department of State, and a Home Office minister was appointed to chair a Ministerial Group on drug problems, on which 12 other departments arc also represented (Home Office, 1988). This role of the Home Office fits in with the increasing emphasis given to international co-operation and national co-ordination in enforcement. However, it is the Department of Health that has led the process of stimulating local services and responses.

Central government pump priming of local health and welfare responses

From 1983 onwards a £17.5 million 'Drugs Initiative' of the Department of Health began attracting bids for the setting up of local drugs services throughout Britain. By 1986, 188 drugs advice and rehabilitation projects had received funds, providing a variety of services such as phonelines, counselling, refcrral, rehabilitation, self-help groups, information gathering and research, etc. This central funding lasted for three years, and was intended as 'pump priming', to encourage local health authorities and town and county councils to pick up the bill from the late 1980s onwards. Research by MacGregor and her colleagues suggests that most services are being funded in this way, in spite of quite severe financial problems facing many local authorities (MacGregor *et al.*, 1988).

The Department of Health has also funded some educational materials for schools as has the Department of Education and Science, which pump-primed local educational authorities by providing four years' part-funding for Drug Education Co-ordinators (basically, specialist drug education advisers). All Local Education Authorities appointed such workers, and some, at least, seem likely to take up the full cost from 1990. In some cases the co-ordinators work closely with Health Education Units (who are part of the health system) and with specialist drugs/HIV officers therein.

The general effect of all this is that central government stimulated the growth of service provision, but from the late 1980s onwards had largely withdrawn from any carry-through funding or leadership role at a local level. The Department of Health and the Department of Education and Science have national research and development projects that provide new educational materials and evaluate the process and outcomes of some local services (e.g. needle exchange), but neither these Departments, nor the Home Office nor the Ministerial Group have put forward any general strategy for action or inter-agency co-ordination at local level. Any advice given has been primarily concerned with encouraging local authorities to draw up their own plans, starting with local studies concerned with the identification and quantification of drug problems. Such a focus does little to suggest what might be a fruitful response to problems; for this, one would have to begin with an analysis of present and potential services and inter-agency co-ordination. Everybody knows that there are problems enough, and knowing that with a higher degree of exactitude does not help in the planning of one's strategic response.

But the attempt to quantify problems on a local basis does help to support central government's policy of encouraging local authorities to take on responsibility for a response. If central government came in with a strategy, saying 'Look, girls and boys, this is what you should do. Here is the recommended strategy', then the local authorities would turn round and say 'Fine—now you fund it'. Central government wants demands for it to fund drug services no more than it wants any responsibility for the shape or outcome of services—hence the focus on local problem surveys. Of course, the surveys must be local, since if they were national then they would have national findings with national funding implications. It is interesting that the expert research advice made available to the government concluded that national surveys are methodologically difficult whereas local surveys are not (Office of Population Censuses and Surveys, personal communication). This is an interesting example of policy-led research consultancy, and would be regarded with some incredulity by experts in other countries.

Overall, then, non-enforcement responses have been dispersed to the peripheries of the state, and have 'gone local', with exhortations towards co-ordination but with no model or strategy to guide them in practice. The rest of this chapter concerns itself with some of the key issues.

Needle exchange and HIV

There is considerable discussion of HIV in other chapters in this book, and so the treatment of this important topic here will be relatively brief. In Britain it is recognised that HIV spreads from injecting drug abusers and from male homosexual groups to others. There are now at least 20 needle exchange schemes in Britain and an evaluation is being carried out by Stimson's team at Goldsmiths College (Stimson *et al.*, 1988). The government's position is to wait until the research is completed before deciding whether or not to encourage more such schemes. Although the balance of opinion among practitioners in the drug field is broadly in favour of the retention and/or extension of the schemes, there is some concern over the possibility that more needles in circulation may mean more needles shared (even with a high return rate). There is concern over the practical problems involved in making clean equipment available on a local level and about how to ensure safe return and destruction of used and possibly infected equipment. Also, there has been some head-scratching over the rationality of a policy of making clean equipment rather more available in the context of a historical decline in clinic prescribing of injectable drugs.

Two kinds of research are of interest in relation to drugs and HIV studies of needle exchange schemes and their clients and studies of the 'hidden sector' of injectors who do not attend such schemes. Preliminary research by Stimson and colleagues suggests that needle exchange schemes vary in their popularity, but can attract a proportion of injectors, most of whom are or were previously in treatment: about two-thirds attend for a second visit and one-third for five visits or more (Stimson *et al.*, 1988). Research into the hidden sector suggests that needle sharing remains quite common in Britain: up to half of injectors appear to get their injection equipment from friends, and half of one sample claimed to have shared with between 11 and 100 people over five years (McDermott, 1988). Very few injectors report stopping sharing altogether in response to HIV, but a small proportion say they share less often or with fewer people. The overall picture, then, given the high likelihood of infection when sharing injection equipment, is that an escalation of infection looks likely. In some areas, such as Liverpool, this process is only just getting under way whereas in other areas, notably Edinburgh, it is estimated that about half of the city's multidrug users are already infected.

Given this situation, urgent attention to policy questions may be advisable. Some radical ideas may be needed. What are the implications for social services, health care and housing of people with HIV and AIDS? Given that injection equipment is, in the context of traditions of sharing, a public health hazard, should all injection equipment be brought under the provisions of drug legislation? If the law is seen as a means of controlling drugs, then why is it not seen as a means of controlling injection equipment? Conversely, if deadly equipment is to remain legal, why should consideration not be given to reducing the controls on non-injectable drugs since the latter are less dangerous than the former? Of course, we know the answers to these questions if we put on our 'common sense' hat. Injection equipment has historically been seen as medical equipment, and this perception continues in spite of HIV, so it is unlikely to be restricted; conversely, illegal drugs are simply illegal (mainly because Britain follows international conventions quite closely), and non-injectables will remain tightly controlled regardless of their relatively low public health risk. It is simply how things are.

Can harm minimisation have legal and social goals, as well as health goals?

Largely because of the advent of HIV there is now considerable interest in harm minimisation, and the topic is a focus for many perplexed and angry feelings (ACMD, 1982, 1984; Dorn, 1987; Newcombe, 1987). The debate has, however, generated some light as well as heat: people have moved on from the recognition that minimising harm is as much an aim for prevention policy as minimising use, and are now asking for greater clarity about what this means in practice. For the majority, the question now is not *whether* but *how*. This brings us to the question about the meaning of harm minimisation.

Unfortunately, harm is sometimes defined in a very limited manner—focusing upon individual drug users and upon the physical harm that may befall them. This has several undesirable consequences:

(a) Harm minimisation as a strategy is confused with collusion with drug users or approval for drug use.
(b) There is neglect of harm to those around the user and the wider society.
(c) There is neglect of types of harm other than harm to health.
(d) It may erroneously be suggested that only health system professionals can make a contribution.
(e) The potential scope of prevention strategy is not grasped.
(f) Criteria by which prevention may be evaluated are not being developed.

In an attempt to address these difficulties, let us offer a provisional definition of the range of things that implicitly are being referred to when we use the short-hand term, 'harm'. Let harm be defined at three levels:

• harm to the individual who uses a drug: let us call this 'damage';
• harm to those in social networks, e.g. family, friends, neighbours, interacting with the user: let us call this 'hurts';

- harm to the broader society—let us call this 'fallout'.

It is useful to have a schema in which these can be related to each other. Figure 11.1 shows the Circle of Harm, which can be used to facilitate discussion and to clarify issues of prevention policy at local levels. For example, the Circle of Harm can be used as a focus for discussion among partners in a group practice, a social services area team, a staff meeting in a local drugs advice project, at various levels in District Health Authorities, or in multidisciplinary settings such as Drugs Advisory Committees.

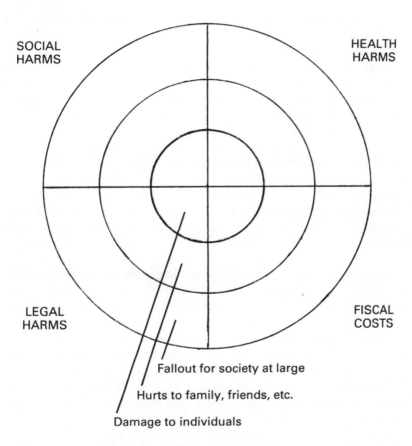

SOCIAL HARMS

HEALTH HARMS

LEGAL HARMS

FISCAL COSTS

Fallout for society at large

Hurts to family, friends, etc.

Damage to individuals

Figure 11.1 The Circle of Harm. *Definition of terms.* Drug-related harm can fall on drug users ('damage'); on their family, friends and others in their immediate social network ('hurts'); and upon other social groups and the society at large ('fallout'). At each of these levels, there may be harm to health, legal harm, social harm and fiscal costs (money costs of the problem itself, and of responses to it). These kinds of harm may result from drug use *per se*; or from the manner and circumstances of use; or from social reactions to users; or from control policies (unwanted 'side-effects' of policies).

Legal, health, social and financial *damage* to users themselves

Think of a small circle and let this be the scope for damage to the individual who uses a legal or illegal drug. This damage may be legal damage, health damage, social damage and/or money problems. (See figure 11.1.)

Legal, health, social and financial *hurts* to those in the family and elsewhere who directly interact with users

If a larger circle is drawn around the individual, the new space enclosed by this circle is the scope for harm to family, friends and others close to the user who are hurt in some way(s) by the use. These negative impacts or 'hurts' may be health, legal or social (e.g. the mother goes on to tranquillisers, the brother gets picked up by police attracted by the user's bad reputation, the sister gets called names by neighbours), and, of course, there may be money problems (theft from the home, loss of parental income due to taking time off work to care for or control the user, etc.).

Legal, health, social and fiscal *fallout* to wider society

Lastly, if a big circle is drawn around the other two, this represents the sphere of dis-benefits falling upon the wider community. Such fallout can be legal, health, social and/or fiscal (e.g. money costs of law enforcement, costs of treatment, costs of the diversion of effort from other social goals, etc.).

This approach makes clear the probability that any given prevention policy or activity would probably have a variety of consequences. Some consequences might be universally desired (e.g. fewer break-ins), some universally reviled (e.g. more deaths) and some approved by some observers but not by others (e.g. fewer prosecutions of people caught in possession of small amounts of drugs). Of course, there would be disputes over the values that should be attached to the observed changes.

For example, let us consider three possible policies on drugs and the control of syringes that may be used in injection, and their effects on AIDS.

Policy A: experimental, varying and partial availability of syringes through so-called '*needle exchange*' schemes.
Policy B: cheap, stable and *easy supply* of syringes in all neighbourhoods in which injection of drugs is known.
Policy C: *repressive controls* aiming to make it more legally hazardous for individuals to possess injection equipment than to possess drugs *per se*

(perhaps by a decrease in penalty for drug possession, alongside new controls on injection equipment).

What might be the consequences of each of these policies in terms of damage to individuals, hurts to families and friends, and fallout for the wider society? Different readers will each have their own ideas about this, and such differences of view are an essential part of the process of arguing through the issues and coming to the best possible local policy. The aim in this chapter is to suggest a common language for discussion of these difficult issues.

Beyond the question of the effectiveness of particular national policies or local programmes (the question, 'Does the policy/programme give us outcomes that may on balance be viewed as desirable?') lies the question of cost effectiveness: 'Does it give us desirable outcomes at a reasonable cost?' A policy is not much good if it returns modest improvements in damage, hurts and/or fallout but at enormous fiscal costs, when the money might have been more productively employed in a different fashion or elsewhere.

Let us approach the issue of the cost effectiveness of prevention policies and programmes by reference to the families, friends and neighbours of drug users. Few people would disagree with the proposition that it is worthwhile to spend a certain amount of money to reduce the various hurts (social, legal, health-related, fiscal) that may fall upon them. The question would be, how much is it worth to reduce these hurts? For example, would it be worth £3000 to make ten old age pensioners less anxious by financing a police operation over two months to move drug dealing away from the building in which they reside? Would this be even more worth while if it could be calculated that, apart from being happier and sleeping better, they did so without the need for prescribed drugs? There might be consequential savings for social services and the health service, and these savings could be set against the cost of the police operation that caused them, so making the exercise of reducing hurts quite cheap or even self-financing. Such an exercise would be cost-effective when viewed at a local level, though there might be a problem of 'displacement' of the problem to another locality.

In summary: a prevention policy or programme may be regarded as cost-effective when and if the value of changes in levels of harm seem worth the fiscal costs of the policy. If health and welfare professionals are to stand their ground in the debates over effectiveness and funding that have characterised the 1980s and may continue into the 1990s, then they may have to consider whether they can make common ground with each other around these issues. This may mean stepping outside their own specialisation and taking a broad perspective that takes account of a range of social, legal and health-related objectives.

Schools and the mass media

Back in the 1960s, and increasingly during the 1970s and 1980s, education was seen as a panacea for drug problems. Education was often called 'primary prevention' on the assumption that it had the power to prevent initial experimentation with drugs, if the right educational methodology could be found. This belief in the power of drug education is now rather threadbare, following a series of evaluations and reviews of drug education that indicate that none of the available methodologies contains drug experimentation at all (De Haes, 1986). This seems to be the case whether one is thinking of scare approaches, pure information approaches, 'person focused' approaches that aim to increase self-esteem and social skills, or mixed educational approaches. The pessimism about effectiveness of drug education in preventing experimentation—or maybe it is a new realism—has led some experts to question the value of preventive education or to record that it should be done only in those contexts in which educators can teach 'safe' or safer drug use (Clements *et al.*, 1988). Fears of condoning drug use may lead educators to confine their activities to social groups in which drug use is already rife, and to keep out of other contexts, such as schools, altogether.

What can health and welfare professionals say and do in relation to education about drugs? First of all, it is important to recognise that the school curriculum and, in particular, the National Curriculum (which became operative in 1989 in England and Wales) offers opportunities much broader than preventing drug use or drug-related harm (though these two aims may also be pursued, if done in ways appropriate to the context). There are opportunities for teachers to adopt *educational* goals in relation to drugs, meaning that they can integrate academic coverage and discussion of drug-related issues into all the subjects of the curriculum from mathematics through English to science. In mathematics, for example, the curriculum could include study of the spread of HIV and extrapolation of its possible future rise, as well as the use of Household Expenditure Survey data on expenditure on alcohol. In English, teachers and pupils could study persuasive communications, biographic accounts or use of language. In the sciences, there is obvious scope for studying the central nervous system, mechanisms of overdose (e.g. through mixing sedative drugs) or routes of infection. In other subjects, there are equally appropriate ways of discussing aspects of drug problems; for example geography can cover regional production (wine lakes in the European Communities, cocaine in South America) and trafficking and trade (arms to Lebanese factions, opium and cannabis to the West). It is not so much that each curricular subject can make its contribution to the solution of the drug problem, but that teaching about aspects of the drug problem can make its contribution to the curriculum, displaying the relevance of education and contributing to the education of future citizens. Materials for this curriculum-based approach are already available (Health Education Council, 1986) and more are on the way. For health and welfare professionals to support (or at least not to obstruct) these developments, they will need to put aside their own everyday perspectives and to listen and learn from other professionals: you cannot simply insert a health systems perspective into an educational context.

A similar modesty is required to work with local media, such as local radio or community arts. In one demonstration project in the South of England in the late 1980s, drugs advice workers were successful in buying air-time on a local radio station to broadcast a short youth-orientated message about interactions between sedative drugs. Listeners were invited to call a phoneline which gave further information (Fraser and Gamble, 1988). In this case the drugs workers had to overcome their professional backgrounds and familiarity with extended one-to-one counselling sessions and to work within the 'rules' of broadcasting. In another example a project in the Midlands of England developed a comic, called Smack in the Eye, which used a variety of comic-strip styles and techniques (some of them rather rude) to get across information about drug-related and sex-related risks (Gilman, 1988). In this case the workers, having noted that comics were an acceptable communications medium in drug-using circles, had to adopt the rules of communication according to comics in order to develop content appropriate for that context.

These three examples of relevant educational approaches—in school, local radio and comics—have one thing in common. The style of address and the content of communications have to be adapted to the context in which one works. There is no one 'line' on education that is valid independent of context. What fits in one context would be out of order in another: imagine, for example, a teacher coming into the waiting room of a GP's surgery or drugs advice project and beginning to conduct a lesson taken from the curriculum of the General Certificate of Secondary Education. Now imagine vice versa, and you have a picture of what to avoid.

Lastly, let us very briefly look at some aspects of the relationship between health and welfare professionals and the mass media. As many professionals have found, sometimes to their chagrin, the mass media are interested only in views that count (in their eyes) as 'news'. Here is a list of questions that you may be asked. 'How bad is the problem/is it getting worse?' 'Can you tell us about a particularly sad case?' 'Would you say that the Government is winning the war against drugs?' And, if you do not want to speak on any of these issues that are of interest to the public, 'Why do you persist in calling yourself an expert? . . . Oh, so you are not? Goodbye!'

Basic rules for working successfully with the media, at local or at national levels, are quite simple. First, you should talk only for 'back-ground', not for 'attribution' on the first contact. Get the journalist to agree to these terms before you go any further; any journalist worth their salt will immediately agree, and you will then know you are dealing with a fellow professional and not a trickster. Secondly, find out what the story or editorial line is in the journalist's eyes, then you can decide if your concerns can possibly fit in such a context. If they do not, apologise and say that you will be available for background on future occasions and ask for a telephone number where you can get back to them in future. But, thirdly, if the editorial line does encompass your concerns, then say something like 'OK, here is an attributable statement', followed by no more than three short sentences that clearly outline your views. Until you have established a longer term relationship with the journalist in question, it is best to avoid any of their follow-on questions and to say that you have finished speaking for attribution and can continue for background only. A good rule of thumb in dealing with the media is that, if you feel excited, you may be about to make a public fool of yourself; ring off, saying that a visitor has just arrived and that you will phone them back, then consult a colleague and make some notes before you do. If all of this sounds paranoid, be reassured, it is not: it is simply professional and can save you much grief (and possibly much flak from colleagues). When working with the mass media—as with all other information and education systems—you have to understand the basic rules and work within them.

Summarising, drug education may have a range of goals, including prevention of experimentation (but that is unlikely to succeed), minimisation of drug-related harm (which may or may not work: we simply do not know) and the advancing of knowledge as a social good in itself. It can be done in a number of contexts, such as school curricula, local and national media, youth work (ISDD, 1988), community education and so on. In each case, the content and style of delivery will be different, depending upon the possibilities and constraints of the context. And in each of these contexts, a reply of 'I don't know' often sounds more impressive than anything else.

Conclusion

The main thrust of this chapter has been towards the proposition that prevention is a more complex and more difficult thing than it might appear.

The only sure-fire prevention would be effective law enforcement or other means of reducing the availability of drugs: no drugs, no drug consumption, no drug-related problems. But, however vigorous may be the efforts of governments in that direction (Home Office, 1988), it seems certain that illicit drugs will continue to be available and to be consumed throughout Britain in the foreseeable future. Health and welfare professionals should accept that, for the time being at least, they will be mopping up in the midst of a downpour and should decline any invitation to burden themselves by taking on a policy/preventive role that they are not equipped to fulfil.

On the other hand, health and welfare professionals can contribute to the prevention of drug-related harm not only in relation to health harms (such as HIV) but also in relation to social and legal harms to families and the wider community. To do this, many have already developed skills in working with other professions and agencies, and this chapter has put forward a simple language of prevention—a set of terms—that hopefully facilitates the process of inter-agency co-ordination. Lastly, involvement in education has been discussed in terms of sensitivity towards the context in which one works, and modesty in relation to the claims to expertise that one may make.

The overall proposition is, perhaps, familiar for health and welfare professionals who are experiencing the 1980s. Let us look for our triumphs not tomorrow but the day after.

References

ACMD (Advisory Council on the Misuse of Drugs) (1982) *Treatment and Rehabilitation* (London: HMSO).
ACMD (Advisory Council on the Misuse of Drugs) (1984) *Prevention* (London: Home Office).
Clements I., Cohen J. and O'Hare P. (1988) Beyond 'Just Say No'. *Druglink*, **3**, 10–11.
De Haes W.F.M. (1986) Drug education? Yes, but how? In *Addictive Behaviours*, ed. Davies J.K. (Edinburgh: Scottish Health Education Group), pp. 35–51.
Dorn N. (1987) U-curve theory of harm-minimisation. *Druglink*, **2**, 14–15.
Fraser A. and Gamble L. (1988) Local radio as a strategy in reducing drug related harm. *Drug Questions Research Register*, issue 4 (London: ISDD).
Gilman M. (1988) Comics as a strategy in reducing drug related harm. *Drug Questions Research Register*, issue 4 (London: ISDD).
Health Education Council, Scottish Education Group, Lifeskills Associates, TACADE, ISDD (1986) *DrugWise Drug Education for Students 14–19* (especially the curriculum guide therein) (London: ISDD).
Home Office (1988) *Tackling Drug Misuse: a Summary of the Government's Strategy* (London: Home Office).
ISDD (Institute for the Study of Drug Dependence) (1988) *High Profile Youth Work Curriculum and Consultation Materials about Drugs* (available in multiples of 20) (London: ISDD).
MacGregor S., Ettorre B. and Coomber R. (1988) Summary of first report: an assessment of the Central Funding Initiative on services for drug misusers (London: Birkbeck College, mimeo), pp. 10–11.
McDermott P. (1988) *A Report of the Mersey AIDS Prevention Unit Health Promotion Department* (Liverpool: Mersey AIDS Prevention Unit), pp. 1–27.
Newcombe R. (1987) High time for harm-reduction. *Druglink*, **2**, 11–12.
Stimson G., Dolan K., Donoghoe M. and Alldritt L. (1988) Syringe exchange 1. *Druglink*, **3**, 10–11.

12
Drugs and the Law

Roger Farmer

Synopsis

Drug dependence has many facets, not least its relationship with the law. For instance, one approach to limiting harm to the individual and society from drug misuse has been to curb by means of legal controls the possession, use and supply of certain drugs. In this chapter the development of drugs legislation in the United Kingdom will be briefly described and this will provide an historical context for an outline of that cornerstone of current law relating to drugs, the 1971 Misuse of Drugs Act. The Mental Health Act as it applies to drug misuse will then be summarised.

Given the overall statistical association between drug misuse and criminal activity, health-care professionals working with drug dependents may be called on to prepare court reports or to give evidence in court. Some guidance for these tasks will be presented. Lastly the complex relationship between drug misuse and crime will be explored and possible reasons for an association discussed.

The origins of drug legislation in the United Kingdom

Not only do patterns of drug use change with time but a society's attitudes to various kinds of drug taking also may alter. Both these factors have influenced the development of legislation relating to psychoactive drugs so that legal controls have tended to grow up piecemeal in response to what were perceived at the time to be crisis situations.

The history of opium use and the introduction of legislation relating to opiate drugs over the last 200 years exemplifies this (Berridge, 1977). Until the mid-nineteenth century there were no legislative controls on drug misuse in the UK so that opium was available over the counter without legal restriction, and dependence on the drug not only went unrecognised as a concept but also only gave rise to problems when supplies diminished for whatever reason. However, concerns over 'infant doping' (i.e. quietening young children with opium preparations), deaths from adults' overdosing, widespread recreational use of opium among the working classes and opium use in the Chinese community, all became more orchestrated and in 1868 the Pharmacy Act was introduced, restricting sales of morphine and opium to pharmacists. The latter part of the nineteenth century and the first half of the twentieth saw reduced levels of opiate use with non-opiate sedatives being used instead. Individuals dependent on opiate drugs during this period were in the main either 'therapeutic' addicts—those who had become dependent usually on morphine while being prescribed it for medical reasons, or 'professional' addicts—often doctors or nurses who had regular access to morphine and had self-medicated.

Concern that troops on leave from the 1914–1918 war were intoxicated on cocaine stimulated the introduction in 1916 of Regulation 40B under the Defence of the Realm Act, making it an offence to possess cocaine and opium. Subsequently the Dangerous Drugs Act of 1920 confined to medical prescriptions the availability of opiate drugs (other than certain very dilute oral prescriptions) as well as cocaine. This act became the basis of subsequent drugs legislation in the UK, and some of its features are still in force.

Uncertainty remained over the situations in which doctors might appropriately prescribe opiate drugs as treatment for addiction, and this role of doctors, suggested by the Dangerous Drugs Act 1920, was reviewed by a departmental committee (the Rolleston Committee) appointed by the then Minister of Health. The report, published in 1926, noted the low prevalence of addiction to heroin and morphine at the time and recommended that such addiction should be regarded as an illness. Recommendations concerning prescribing were that it would be appropriate to prescribe morphine or heroin to addicts: (a) when 'undergoing treatment for the cure of addiction by the gradual withdrawal method'; (b) 'after every effort has been made for the cure of the addiction, the drug cannot be completely withdrawn . . .'.

These guidelines became the basis of the so-called 'British system' of managing opiate addiction by maintenance prescribing, i.e. providing prescriptions for indefinite periods of time with relatively little coaxing to relinquish the drug habit and often a very lengthy wait until the addict might himself become 'ready' to reduce and ultimately give up his drug taking.

The next significant review of policy was carried out by the Brain Committee which, in its 1960 report, endorsed the views of the Rolleston Committee that addiction was best viewed as a medical condition and that treatment was most appropriately accomplished in suitable institutions.

However, during the 1960s there was a dramatic rise in the number of those known to be dependent on dangerous drugs, particularly heroin. These new heroin addicts were quite different from the therapeutic and professional opiate addicts previously recognised, being younger and often polydrug users. An associated source of concern was a rapidly expanding black market for drugs. In other words the whole complexion of drug misuse in the United Kingdom had changed. The Brain Committee was reconvened to reassess the situation and to review its advice especially with regard to the prescribing of addictive drugs.

The second Brain report, published in 1965, gave rise to many of our current controls and systems for delivering treatment. The Committee reported that a small number of doctors were overprescribing addictive drugs, and proposed that the number of doctors authorised to prescribe heroin and cocaine for the treatment of addiction should be strictly limited. This proposal was accepted by the government of the day as was a system of notification of addicts to the Home Office. Another recommendation concerned the setting up of a range of treatment facilities, and this led to the establishment of special treatment centres attached to hospitals.

The Misuse of Drugs Act 1971

This Act (which came into force from July 1973) consolidated all the existing legislation with some changes, so that, for instance, it replaced the Dangerous Drugs Act of 1965, the Dangerous Drugs Act of 1967 (which had implemented the urgent recommendations of the Second Brain Report), and the Drugs (Prevention of Misuse) Act of 1964 which had addressed the control of amphetamines, methaqualone and LSD. The main provisions of certain sections of the Act, which runs to a total of 38 sections, are as follows:

Section 1 establishes the Advisory Council on the Misuse of Drugs as a multidisciplinary body with the remit of keeping under review the misuse of drugs and of advising ministers on subjects covered by the Act.

Section 2 places drugs to be controlled into three categories:

Class A includes the major natural and synthetic opiates (specified by name), cocaine, LSD, injectable amphetamines and cannabinol.

Class B includes oral amphetamines, cannabis plant material and cannabis resin, codeine and phenmetrazine. Certain barbiturates have since been included.

Class C includes methaqualone and certain amphetamine-like drugs.

This section also permits the removal or addition of any drug from the Schedule or for a drug to be transferred from one class to another by an Order in Council, i.e. without the need for new legislation, so that, for example, certain barbiturates were included as Class B drugs.

Sections 4 and 5 set out the offences of supply, possession and possession with intent to supply.

Section 25 specifies the maximum penalties for offences under the Act, which depend on the class of drugs involved, so that offences involving

Class A drugs carry the most severe penalties and those concerning Class C drugs the least severe. Recent legislation has increased the penalties for trafficking in Class A drugs to life imprisonment, and legal measures have been introduced to deprive drug traffickers of their proceeds from this source by confiscating their assets.

Section 10 empowers the Home Secretary to make regulations to prevent the misuse of controlled drugs. The most important of these regulations is the Misuse of Drugs (Notification of and Supply to Addicts) Regulations 1973. These require any doctor to notify the Chief Medical Officer of the Home Office any patient whom he considers to be or has reasonable grounds to suspect is addicted to any of the following controlled drugs: cocaine, dextromoramide (Palfium), diamorphine, dipipanone (Pipadone), hydrocodone (Hycodan), hydromorphone (Dilaudid), levorphanol, (Dromoran), methadone, morphine, opium, oxycodone (Percodan), pethidine (meperidine: Demerol), phenazocine (Narphen) and piritramide. The notifications provide useful epidemiological data on trends in drug misuse although the numbers notified have been gross underestimates of the actual numbers of drug-dependent individuals.

Under the same Regulations the prescribing of heroin and cocaine for addiction is prohibited except under licence from the Home Secretary. Flexibility of control over prescribing is enabled by the power to bring a drug under immediate control on the recommendation of the Advisory Council on the Misuse of Drugs alone, and following concern over increasing misuse of dipipanone (Diconal; Pipadone) this drug was added to the list on 1 April 1984. These three drugs (heroin, cocaine and dipipanone) may of course be prescribed as treatment of organic disease or injury by any doctor. It is only their prescription as treatment for addiction which is restricted.

If any doctor is convicted under the Act or is considered to be prescribing controlled drugs in an irresponsible way, his right to prescribe controlled drugs may be withdrawn by direction of the Home Secretary. The Act and the associated Regulations establish a system of tribunals to advise the Home Secretary, but between 1974 and 1982 only nine tribunals were held and it has been suggested that a rather narrow legalistic approach may have been adopted so that only cases with clear evidence of grossly irresponsible prescribing were referred to tribunals (Advisory Council on the Misuse of Drugs, 1982).

Thus the Misuse of Drugs Act, in spite of its complexity, has rationalised drugs legislation to some extent, but how does drug dependence relate to the present Mental Health Act?

The Mental Health Act 1983

Mental disorder is defined under this Act as 'mental illness, arrested or incomplete development of mind, psychopathic disorder and any other disorder or disability of mind' (s1(2)). Although the phrase 'any other disorder or disability of mind' means that the term mental disorder potentially encompasses a broad spectrum of behaviour, the Act specifically stipulates that someone may not be classified as mentally disordered 'by reason only of promiscuity or other immoral conduct, sexual deviancy or dependence on alcohol or drugs' (s1(3)).

This means that the provisions of the Act may not be applied to someone who is simply dependent on drugs. However, drug taking may give rise to certain forms of mental disorder as defined under the Act. For example, prolonged use of amphetamines may cause a psychotic illness ('amphetamine psychosis') which would constitute a form of mental illness under the terms of the Act so that various sections of the Act might be applied to someone suffering from that condition if the other criteria were met. Also, of course, certain psychiatric conditions which would be included as forms of mental disorder according to the Act often coexist with drug dependence, e.g. psychopathic disorder. In this case a section might be applicable because the patient suffers from mental disorder accompanying the drug dependence.

Four sub-categories of mental disorder are specified in the Act: mental illness, severe mental impairment, mental impairment and psychopathic disorder, but only three are defined.

Mental illness

This term is not defined.

Severe mental impairment

According to the Act this is 'a state of arrested or incomplete development of mind which includes severe impairment of intelligence and social functioning and is associated with abnormally aggressive or seriously irresponsible conduct' (s1(2)).

Mental impairment

This term is defined in exactly the same way as severe mental impairment except that it covers 'significant' as opposed to 'severe' impairment of intelligence and social functioning (s1(2)). The legal distinction between *severe* and *significant* is far from clear.

Psychopathic disorder

This term means 'a persistent disorder or disability of mind (whether or not including significant impairment of intelligence) which results in abnormally aggressive or seriously irresponsible conduct' (s1(2)).

In summary, therefore, the provisions of the Mental Health Act do not apply to someone with drug dependence which is not complicated by or does not coexist with mental disorder. The second Brain Report proposed that there should be legal provision to compulsorily detain in treatment centres patients withdrawing from drugs. However, this recommendation of the report was the only one of its proposals not to be implemented and probably few would now regard compulsory treatment for drug dependence as justifiable on grounds of ethics or efficacy.

Writing reports for the courts

Health-care professionals involved in the management of drug misusers, particularly doctors, probation officers and social workers, may be called on to provide reports for the courts. Such reports constitute a vital link between such professionals and the legal system, and writing them is one of their most important tasks. The guidelines which will be presented below are for the preparation of medical or psychiatric reports, but much of the advice will usefully apply to other kinds of report such as social enquiry reports. The examples given are meant to be parts of a medical report prepared by a doctor not specialising in the field of drug dependence, such as a general practitioner.

There are certain desirable features of court reports. They should be clear, concise, free from technical expressions and written in standard English, i.e. in prose and not in note form. The author should aim to reach definite conclusions and make realistic recommendations. Value judgements and, most certainly, pejorative comments should be avoided.

Reports may be read by a variety of people including judges, magistrates, barristers and solicitors, but none is likely to possess detailed medical or psychiatric knowledge. So medical jargon should be eschewed, or if a medical term is used, an attempt should be made to explain it in layman's language. The length of a report should be consistent with the report's being sufficiently informative but yet easily read and understood. When information has been provided by the patient alone without any substantiation, it is wise to qualify statements in the report with words and phrases like 'apparently', 'I believe', 'according to the patient', etc. When alluding to the alleged offence, care should be taken not to prejudice the trial. Furthermore it is important to have obtained the patient's valid consent for any report to be written.

I favour a relatively standardised format with use of headings to assist the reader find his way about a report. A possible scheme is therefore as follows:

(1) Introduction

This should make clear just what the report is based on.

Example
John Smith is a 26-year-old single man who is currently unemployed. This report is based on three interviews with him between 12 February and 14 March 1988. I have also read the report of his probation officer, Stephen Green, dated 17 March 1988.

(2) Drug-taking history

Usually a concise chronological outline of a patient's past and present use of drugs is most suitable. Changes in pattern of drug use should be mentioned, including, for example, when injecting was adopted as a route of administration or when the use of a particular drug became regular. Any evidence of dependence should be included, as should any previous treatment for drug problems.

Example
John Smith's first use of non-prescribed drugs was when he smoked cannabis at the age of 16 years. Over the next four years he apparently tried various other drugs including diazepam, dexamphetamine and cocaine. I gather he first experimented with heroin by smoking it when he was 20 years old and first injected this drug a year later. Its use became progressively more frequent and heavier, and in February 1988, when I first saw him, I believe he was injecting about one gram of street heroin daily. By that time it seems obtaining and taking the drug was one of the most significant parts of his life and he was going to extreme lengths to obtain the drug. He described experiencing the characteristic withdrawal discomfort when he missed a dose of the drug. I believe he has usually obtained clean needles and syringes from chemists but has shared used needles and syringes three times during the last six months. Mr Smith has never as far as I know approached any drug treatment agency.

(3) Family history and (4) Personal history

In the next two sections background family and personal history should be given. It is rarely necessary to give this in much detail, and if the information has already been provided for the court in another report this should be pointed out.

Example
The report by Stephen Green, probation officer, dated 17 March 1988, includes the family and personal history, so I shall not repeat it.

(5) Mental state

This should briefly summarise the findings. Long lists of negative findings should not be given.

Example
When I interviewed Mr Smith on 14 March 1988, he seemed willing and able to give a good account of his situation. He was not depressed and I thought he was of average intelligence.

If appropriate, findings on physical examination should be appended.

Example
There were fresh injection marks on both arms and an abscess on the front of his lower arm on 12 February 1988, but on 14 March 1988 only old scars were seen.

(6) Summary

This should bring together salient factors from the history with opinions and any recommendations.

Example
There is a two-year history of dependence on heroin. Obtaining and taking the drug became a central aspect of the patient's life, he needed to take more of the drug to achieve the same effects, and he suffered the characteristic withdrawal symptoms when his dose diminished.

Mr Smith was working in a setting where heroin was easily available when he was first introduced to its use by a work colleague. Use of heroin has apparently buffered him from the demands of life which he has always had difficulty coping with, and its continued use has probably been perpetuated by a desire to avoid unpleasant withdrawal effects.

Given the chronicity of the patient's drug misuse and the severity of his dependence on heroin I think he would best be managed at least initially by a unit specialising in the treatment of drug dependence. St George's Hospital Drug Dependence Unit has kindly agreed to assess Mr Smith with a view to treating him, and the court might consider dealing with this case by deferring sentencing for four months in order to assess the success of any treatment which might be offered for Mr Smith's drug dependence.

(7) Signature

This should include your full name, qualifications and professional status.

In a report the court is looking for a professional opinion as to the nature and extent of any drug problem. It will also expect some indication of what treatment might be appropriate and if possible where this could be provided. The court is also likely to be grateful for practical suggestions as to how someone might be best disposed of by the court, taking into account the needs of the patient and society.

In the witness box

The subject of giving evidence in court is mostly beyond the scope of this chapter but a few points are perhaps worth making. First, as uncertainty over the correct title for the judge or magistrate will not help one's self-confidence, table 12.1 shows the correct titles according to the type of court.

Table 12.1   Correct titles for judges or magistrates

Court	Title
Appeal Court High Court Central Criminal Court	My Lord, My Lady
Crown Court County Court	Your Honour
Magistrates' Courts	Your Worship(s)
	Barristers must use Sir, Madam or Ma'am

It is not always appreciated that all evidence should be directed to the judge or magistrates. By facing the judge to answer questions posed by the barrister, and only turning back towards the barrister when one feels satisfied with one's answer and ready to accept another question, some witnesses feel they can exercise more control over the proceedings. The time taken turning back to face the judge may also help one prepare a response to a question. It should be noted that, although the witness has to look at the judge, he is not obliged to reciprocate and because we normally expect eye contact from our listeners this can be initially disconcerting.

Evidence should be clearly delivered and should be as precise as possible avoiding the use of jargon or technical terms, particularly as one may be asked to explain them!

Drug misuse and crime

One of the few things that can be said with certainty about the relationship between drug misuse and crime is that it is complex.

The popular assumption is that heroin use leads to crime and that heroin users, particularly if dependent, turn to criminal activities, especially property crime, in order to finance their habit. The reality, however, appears to be less simple, with many factors bearing on the relationship, including the age of the drug user, the chronicity of his drug use and the severity of any dependence. It is also worth pointing out that, since possession of non-prescribed opiates is itself an offence, the relationship discussed here is that between opiate use and other forms of criminal activity.

An association certainly exists between opiate use and criminality. In the USA opiate dependents are not only often involved in criminal behaviour on a daily basis, but many of their offences are serious. The magnitude of the crime problem associated with opiate dependence must therefore be assessed in terms of both the frequency and the severity of criminal activity. In the USA about 500 000 addicts commit more than 50 million crimes per year (Nurco, 1987), and a changing pattern of crime by opiate dependents has been noted with an increase in violent crime. Whereas in the 1950s crimes were usually petty and usually against property rather than persons, in the 1960s a trend towards more violent crime began so that, since the late 1970s, crime committed by regular opiate users has been characterised by violence and the use of firearms.

The British scene, however, remains rather different and on the whole opiate users here are not involved in serious crimes to support their drug habit. The explanation for this difference remains unclear, but contributing factors may be the likelihood that those who become involved in drug use in the USA come more often from very deprived urban environments with subcultures of violence or from alienated social minorities; black market drugs are cheaper in Britain so that more serious crime is unnecessary to finance a drug habit, and welfare benefits in Britain help to subsidise the regular acquisition of drugs without resort to serious crime.

However, an association between crime and drug dependence is not the same as a causal link. It seems, for instance, that for many opiate users criminal activity predates drug use. In Britain about two-thirds of male opiate users have been convicted of offences before notification of drug addiction to the Home Office (Mott, 1981), although clearly notification often occurs well into someone's drug-using career. Also, drug use may be but one criminal aspect of a delinquent lifestyle. For some individuals drugs may even be used as a means of celebrating the accomplishment of a criminal act.

If the financing of a drug habit does not derive from criminal activity, where might it come from? The irregular or less dependent user, particularly, may obtain money from legitimate sources such as state benefits, relatives or friends, and employment. Some drug users restrict their criminal activities to being involved in the distribution of street drugs, usually by buying and selling illicit drugs.

The evidence for a causal link between opiate use and crime appears strongest for the more severely dependent individual. Longitudinal studies in the USA, for instance, have demonstrated levels of crime committed during periods of dependent drug use far exceeding those committed during periods off drugs. However, elucidation of the extent of the causal link will depend on longitudinal studies which begin before drug use has occurred.

Drugs and the law in perspective

In this chapter some aspects of the two-way relationship between drug misuse and the legal system have been presented, particularly society's attempts to curb drug use, which it has considered contrary to public interest, and the interaction of drug misusers with the legal processes. Certain functions of health-care professionals with respect to the legal system have also been described. The legal and therapeutic approaches to drug misuse both seem valid for prevention, as well as having merits for helping the individual and protecting society, but it is the balance of the two which will continue to be debated.

References

Advisory Council on the Misuse of Drugs (1982) *Treatment and Rehabilitation* (London: Department of Health and Social Security).
Berridge V. (1977) Opium and the historical perspective. *Lancet*, **ii**, 78–80.
Mott J. (1981) Criminal involvement and penal response. In *Drug Problems in Britain: A Review of Ten Years*, eds Edwards G. and Busch C. (London: Academic Press), pp. 217–244.
Nurco D.N. (1987) Drug addiction and crime: a complicated issue. *Br. J. Addiction*, **82**, 7–10.

Bibliography

Berridge V. and Edwards G. (1981) *Opium and the People* (Harmondsworth: Penguin Books).
Bucknell P. and Ghodse H. (1986) *Misuse of Drugs: Criminal Law Library No. 2* (London: Waterlow).
Carson D. (1985) Doctors in the witness box. *Br. J. Hosp. Med.*, **33**, 283–286.
Edwards G. and Busch C. (eds) (1981) *Drug Problems in Britain: A Review of Ten Years* (London: Academic Press).
Gostin L. (1983) *A Practical Guide to Mental Health Law. The Mental Health Act 1983 and Related Legislation* (London: MIND).

Index

255